One Foot in
HEAVEN

The Story of Bob
Lindsey of Jerusalem

Kenneth R. Mullican, Jr.
AND
Loren C. Turnage

PublishAmerica
Baltimore

First printing

Unless otherwise noted, all Scripture quotations in this publication are from the Holy Bible, New American Standard Version, © Copyright The Lockman Foundation, 1960, 1962, 1963, 1968, 1971, 1972, 1973, 1975, 1977. Used by Permission of The Lockman Foundation.

ISBN: 1-4137-6381-2 (softcover)
ISBN: 978-1-4489-0251-4 (hardcover)
PUBLISHED BY PUBLISHAMERICA, LLLP
www.publishamerica.com
Baltimore

Printed in the United States of America

For Margaret Lutz Lindsey, who is an integral part of the story,and without whose willingness to share intimate details, letters, and photographs, this story could not have been written.

CONTENTS

FOREWORD

The death on May 31, 1995 at age seventy-seven of Robert L. Lindsey, pastor, synoptic researcher, pioneer translator of the gospels into Modern Hebrew, and doyen of the Jerusalem School of Synoptic Research, was received with a great sense of loss by those who knew and loved him. His colleagues and students remember Dr. Lindsey as a giving, selfless individual and a dedicated biblical scholar. His Christian students and friends also remember a pastor named Bob who, always aiming at helping the congregants put Jesus' teachings into practice, infused his sermons with the refreshing insights of Jerusalem-based scholarship.

When I came to Israel in 1963 to begin graduate studies at the Hebrew University of Jerusalem, Dr. Lindsey was forty-five years old. He and his family had moved recently from Tiberias to Jerusalem. It had been in Tiberias, beside the Sea of Galilee, eighteen months before, that he had stumbled upon the key to the synoptic problem's solution: Luke's Gospel was not dependent upon Mark's.

In Jerusalem, "Bob" Lindsey became my pastor, my mentor, and my second father. As pastor of the Narkis Street Baptist Church, in the Rehaviah neighborhood of Jerusalem, Bob was my spiritual leader for twenty-four years (from 1963 until his retirement in 1987). Eventually, I served under him as one of the congregation's elders. Listening to his sermons, adult Bible class lessons, and through hundreds of private lessons, I absorbed some of his immense knowledge of Jesus.

Only twice during my first seventeen years in Israel could I afford a visit to my parents in the United States. Bob and his wife, Margaret, became my surrogate parents. When Josa and I were married in 1969, Bob and Margaret not only provided us with their cabin overlooking the Sea of Galilee for our honeymoon, but Bob chauffeured us there from Jerusalem! That kind deed took more than five hours of driving.

Now that Bob is gone, I feel orphaned, much like the famous scholar, Rabbi Akiva, upon the death of his teacher, Eliezer ben Hyrcanus. When Akiva met the men carrying Eliezer's body from Caesarea to Lydda, he rent his garments, tore his hair, and began to weep and cry out: "Woe is me, my master, because of you! Woe is me, my teacher, because of you! You have left the whole generation fatherless!" At Eliezer's funeral, Akiva eulogized him, "My father! My father! The chariots and horsemen of Israel! I have many coins, but no money changer to exchange them," that is, "I have many questions, but no teacher to answer them."

I have accepted the reality—Bob is no longer here. I have realized, reluctantly, that he was not mine permanently. Beruriah, the brilliant scholar of the second century A.D., had the painful task of telling her husband, Rabbi Meir, that their two sons had died. Before breaking the awful news to him, she prepared him: "Some time ago," she said, "a certain man asked me to hold a pledge in trust for him. Now he wants it back. Should we return it?"

"One who is entrusted with a pledge," he answered, "must return it to its owner upon demand."

Then Beruriah informed Meir of the tragedy. Rabbi Meir wept and cried out, but Beruriah reminded him of his own recent advice. Rabbi Meir ceased his wailing and said: "The Lord has given. The Lord has taken away. Blessed be the name of the Lord."

Like Rabbi Akiva, I have grieved the loss of my teacher; but like Beruriah, I know that Bob is now with the Lord. Moreover, I am further comforted because his scholarly work continues—through the disciples he raised up, through a research institute, the Jerusalem School of Synoptic Research, and through Jerusalem Perspective Online (*www.JerusalemPerspective.com*), which publishes the results of his students' and colleagues' research.

Indeed, Robert Lindsey continues to impact the lives of countless individuals. He raised up a circle of disciples, and now they too are raising up disciples. The movement he birthed continues to expand quietly—like a small seed! Robert L. Lindsey's discoveries will force a revolution in New Testament scholarship. One day they will topple the synoptic theories now held by a majority of scholars. Generations may pass before the correctness of his approach becomes evident to the wider circle of New Testament scholars, but happily, those of us who have been trained in Lindsey's methodology can already enjoy the fruit.

Baruch dayan ha'emet! Blessed be the Faithful Judge!

David Bivin
Jerusalem, Israel
April 2004

PREFACE

One Foot in Heaven is the story of Robert L. "Bob" Lindsey's more than four decades in Palestine and Israel, most of which time he served as pastor of a Baptist Church in Jerusalem. No one loved the land of the Bible and the people of the land, including Jews, Arabs, and expatriates, more than Bob Lindsey. With strong faith and a sense of humor, he faced the challenges of wars, fire-bombing by religious radicals, and losing his left foot from an antipersonnel mine explosion while helping an Arab youth return to Israel. On an occasion when Bob was not feeling well, his son-in-law Ken Mullican remarked, "You're moving like you have one foot in the grave!" Bob replied with a grin, "No, not one foot in the grave—I have one foot in heaven!"

Bob was known and respected by countless individuals whose names do not appear on the pages of this book. Those who were selected by the authors were chosen primarily because their interaction with Bob demonstrates some aspect of Bob's character and secondarily because sufficient documentation of their relationship with Bob was available.

The researching of the book proved to be an interesting and inspiring process as the authors discovered new information about Bob's life. Attempting to accurately portray someone's life with selected moments and relationships, however, is a daunting task. He was a serious but relaxed, fun-loving but caring, disciplined but impulsive, Greek and Hebrew scholar and practical pastor, and he enjoyed interacting with people of every walk of life. His intriguing story should be enjoyed by a wide range of readers.

CHAPTER 1

NO MAN'S LAND

Shadowy figures moved silently among the war-torn buildings lining the Jordanian side of the narrow strip of no man's land separating Arab East Jerusalem from Jewish West Jerusalem. They were not far from Mandelbaum Gate, a checkpoint near the ancient, walled city. A slender American who appeared younger than his forty-four years was accompanied by a fifteen-year-old Palestinian youth. The night of September 13, 1961, was cool (due to the elevation of Jerusalem) and dry; no rain had fallen in more than five months; the autumn rains had not yet begun in the Holy Land.

As a cloud passed before the moon, the pair carefully continued picking their way among the debris. They had to be extremely careful—every sound seemed to be magnified in the night and soldiers on both sides of the border could be listening. They ducked into the shadows as the moon emerged from behind the passing cloud. The quiet was shattered by a dog barking nearby. A small child howled his displeasure and a voice shouted angrily in Arabic, *"Ouscut, ya kelb! Ouscut!"* ("Shut up, dog! Shut up!"). The muffled voices of the soldiers on the Israeli side of the checkpoint, punctuated by laughter, floated across the narrow strip. Only a little further and the pair would be able to reach a place where they could slip undetected across to the Israeli side. They were ready to proceed as soon as the moon passed behind the clouds.

Suddenly the two stiffened when they heard the clicks of weapons as a Jordanian Legionnaire patrol prepared to fire. "We've been spotted!" the American whispered in alarm to the youth. "We've got to go back! Keep low and stay close to me!" Bending as low to the ground as they could, the two retreated quickly in the direction from which they had come.

Without warning the world exploded! In spite of the intense ringing in his ears, the American heard, from seemingly far away, soldiers shouting from both sides of the border. Slowly, reality began to dawn and he realized that he had detonated one of the dozens of antipersonnel mines planted in the desolate no man's land. As his mind began to clear, his first thought was for the safety of his young charge. "Edward! Edward! Where are you?" he shouted.

"Over here, Uncle Bob! I can't see! I can't see!"

"Oh, dear God, no!" moaned Bob. Mercifully, his body's initial release of endorphins had numbed Bob's wound so that he was not yet aware of the extent of the damage to his mangled foot. He was aware, however, that he was bleeding profusely and that unless he was able to stop the bleeding, he would not be able to get them out of there. Even in their traumatized state, it was clear to the wounded pair that they were going to have to get out of the minefield themselves—no one was coming after them. It was obvious that neither the Jordanians nor the Israelis were going to venture into a minefield in the dark and they could be dead by morning. Breathing a prayer, Bob calmly removed his belt and used it as a tourniquet. He couldn't tell if it was working or not—clouds obscured the moon, and there was blood everywhere.

The Israelis, speaking Hebrew, were urging them forward, while the Jordanians, speaking Arabic, were threatening to shoot them unless they returned to the Jordanian side. Although Bob and Edward understood both Arabic and Hebrew, at first they answered neither, since they feared speaking either Arabic or Hebrew might cause the opposing side to shoot them. As Bob crawled over to Edward, he fought waves of nausea and the urge to slip into unconsciousness as the initial numbness of his wound wore off. "Edward, I'm so sorry—I'm so sorry!"

"It's ok, Uncle Bob," Edward moaned. "It's ok."

The Jordanian soldiers continued to threaten and to demand that they return to the Jordanian side. "I don't think we have any choice but to try to crawl back to Jordan," Bob concluded sadly. "There is too much chance of being shot by the Jordanians or of crawling into another mine before reaching Israel. Can you see well enough to follow me as I crawl?"

"I think so," responded Edward weakly. "I can see a little bit out of

14

one eye."

At this point Bob shouted in English, "Don't shoot! We need help!" When it was apparent that the wounded pair was turning back to Jordan, they were instructed to lie still while the Jordanians decided the best course of action. As they lay waiting for directions to crawl out of the minefield, Edward suddenly asked, "Uncle Bob?"

"Yeah, Edward?"

"How's Barbara doing?" Edward had shown more than a brotherly interest in Bob's second daughter for some time.

"Much better than we're doing at the moment, I trust," Bob responded wryly.

After what seemed to be an eternity, Jordanian soldiers began to shout directions for crawling out of the minefield. As they began to crawl, Bob's belt slipped and blood spurted from the severed arteries. He quickly secured it again, a routine he was forced to repeat several times. They then continued the painful, circuitous route toward captivity. As the Jordanian soldiers carried on a lively discussion as to the best route through the minefield, the pair crawled slowly forward, inch by inch, half expecting to hear another deafening roar, that, this time, would end it all. Finally, more than two hours after the explosion, they exited the minefield and crawled into the waiting arms of the Jordanian Legionnaires.

Bob groaned as the army truck navigated the rough, narrow streets traveling the short distance to the hospital. He hardly dared to think of the enormous, international repercussions of his impulsive attempt to return the Arab youth to the Baptist Center in the Central Sharon Plain near Petah Tikva, the only home Edward had ever really known. What effect would this incident have on Bob's wife and six children? What effect would it have on Baptist work in Israel? Would all the Baptists serving in Israel be forced to leave because of this incident, or would only he and his family have to leave? That is, if he ever got out of prison. What about the Baptists serving in Jordan? How would the incident affect them and their work? And what about Edward? Would he be blind or partially blind? A great, dark cloud of uncertainty and regret settled over Bob Lindsey as he lay in the hospital awaiting surgery on his mangled left foot. Instinctively, he desperately cried out to God, "Lord, you know my heart. Have mercy on Edward and me and those we hold dear. Somehow, Lord, bring good out of it."

CHAPTER 2
EDWARD AND UNCLE BOB

Fifteen-year-old Edward Salim Zoumout had been a ward of the George W. Truett Children's Home in Nazareth since he was eleven months old. As his Arab Christian parents fled Nazareth for Beirut in 1948 to escape the coming Arab-Jewish War, they left the baby in the care of Kate Ellen Gruver, director of the children's home. The home had been set up to care primarily for Arab children orphaned by the conflict. The children grew up calling the Baptist workers by their first name preceded by "uncle" or "aunt." To the children in the Truett Home, Bob Lindsey was, therefore, "Uncle Bob."

Because family figured so prominently in both Christian and Muslim Arab culture, orphans tended to be the focus of contempt and the butt of jokes. Therefore, the decision was made to move the children's home from the Arab city of Nazareth to a farm known as *Kfar Ha-Baptistim* (Baptist Center, literally "Village of the Baptists") near the city of Petah Tikva. The farm was surrounded by Jewish *kibbutzim* and *moshavim* (communes and cooperatives). There the orphans could have their own private school and the work on the farm offered opportunities for developing acceptance, responsibility, and character. There also would be the opportunity to experience the satisfaction of working together to care for animals and crops—the experience of being needed, of being an integral part of something important. It gave a sense of worth, a sense of family. The school later would be open to children of Baptists and others serving in Israel, as well as other children, who would board at the school.

Milton and Martha Murphey (known affectionately as "Uncle Murph" and "Aunt Marty") were in charge of the home when it moved to the Baptist Center, which everyone simply called "the farm." Initially the classes were in Arabic but later there was quite an eclectic mix in the teaching staff and curriculum. Baptists came from America for short-term and long-term service as teachers; still other teachers were recruited locally. Therefore, physics might be taught in Hebrew, world history in English, and agriculture in Arabic. The children, both orphans and boarding students, were treated as one large family. There were the usual growing pains associated with family relationships, but in spite of any shortcomings, the farm succeeded in providing a sense of belonging to other people and to a place, as well as a sense of being loved for oneself—both so vital to one's sense of well being.

Martha Murphey remembers Edward Zoumout as being:

> ...somewhat shy, although he didn't really appear so with the other home kids and boarding students. He was also somewhat of a loner—he participated in activities, but I think he was more comfortable observing from a distance. He was studious but would not have been considered a great "brain." He loved to play the piano, but not for an audience. I believe his favorite tune was "Autumn Leaves"—at least, he played it a lot and I was glad because it was one of my favorites too.

In 1956, Bob, his wife Margaret (pregnant with their sixth child), and their five children moved from Jerusalem to the farm where the Lindseys assumed leadership, while the Murpheys and their children went for a year of language study followed by a year of furlough in America. It was during this time that Edward, and the other orphans, bonded with "Uncle Bob." Bob's reaction to the strict discipline of his own childhood had resulted in a lighter approach to parenthood. This coupled with his unassuming, energetic, fun-loving, impulsive nature made him an immediate hit with the children. Fond memories of camping trips at the site of ancient ruins, singing around the campfire, fishing trips, contests, movies in the multipurpose room (affectionately know as "the playroom")—these are the legacy of the Lindseys' tenure as "parents" at the farm. Chores became fun with Uncle Bob holding the reins. For example, a favorite memory of the "home kids" is coming in from the field with the tractor pulling a wagon load of peanuts, singing "Bringing in *botnim*, bringing in *botnim*, we shall come rejoicing, bringing in *botnim*" with *botnim* (peanuts) substituted for "sheaves" in the old hymn.

Shortly before Christmas of 1960, when Edward was fifteen years old, the Murpheys received a letter from Edward's father, who was now living in Salt, Jordan, a city located east of the Jordan River about fifteen kilometers northwest of Amman. He requested that Edward, whom he had not seen since he was eleven months old, be permitted to visit him at the Christmas season. They also received a letter from the Cannon of St. George's Anglican Church in East Jerusalem, vouching for the character of Edward's father. After considerable discussion and soul searching, the Murpheys agreed to the visit because of their sympathy with Edward's biological parents' desire to be reunited with their son and because of the potential emotional benefit for Edward. Noteworthy is the fact that when the paperwork was finished and the plans were made, Edward still had no desire to visit his father since he had no memory of him. With encouragement, however, he finally consented to go.

At the season of the Eastern Orthodox Christmas, on Friday, January 6, 1961, Margaret Lindsey, the Murpheys, and Dale and Anita Thorne (teachers at the school) accompanied a somewhat apprehensive Edward Zoumout through Mandelbaum Gate to meet his father. Murph had purchased fresh fish for Edward to take as a gift to his father, thinking fresh fish would be a welcome treat. (Edward later related his disgust at his father's procrastination that resulted in the fish spoiling before they could be cooked.) When they had crossed to the Jordanian side, they proceeded to Christ Church Hostel in the Old City. From there they telephoned Edward's father who came to Jerusalem to pick up Edward. When he arrived, Mr. Zoumout seemed excited to meet his son, but Edward remained somewhat reserved.

Since the authorities required the visitors to leave before the expiration of their three day visa, arrangements were carefully agreed upon to meet back at Christ Church Hostel at 5:00 P.M. on Sunday. Margaret and her colleagues occupied their time shopping and site-seeing, including a visit to the ancient city of Petra east of the Jordan River.

When Edward and his father failed to appear at the agreed upon time, the party was frantic. Hadn't Edward's father repeatedly assured them of his reliability and promised to return with Edward at the appointed time? Perhaps he truly was returning with Edward but had been unavoidably delayed? Perhaps there had been an accident? Perhaps he never intended to return at all? At last they went to Mandelbaum Gate where they waited. Finally, they called the pastor at St. George's, telling him that Edward still hadn't come and that they had to cross over into Israel at 8:00 P.M. They asked the pastor to contact Mr. Zoumout and see what he could do to help Edward return to Israel. Unknown to the Baptist workers or to Edward, Mr. Zoumout had secured a document from the Jordanian government giving his son permission to remain with him in Jordan. Indeed, he never had intended to return with Edward.

Although extremely anxious about Edward's well being and reluctant to return to Israel without him, they concluded that they had no other choice. A visa could not be extended simply because a member of the party did not show up in time—whether it involved a family member or not. If they did not leave before the deadline, they would be in Jordan illegally and would be subject to arrest. At best, they would be barred from future visits to the country. With their minds swirling with unanswered questions and their hearts heavy with worry, the party crossed back into Israel as their visas expired.

After they returned home, the Murpheys discovered that Edward had confided in some of the other children that he feared that his father would not permit him to return. About a week later the Murpheys received a letter from Edward that was delivered by a Catholic priest crossing into Israel from Jordan. (There was no direct mail or telephone service between Israel and Jordan at that time.) In writing about receiving the letter, Martha Murphey stated, "…it about broke our heart. It started out by saying, 'Dear Mother and Father,' and all through the letter he said, 'Get me back to Israel,' and told about how his father had lied to us as he had had no intention of bringing him back to us."

Edward wrote that when the time had come to return to Israel, his father had refused him permission. He also had discovered that his mother was in a mental institution. When his father threatened him with a knife during a dispute, he ran away to Jerusalem and was taken in at a French Catholic School. Although they treated him kindly, he was extremely unhappy because he so missed the children and adults at the farm who were the only family he had ever known.

The situation in which Edward Zoumout found himself was troubling to all those connected with the farm, but particularly so to Bob Lindsey even though the Lindseys were now living in Tiberias. Immediately, Bob and others began to explore every avenue available to secure the return of Edward to the farm. In a letter of March 17, 1961, Martha Murphey wrote about Edward's situation.

> We haven't gotten Edward back yet. We are trying to contact a lawyer on the other side to take care of things so that we will be able to bring him back with us when we go to Jordan at Easter (2nd Easter, Greek Orthodox). He says that he gets so disgusted with the boys in the school there. They curse all the time and he says that he sure is glad that he has had the training that he has had. He says the boy that he sits with in class never brushes his teeth and he can't stand to smell his breath. It is so funny to hear Edward talk like this for we always had a hard time getting him to take a bath and to brush his teeth and to be tidy. He also cursed up till the time he accepted the Lord before leaving here. We are praying that this will all turn out well in the end, but right now Edward plus all the kids here are learning a very worthwhile lesson. He wrote not to send him anything but his Bible. I think that he is being tested in his faith by the Catholic fathers. (His father has abandoned him and, thanks to Father Patrick, he is in a Friars' School there.)

Since Christians were permitted to cross over into Jordan during the season of Easter as well as at Christmas, Dale and Anita Thorne, along with two other couples, crossed over on Friday April 20, 1962, during the celebration of Easter by the Western Church. The Thornes first met with a Jordanian lawyer who was related to one of the teachers at the Baptist School in Nazareth. The lawyer then took them to the Catholic School where Edward had been staying. They at first denied knowing him, but finally they admitted that he had been there but had been picked up by the police for some reason. He was now in prison at the Citadel (commonly known as "the Tower of David") by Jaffa Gate in the Old City. The lawyer knew the prison warden who permitted them to visit Edward for a short time and to give him his Bible and some letters they had brought with them.

A week later, at the Eastern Orthodox Easter, Bob Lindsey and Milton and Martha Murphey crossed into Jordan through Mandelbaum Gate and traveled to Salt to visit Edward's father. By this time, Edward had been released from prison (after eighteen days there) and had returned to the Catholic school where he worked in the dining hall. They discussed the matter at length with Mr. Zoumout, asking that he give his son permission to return to the children's home, but he adamantly refused. They then conferred with the Jordanian lawyer that had assisted the Thornes in visiting Edward. The lawyer filed a petition with the court on behalf of Edward and the home. Although the home was Edward's legal guardian, the Jordanian authorities failed to rule favorably on the petition that would grant him the right to return to Israel. Under Palestinian law, a parent could reclaim a child at any time, no matter what documents he or she may have signed transferring custody of the child. Evidently, the Jordanian court still interpreted the law as valid. There was no consideration of the fact that Edward had experienced no contact with his parents since he was eleven months of age. Nor was consideration given to the fact that, to Edward, the orphans and caregivers at the farm were his only real family.

In writing of Edward's situation, Margaret Lindsey later recalled:

> We tried everything under the sun to get him back, but in vain. Finally a Catholic priest who had the privilege of going back and forth began bringing letters and we realized what a terrible time the boy was having. His father tried to exploit him in the most horrible ways, beat him constantly and threatened his life. Finally, the Catholics took him into a school of theirs [where he lived, studied, and was employed in the school restaurant] but he was miserable and kept writing these heartbreaking letters. The school year was starting and the Catholics, not having any real responsibility for him, said he couldn't continue, so he had no refuge from his father in view.

Margaret also later recalled a significant conversation with Bob about Edward, who had become like a son to them. One evening, after reading a letter from Edward pleading for their help in getting him back home to the farm, Bob mused, "People are always smuggling things back and forth across the border. If someone would show Edward how, he could slip over the border himself—or someone could smuggle him out."

Chapter 3

Missing

Margaret Lindsey was serving breakfast to her three younger children, Danny, Robert, and Debbie at their rented home in Tiberias overlooking Lake Kinneret (Sea of Galilee). Her three older children, David, Lenore, and Barbara, were boarding students at the farm. The morning routine was interrupted by a knock on the door. It was someone delivering a telegram from Frank Hooper, a Baptist colleague in Jerusalem:

BOB'S CAR FOUND NEAR NO MAN'S LAND
CALL FRANK

Since the Lindseys had no telephone, Margaret quickly went to the nearby Scottish Hospital to use their telephone. When she got Frank on the line, the first thing he said was, "Do you know where Bob is?"

Margaret replied, "I thought he was with you."

Frank replied, "I don't know where Bob is either. He never showed up for our executive committee meeting. But his friend Elie, the painter, spotted Bob's car parked in Musrara near Mandelbaum Gate with the keys still in it."

Immediately, Margaret recalled Bob's earlier comment that someone should smuggle Edward out of Jordan. "I'll bet anything that he went over to get Edward," she told Frank.

Bob had left Tiberias the previous day for a two-day trip that would end in Jerusalem with an executive committee meeting of the United Christian Council in Israel (UCCI). He first drove by the farm and visited his three older children. Continuing on to Netanya on the Mediterranean coast, he visited some Baptist colleagues in Hebrew language study. Elizabeth (Betty) Smith recalls:

Ours was one of the homes Bob visited in Netanya that day. We had returned from our first furlough and moved from Jerusalem to be near a good Hebrew study center. We were at last free to study Hebrew at Ulpan Akiva along with the new couples, the Reeds [Marcus and Ruth] and the Laniers [Chandler and Sallie]. Bob occasionally dropped in unannounced but never left without personal words of encouragement to "hang in there" and conquer the language as the only way to enjoy the Land and to feel satisfaction in ministering to the people. As the months went by, Bob often gathered the six Hebrew students and gave us his impromptu lessons using vocabulary he knew we would need as Baptist representatives — words and phrases that we would not ever get in an ulpan class. He was a stimulating teacher.

In Netanya he met with the three couples and taught one of his supplementary Hebrew language sessions. After encouraging them to keep up the good work, he spent the night with the Laniers. Following a restless night in which he didn't sleep well because of his preoccupation with the Edward Zoumout dilemma, he arose early without his disturbing his hosts. As far as the Laniers knew, Bob was heading to Jerusalem for an executive committee meeting of the UCCI. It was later learned, however, that he left Netanya and drove north along the coast to Haifa where he met Anson and Pat Rainey who were spending the night in the Baptist apartment there. Anson, a Ph.D. candidate from Brandeis University, had completed a year at the Hebrew University in Jerusalem as a special student in archaeology and ancient languages. Bob and Anson had met at Brandeis prior to Anson's coming to Israel for study. Bob had been impressed with the young graduate student and, when Anson had arrived in Israel, Bob had enlisted him to assist in his synoptic gospel research. Long before the day of computers, Anson laboriously color-coded key words and phrases in Matthew, Mark, and Luke in a copy of Huck's Synopsis. The Raineys were now returning to the United States where Anson would complete his studies at Brandeis. They had breakfast together and then Bob drove them to the port before leaving for Jerusalem.

Within the hour, Herman and June Petty arrived from Nazareth to take Margaret and the three younger children to Baptist Village as the search for Bob continued. When Margaret and the Pettys entered the "playroom" at the farm, several colleagues and friends were waiting. There Margaret learned that the first clue of Bob's whereabouts had come that morning from an Arabic radio newscast and Arabic newspaper report in East Jerusalem. Both reported that an American minister and an Arab boy had been injured in the early morning hours in an antipersonnel mine explosion in no man's land between East and West Jerusalem. Everyone assumed that it was Bob and Edward who had been injured in the blast, but no one knew the extent of their injuries.

Margaret left Danny and Robert at the farm with the three older Lindsey children, while the Pettys drove her and Debbie to the Hooper's house in Jerusalem. On the ride to Jerusalem, as her mind raced with a thousand unanswered questions, she felt a strange sense of comfort as she recalled her unusual encounter of the previous evening. With Bob out of town, she had put the three younger children to bed and was feeling restless. The weather was very hot and she had bursitis pain in one shoulder, she was feeling lonely and somewhat discouraged, and she was thinking about Edward. She decided to go out on the upstairs veranda and sleep where it was cooler since the veranda faced the lake and caught any breeze that might come from over the water. Feeling very much in need of divine intervention, she said simply, "Lord, this pain in my shoulder needs help." Although the night was pitch black, suddenly there appeared a beautiful sparkling light over the lake, and she could see all the way across to the opposite shore. Gradually, the luminescence faded and disappeared, but she continued to feel strongly the loving presence of the Lord giving her strength and peace. She slept well the rest of the night, not knowing how much she was going to need that strength and peace in the coming days and weeks.

In the meantime, Lucian Kinsolving, American Consul in Jerusalem, Jordan, visited Bob and Edward who were under guard in the hospital. He then relayed information to A. B. Casoli, American Consul in Jerusalem, Israel, less than a mile away. Margaret and her friends learned from the consulate that Bob had lost a foot and that Edward's eyes were injured, but that their lives were not in danger. Margaret immediately applied for a permit to cross to East Jerusalem to visit

Bob.

During the anxious period of waiting, she occupied herself with caring for Debbie and in praying for Bob and Edward. But she also had a lot of time to think—to wonder what the future held for the family and for the work in Israel and Jordan. And she also had time to remember—to gently caress the memories of that serious but relaxed, fun-loving but caring, disciplined but impulsive young man with the ready smile with whom she had fallen so helplessly, hopelessly in love more than two decades before.

CHAPTER 4

THE MAN I WILL MARRY

Yokahama, Japan, was bustling with activity as two young Americans stood in the long line in the American Express office. They had never met and they had no way of knowing that there was converging upon them at that very moment a rare, singular, and providential episode of life, to which everything that happened in the future would be directly related. All the ingredients were present: August 15, 1940; Yokahama, Japan; the American Express office; and their being in that particular line.

One of the players in this life drama was Bob Lindsey from Norman, Oklahoma. Within a month after graduating from the University of Oklahoma with a BA in Classical Greek, he arrived in Palestine with the goal of learning to speak and read Modern Hebrew. He carried with him letters of introduction from W. B. Bizzell, President of the University of Oklahoma and from Josh Lee, United States Senator from Oklahoma. President Bizzell's letter, on official letterhead stationary complete with ribbons and an embossed seal of the university is indicative of the high esteem with which Bob was held by many in his home town:

January 18, 1939

To Whom It May Concern:

This letter will serve to introduce Mr. Robert L. Lindsey, a student in the University of Oklahoma, who is visiting your country. I know Mr. Lindsey well and regard him very highly. He is the son of the comptroller of the University of Oklahoma, and one of the finest young men whom I know.

Mr. Lindsey is a young man of the highest character and he is worthy of every confidence that may be imposed in him. Any courtesy extended to him will be greatly appreciated by me.

Very sincerely yours,
(Signed)
W. B. Bizzell, President

Soon after his arrival in Jerusalem, Bob made arrangements for lodging with a Jewish Christian family of Orthodox Jewish background, Zebulon and Ruth Weinstock. "Zeb" had come to Palestine from Hungary as an infant; Ruth was too young at the time to remember her immigration from Egypt. Bob ate at their table and slept on a couch in the room that served both as their living and dining room. Their beautiful three-year-old daughter, Aviva, was a *sabra* (literally, "prickly pear cactus"; a term used in Hebrew to describe one born in Palestine, later in the state of Israel—prickly on the outside but sweet inside—as is the cactus fruit). The Weinstocks opened to Bob their hearts as well as their home and soon were like his parents and little sister.

Living with the Weinstocks was a great asset to his Hebrew language studies. The family spoke Hebrew and only Zeb spoke a little English. When Bob enrolled in Hebrew language classes at the Hebrew University, Zeb enthusiastically helped him with the language in the evening. During the day, when he was not in class or studying, Bob practiced his Hebrew with the neighbors and in local markets and shops. His curiosity as well as his genuine interest in people rendered him fearless in making conversation with strangers. In addition to Hebrew, he studied archaeology, topography, and Hebrew Bible.

He wrote of his experience of living with the Weinstocks:

I particularly felt I must learn Hebrew as it was the tongue being spoken by all the youth of Jewish Palestine, and it was the mother tongue of both of these people [the Weinstocks]. The experience of living in Jerusalem proved fruitful in many ways but in none more than that I came to know what were the difficulties and problems of the average Jewish Christian firsthand. My sympathies with such people made me feel I should dedicate my life to this land.

This handsome young man of slender build and ready smile quickly endeared himself to Jews, Arabs, and expatriates as well. As he wandered the streets, shops, and markets of Jerusalem, he compiled his own list of words and phrases, studied syntax, and worked hard at pronouncing sounds not used in English. It was always a special joy to hear little Aviva's greeting when he returned to the apartment. As Bob entered, she would shout, *"Henay Bob!"* which meant literally, "Behold Bob!" or "Here is Bob!" Thus, he very quickly learned this common biblical word, "behold." When he felt sufficiently confident with spoken Hebrew, Bob left the Weinstock's home for three months to work at Kibbutz Ginegar, south of Nazareth. By the time of his departure, Bob could read, write, and speak Hebrew quite well.

Bob enjoyed exploring Jerusalem and the surrounding villages on his bicycle. Because of the tension between Arabs and Jews, however, when he visited an Arab area he normally wore the typical Arab headdress, the *kafiya*. He considered that his most valuable experiences were the many hours he spent talking with Jewish and Arab youth. He put tremendous effort into learning what they thought about the issues of life, culture and religion.

These were turbulent times in Palestine. On one occasion Bob cringed when he saw the bodies of two British soldiers killed by an explosion in front of the Baptist Chapel on Henrietta Szold Street where he attended church services. He never learned whether the explosion was intended for the soldiers or for Jews. (The Baptist Chapel was located in the Jewish section of West Jerusalem.) The British had been attempting to maintain peace while governing Palestine under a mandate from the League of Nations following World War I. Under pressure from oil-producing Arab states, Britain had issued the so-called White Paper, limiting Jewish immigration to Palestine. Thus, the flood of Jewish immigrants from Europe to Palestine during the early thirties nearly dried up after May of 1939.

The Jews of Palestine viewed the British action as turning the Jewish National Homeland into a ghetto with locked doors under Arab rule. The Jewish *Haganah* (defense force) was organized to protect Jewish settlements from attack by Arabs, but in order to bring about change, some factions were also prepared to attack telephone lines, railroads, and British government installations. In addition, the Arabs had their own nationalistic aspirations, so they likewise chafed under British occupation.

When it was time for him to return to the United States, Bob, at the urging of a travel agent in Jerusalem, elected to take an alternative route through the Far East. Because of the war in Europe, travel through the Mediterranean and Atlantic was considered extremely dangerous. When Germany annexed Austria and Czechoslovakia and marched on Poland, Great Britain and France declared war on Germany. Hitler's forces invaded France, Belgium, and the Netherlands, and Italy entered the war on the side of Germany. Thus, world events prompted a decision that would provide a memorable conclusion to Bob's sixteen-month adventure in Palestine and set in motion a chain of events that he would cherish the rest of his life.

Leaving Palestine, Bob traveled through Syria and Iraq to the Persian Gulf. There he took a ship through the Straits of Hormuz and across the Arabian Sea to India where he spent a couple of weeks. From India he sailed to Singapore, Hong Kong, and finally to Yokahama. There he planned to book passage on the Japanese steamer *S.S. Heian Maru*, scheduled to sail for Seattle on August 17. Upon his arrival in Yokahama, he went to the American Express office to pick up any letters or telegrams and stood in line waiting his turn.

Without his being aware, a petite twenty-one-year-old American girl named Margaret Lutz was standing behind him. She was not superstitious and normally did not have premonitions, but as she looked at the back of Bob's head, she had a premonition: "This young man is the one I will marry." She quickly tried to dismiss this ridiculous idea, but as he finished his business and turned to walk away, she found herself looking up into the striking hazel eyes of a travel-worn young man. He was wearing a pith sun helmet and she thought he must have come from India or some such place. He smiled, and then walked out—and she thought, "Well, that's that." But a few minutes later, he walked in again and stood inside the door, looking a little puzzled. As she finished her business at the counter and went to join her mother and the others in her party, she noticed he was standing near her mother.

"Excuse me," she heard him say in his Oklahoma accent, "but I understood you to say something about Korea. I am interested in the situation there, and would like to know something more about it." With that he introduced himself to Margaret's mother, Lenore Lutz, and she in turn, introduced him to Margaret and the rest of the party.

Bob's first impression of Margaret was that "she looked silly" because she was wearing a fancy hat and lipstick. He was used to the girls in Palestine who, at that time, did not wear makeup. Margaret's impression of Bob, on the other hand, was that he was quite handsome. But his first impression was soon eclipsed by his fascination with her unique personality and depth of character, coupled with her beauty.

In the conversation that followed, they realized that they both planned to sail on the same ship to America in two days. Bob was waiting for his father to wire money for the voyage. Prior to the ship's sailing, Mrs. Lutz and her party planned to go on an outing to Nikko where they would meet some friends. Bob, on the other hand, planned to spend some time in Tokyo.

While waiting at the station for the train, one of Margaret's girl friends whispered to her, "Seems like an interesting person, doesn't he? I hope he manages to get on our boat."

Annoyed at the confusing emotions welling up within her, Margaret replied casually, "Oh, I guess he's all right."

They sat near each other on the train to Tokyo and easily fell into conversation. As they pulled into the station where Bob planned to get off, they sat silently looking at each other. Finally Margaret said, "Well—"

Bob shifted awkwardly in his seat as he quickly glanced out the window and said, "Well—"

After a slight hesitation, she ventured, "If you'd like to come with us to Nikko—?" But by that time the train had pulled out of the Tokyo station and they were on their way to Nikko. The more she tried to dismiss the premonition she had experienced in line at the American Express office, the more she found herself becoming interested in this young Oklahoman.

CHAPTER 5

NIKKO THE BEAUTIFUL

When the party changed trains on the way to Nikko, there was a breathtaking moment when Margaret thought she would never see Bob again. Bob stopped to buy a ticket while the others, already having their tickets, ran to catch the train as it was about to pull out of the station. The entire party was securely seated on the train for several minutes, and with every strange Japanese announcement, she was sure the train would leave without him. She kept saying to herself, "If he would only get here—if he would only come on!" Frantically stepping out onto the platform to see if he was coming, she succeeded only in losing her seat to a rather large Japanese man in a *kimono*.

Bob did board the train as it was leaving the station. The ninety-mile train ride through the afternoon offered an opportunity for the two young people to become better acquainted. Above the roar of the electric train, the clack-clack of wooden-soled shoes, and the staccato tones of Japanese conversation, they shared life experiences. They learned how much they had in common, even though they were of different church affiliations and had been reared in different countries.

Bob learned that Margaret's parents were Presbyterians serving in Pyongyang, Korea. Her father, Dexter Lutz, with a Ph.D. in agriculture, did not preach *per se*, but taught in Korean mission schools and gave personal witness in rural churches. His main work, however, was in helping the farmers to raise better crops. He taught improved methods of fertilization, introduced apple growing, introduced a short season variety of potatoes that could be grown as a second crop after the rice was harvested, and also published a farmer's journal. Mrs. Lutz taught voice at the mission school and was responsible for numerous musical productions. In later years she would be renowned for her work with a Korean blind children's choir.

Margaret had come home to Korea from college for the summer where she had enjoyed a good vacation with family and friends. A highlight of the summer had been a trip to Peking (now Beijing), China. She was returning to the United States for her senior year at Beaver College in Philadelphia. Her mother and sister Betty had come as far as Yokahama in order to spend more time with her, see her off, and then to return to their home in Pyongyang. After graduating from college, she planned further study and then to enter some sort of church-related work.

Margaret learned that his full name was Robert Lisle Lindsey, but everyone called him "Bob." He was born on August 16, 1917 in Norman, Oklahoma, to Josiah Lawrence Lindsey and Elsie Lisle Lindsey. His father, known as "J. L." or "Judge," had been the comptroller of the University of Oklahoma since 1911 when he assumed the position at 29 years of age (a position he would hold for thirty-six years). When Bob was two, his sister (and only sibling), Mary Virginia, was born. J. L. and several friends bought some land west of the university that they developed for new residences. When the planning commission mapped the streets, the main east-west thoroughfare for the area, Lindsey Avenue, was named in honor of J. L. Lindsey.

She also learned that after graduation from the University of Oklahoma he had gone to Palestine to study Hebrew and that he was on his way back to the United States to enter a Baptist seminary and planned to become a minister.

Of such was the conversation as the train roared its way through the picturesque countryside, although the new acquaintances seemed only vaguely aware of anything other than each other. Margaret seemed to want to absorb everything he had to share and to share her life experiences with him as well. He felt strangely comfortable as they talked. She seemed different from the other girls he had known. She was quite determined to be her own person—and he liked that! On the other hand, she had tried unsuccessfully, to convince herself that there was no such thing as "love at first sight."

The village of Nikko was absolutely beautiful. *Kikko* in the

Japanese language means "beautiful," and the Japanese had a saying that "one cannot say *kikko* until one has seen *Nikko."* Arriving at the hotel too late for dinner, the party dined on tea and fruit. As they were eating, Bob confided to the Lutzes that he had a problem. He had expected his father to wire him money to pay for the voyage to America, but it had not yet arrived. Personal checks were not accepted (and credit cards did not yet exist). Margaret and her mother did not have the money, but knew others in their party that might have it to lend and promised to ask their friends.

A little before midnight, the Lutzes went upstairs to their room. Bob was too excited to sleep so he walked out into the garden. Before retiring to bed, Margaret wrote in her diary: "Met Bob Lindsey who attached to the party, and we stuck together a bit."

The Lutzes and their party had not been upstairs long when the thin paper walls, doors, and windows of the hotel began to rustle strangely. All the guests ran out into the hall, some pulling on dressing gowns. Everyone was chattering excitedly and clinging to each other, as a second tremor shook the building. The floor and walls swayed and, for a few moments, everyone entertained only visions of being buried under an avalanche of debris. And then suddenly it stopped. There was such silence and absolute calm that it was difficult to believe that there had been an earthquake.

The calm was shattered by Bob Lindsey bounding up the stairs three at a time. "What an earthquake! How did it feel up here? I was outside and at first I thought it was the sound of a thousand doves taking flight! I've never been in an earthquake before and the tremor ceased before I could realize what had happened. Then when the second tremor occurred, I realized the same fluttering noise I had heard earlier was coming from the paper in the windows! Now there's a full moon outside and it's perfectly gorgeous!" No one felt like sleeping at that point, so everyone filed outside into the garden.

It was like a dream outside the hotel in the moonlight. No sign of any sort of disturbance was evident. The hotel with its delightful Japanese architecture seemed almost a part of the wooded mountains that rose behind it. The air was perfumed with the fragrance of pine trees. They could hear the falls splashing nearby, and could barely make out the outline of the famous Red Lacquer Bridge.

When someone noticed that the time was now midnight, Bob

volunteered that it was now August 16 and this was his twenty-third birthday. Impulsively, although feeling rather foolish, Margaret led the group in singing "Happy Birthday" to him. As the others went back inside, Bob and Margaret lingered beside a picturesque lily pool cut into the stone, illuminated only by the moonlight and the filtered light coming from the papered windows of the hotel. They seemed to have so much to talk about and, as they walked about the garden, they discovered a path going up the mountain. It was a crazy idea, but the adventurous duo decided that they would climb to the top.

The night was bathed in moonlight that illumined the soft mist as they climbed higher up the mountain. Their shoes and socks soon were soaked from the heavy dew on the tall grass hanging over the trail. Like all mountains, it proved to be higher than either of them had suspected. Far below they could see the twinkling lights of a village. By the time they reached the top they had lost not only the trail but also all concept of time. They walked, lost in conversation, attempting to discover past experiences and future dreams, each of the other.

Little did they dream of the commotion that their adventure had caused back at the hotel. After all the others had gone back inside, the clerk had asked Mrs. Lutz, "Your party all in, madam?"

"Why no," she said, "Two of them are still out. They went for a walk."

"Very bad, very bad—must come back!"

"Why? What's the matter?" she asked, puzzled.

"Must go get them! Crown Prince here in villa, across river! Very bad for American to be out! Might walk over there! Many soldiers!" he explained excitedly in broken English. It was indeed dangerous for Americans to be out walking at night since there was such national tension between America and Japan. "Must find them! Must call police!" he persisted.

But neither the police nor one of the men from their party was successful in finding the carefree pair and so the search eventually was called off. When the climbers decided to return to the hotel, they discovered that the heavy mist had made everything cold and damp. Having lost the trail that they had followed on the way up, they now slid down rocks and steep banks, hanging onto branches and bushes, too out of breath in the scramble to talk much. They also were never quite sure whether in the next instant they might step off a precipice. Bob led the way and Margaret trailed along, trying to keep her footing in the slippery darkness.

The trip down the mountain was much quicker than the trip up, but upon reaching the bottom they discovered that the hotel was not where it should be—they had descended the side of the mountain opposite from their ascent. Making their way around the base of the small mountain, it was nearly 4:00 A.M. when they arrived back at the hotel. From the terrace they could see two figures standing in the lighted doorway: Margaret's mother and Dr. McAnlis, a dentist who served in Korea with the Lutzes. Mrs. Lutz was in tears. "Oh, here you are at last!" she sobbed. "We were so afraid! Didn't you know it was dangerous?"

Bob's heart sank within him! What would a mother think of a young man she had just met taking her daughter out to wander for four hours on a mountain? Dr. McAnlis was quite angry, but to Bob's surprise, Mrs. Lutz was more relieved than angry and even apologized for having been so worried!

Realizing the disturbance they had caused, they both apologized profusely—but could hardly feel sorry for something that had been so meaningful.

When she got back to her room, Margaret wrote again in her diary about the earthquake and about their night walk. She concluded with: "We had a wonderful talk—he is so spiritual. Best was his singing some songs in Hebrew."

Chapter 6

A Shipboard Romance

When they returned to Yokahama, they learned that the money for which Bob was waiting had not come. So Mrs. Lutz asked among her friends and found sufficient money to loan Bob for the voyage. But there was still the problem of exchanging the local currency, since the ticket could only be purchased in U.S. or Canadian dollars. All morning they went from bank to bank, but the answer was the same, "No American money—try some other place." At noon, Margaret returned to the American Express office and told Bob of their failure to get the money exchanged. She appealed to the sympathetic clerk who suggested that a certain Canadian man, who was to arrive at one o'clock, might be able to help. The ship was scheduled to sail at 3:00 P.M. so the Canadian was their last possible hope. Margaret reluctantly prepared to sail with her friends, praying that Bob would be able to sail with them.

The Canadian arrived precisely at 1:00 P.M. and agreed to make the exchange. Bob then rushed off to the steamship office to purchase his ticket. With no minutes to spare, he arrived on board as the cry, "All ashore!" was given. He quickly took some movies of Margaret saying good-by to her mother and sister Betty as they prepared to disembark.

Colorful streamers stretched from ship to shore and music played as Bob and Margaret joined the throng at the rail. "Good-by! Good-by" they called and waved as the Japanese ocean liner *S.S. Heian Maru* was tugged from the pier. They continued waving until they were exhausted. Silently gazing at the shrinking shoreline, they pondered the recent events and the Providence that had placed them side by side at the ship's railing. Whatever the future held, they had learned that one thing they both possessed was a willingness to be daring and impulsive. If they did have a future together, it promised to be anything but dull!

Her late night diary entries chronicle the beginning of the shipboard romance:

> August 17, 1940.
> Sailing date! From this utterly perfect trip God has been so good to me that I can hardly contain it. We nearly didn't get enough money to get Bob on the boat, but we did. Did some shopping and sailed. Bob took movies of us. We were late on deck in the moonlight.
>
> August 18, 1940.
> This morning we had a service on board with Mr. Henderson preaching and Bob leading the singing and me playing the piano. Then Bob wanted to have a young people's meeting tonight, but there's no cooperation from the kids and definite antipathy against him— crazy!!!
>
> August 19, 1940.
> Last night we talked clear up on the very front of the boat where it was thrilling. Bob made things come alive on the boat and had practically everyone out doing the Hora with his accordion. It is danced in circles, lines and chains and is full of jumps and everyone claps. It was loads of fun. In the evening we listened to music in 1st class.

(This was in spite of the fact that they both held tourist class tickets.) The same day she wrote to her family in Korea:

> Today, in the afternoon things suddenly came to life on the boat and Bob did it. I don't know how but suddenly the whole bunch of college kids and a few younger, and the boat is crowded with them, were on deck doing a Jewish folk dance. We had more fun, and he managed the whole thing—everyone did what he said,

and after several hours of it (!!) when we had done a lot of different kinds of folk dancing, they were ready to eat out of his hand. What a leader he is!

Fran said to me later, "You know, I didn't like Bob a bit at first, but now I think he's perfectly swell. I guess he's the kind that grows on you." He really has an amazing ability for leadership and making friends! He played his accordion for all of it. We did the Virginia Reel, too. All the older people and the officers were out on deck watching the proceedings!

Tonight Bob and I went up to First Class Lounge where an awfully nice man was playing classical music on the electric vic. We sat and listened an hour—it was wonderful, and then down for part of the movies—which was a bunch of newsreels mostly.

Then we got our Bibles and his Hebrew O.T. and found ourselves a corner and had a marvelous study of Psalm 46 for about an hour. He makes so much come to life that I couldn't see before, partly because of using the Hebrew directly. Must go to bed now—my eyes are bloodshot. Love you all so much.

Four days into the voyage, the evening of August 20, they realized that they were in love. She confided in her diary:

Tonight Bob told me he loved me. Somehow I don't want to spoil that shining hour by ever thinking of another thing. I'm so happy but so bewildered by it all that I hardly know whether I love him or not. It knocked me off my feet, but he was so wonderful and something began to happen—to grow that minute—it all seems so right—so completely from God.

Before they reached Seattle, Bob and Margaret talked of marriage, but told no one. (Margaret also chose not to tell Bob about her premonition at the American Express office.) They decided that Margaret would complete her last year of college, while Bob would start his studies at Southern Baptist Seminary in Louisville, Kentucky. They would marry in the summer following completion of the school year.

As they stood at the rail while the tugs maneuvered the ship up to the pier in Seattle, Margaret felt considerable apprehension as she thought of meeting Bob's family. Bob also prepared himself to introduce Margaret to his parents, knowing well that his mother had already picked out a local Norman girl for him to marry.

Bob's parents, J.L. and Elsie, and his sister Mary Virginia took the family car to Seattle to welcome Bob back. On the way Mary Virginia jokingly said to her parents, "I'll bet Bob will have found a Jewish girl and brought her back." The Lindseys now stood among the swarming crowd of people on the pier and tried to catch a glimpse of Bob at the ship's rail high above them. When they did locate each other and waved, the Lindsey family was quite surprised to see dark-eyed, dark-haired Margaret, who was standing beside Bob, and waving also. Smiling smugly, Mary Virginia said to her parents, "I told you—see that Jewish girl with Bob?"

CHAPTER 7

MEETING THE FAMILY

From the railroad station in Oklahoma City on September 3, 1940, Margaret began a letter to her family in Pyongyang about the trip back to Oklahoma with Bob and his family and about spending a few days in their home. From Oklahoma she would travel by train to Philadelphia to complete her senior year at Beaver College.

> Being with Bob is a great adventure. He does the most amazing things—like going places he's never been, and making friends, meeting people without the slightest hesitation, and always there's something marvelous coming out of it. I'm learning so much. I realize how much I've missed in life by being reserved and self-conscious. We're a perfect pair—I hold him down a bit which is good because he tends to be too forward, but he gets me into places where I ought to be but where my nature rebels at pushing in!
>
> I was quite a shock to his family and knowing his mother now, I understand why we've got to go slow in letting them know how serious it is. Bob has told his preacher (Edgar Hallock) and Edgar, Jr. (his best friend, the preacher's son), but I imagine his family will be about the last to know!
>
> Anyhow, they were very glad to have me drive back with them. As a surprise to Bob they had a lovely big, new Buick, bought before the trip. Complete with radio, cooling & heating system and all you could want.
>
> By the way, everybody got paid back immediately the money that Bob borrowed for his ticket so that all turned out ok.

Since Margaret had previously arranged for her baggage to be transferred from the ship and go by rail to Philadelphia, she was unable to retrieve it when she changed her plans and went by car to Oklahoma. Regarding the matter she wrote:

> I had the little zipper bag with me, for which I've been glad. It's been swell not to have baggage, even though I did have to wear Mary's clothes once in a while. We're exactly the same size and she's about 3 months younger than I am. She has lovely red hair and is good looking, dresses beautifully and belongs to the most outstanding sorority on the campus of Okla. U. She is entirely different from Bob. She's quite defiant in her attitude toward his kind of Christianity. I had some pretty good talks with her about it all. I think it would be best if her mother would let her go to a different church, maybe another denomination, at least where Bob isn't so active and so beloved. However, no one can tell Mrs. Lindsey anything. She's so autocratic.
>
> Mary & I got started talking when in Portland, our first stop. We stopped at an auto camp, left Mr. & Mrs. Lindsey there and we three went into a big hotel where Bob had arranged to meet a group of his friends who had been in the original group that he went to Palestine with.
>
> We let him out and Mary and I drove around hunting for a place to park. We got to talking and drove for about an hour before we went in. Mary immediately asked me if I'd mind if she'd smoke. Of course I said no, that I was used to it, but even so my own attitude toward smoking, etc. had changed somewhat this summer. She said Bob and her mother didn't know she did. She said that her mother used to say she wouldn't have her in the house or family if she did, so, hers being a rebellious nature, she immediately wanted to. Some parents are so foolish. Mary's

really a swell girl and I like her loads, only she is completely different from Bob. She and Bob have a nice relationship. They're each very tolerant of the other. Mary has a redheaded temper though.

Mrs. Lindsey has a heart of gold and she'd do anything for anyone, but in order to get along with her it has to be understood that she's boss and that she's always right. She'll get on the warpath and rave. She won't mean half of what she says, but it's sure hard to take. She isn't well and is awfully nervous. Mother, I have to laugh when I think how perfectly swell and sweet you were that nite at Nikko. Mrs. Lindsey would have had everyone in the hotel up and she would have laid us out so when we got in that you would have heard her all over the building. I'm still sorry as can be when I think how we worried you. I appreciate you even more if possible after knowing her. Yet she's swell underneath and I can't help liking her a lot in spite of her. She'd mother anyone, but she wants to do it her way.

Mr. Lindsey is a shining example of loving patience. He's a peach. Strong, quiet, humorous, and kind of soothingly tolerant of Mrs. Lindsey. He lets "Mother" have her way, or at least lets her think so!

When Bob took me by Mary's sorority house to pick her up, he honked and then called up, asking for Mary in a very English accent, sounding perfectly ridiculous. We heard about 10 girls go into hysterics and Mary called to us to come in. That house is perfectly gorgeous. We don't have anything at Beaver to begin to touch it. I was simply overawed. We met some girls downstairs & then Mary took me all over the house and I met everybody. It was "super" and I met some darling girls. Shoot—I do prefer these western people so much.

Margaret's visit to Bob's home town would not have been complete without meeting the young woman that Mrs. Lindsey had already picked out for her daughter-in-law. Of "the other woman" Margaret wrote,

Ruth Elanor was there in all her glory. She was to speak the main part of the evening meeting—"Problems Facing Young People" or something to that effect. I feel so insignificant beside her—she's such a big shot—but I've got one thing way over her & that's one Bob Lindsey!

Her letter concludes:

We went from there into Oklahoma City to get my ticket fixed up and I was to leave at 11:50 this morning. Last night when we finally got away after tending to a lot of business, we took Mary to the house, went to mail letters, then to Hallock's to arrange for Bob's ordination which is to take place Sunday after next.

Then we got Mary, took her home, and drove around a little longer since it was our last night together and we had a lot to talk about. It was at the most no more than 11:00 when we came in, but I wish you could have heard Mrs. Lindsey this morning! She was furious! I never heard such going on in my life. She started at me before Bob came out and then she lit into him. She was on a rampage all day, at least till I left.

She said the awfullest things about Bob which of course, she didn't mean. She got off on a tangent about how he wasn't to do anything but work and tend to business this year and she didn't want any fooling around and monkey business. She kept stressing that he was to take no trips but to come home for Christmas. It was a bunch of kind of broad hints to which I made no comebacks. She has made it hard for him to earn his own money by insisting on giving it to him, & then she turns around and says he's no good because he doesn't earn his own. Honestly I can't understand the woman. Anyhow he's now much more in a position to do something about it. He's holding meetings this week & next in Oklahoma City every night. We went around making arrangements today when I didn't get the 11:50 train due to washouts. I got the 3:20, which I'm on now. Bob had to go back a little sooner because he had arranged to pick up Mary at a certain time. (This is a gorgeous train, lovely seats, radio, stewardess, everything!)

Mother, dear, the letter last day out was such a s'prise—I loved it. I don't know what to do about the check. You shouldn't have given it to me. Shall I put that much back in your account? 'Cause you see, Bob did pay me back!

I've written a book! Oh I forgot to say we looked at diamonds too and it was such a thrill to me. I don't know that anything will materialize very soon along that line, though at least we know what we want!

I'm positively getting writer's cramp & I'm sure you're tired reading.

Love you all so much—
Margie

CHAPTER 8
WITH THIS RING I THEE WED

Being in the dark about the depth of her son's relationship with Margaret, Mrs. Lindsey candidly encouraged her not to become serious with Bob. She told Margaret that Bob was always going to be a (financially) poor preacher. He would be extremely busy in seminary and would not have time to travel to visit her. Furthermore, she concluded, "In the seminary he will meet and marry a nice Baptist girl."

On September 15, 1940, Bob was ordained to the ministry in the First Baptist Church of Norman. He then went to Louisville, Kentucky, where he entered Southern Baptist Theological Seminary. Bob and Margaret corresponded frequently, and their relationship continued with its ups and downs as Margaret sorted through her feelings.

After her whirlwind romance with Bob, Margaret discovered upon her return to Beaver College that she faced a romantic dilemma. In a letter dated October 6, 1940, she wrote to her family in Korea:

> I think I told you perhaps, that I had been somewhat confused by the letter from Carleton. That was only the beginning. I've been deluged with letters from him which have served to stir up old affections, feelings, hopes, which were so strong at one time, that although I thought this summer that I had put them away entirely because I had to, now that this has happened they are returning to get me very mixed up. I feel quite definitely, still, that all that happened with Bob was

the Lord's leading and doing, and perhaps this is rebellion on my part. At any rate I have been, during the past two weeks, in a very confused state of mind. It's rather maddening, too, that it doesn't bother Bob in the least. He says he understands perfectly, and he's going to wait till this "temporary revival of old affection" passes. He is so sure that we're meant to be together that he isn't worrying about it. It almost makes me want to throw things and "show him" and everything else, and yet underneath I know perfectly well that he's right.

It also didn't help to get a long letter from Joe, who according to this, although I suspected he was serious about me, was more so and counting on more than I'd ever realized. He was doing some settlement work in New York this summer and made some contacts which gave him a rather changed viewpoint on life. Particularly, he said he had come to my way of thinking on a lot of subjects we had argued about. You know he was becoming very liberal last year, and I always told him exactly what I believed. Mother, does it amuse you a little that I was worried about what I was last summer? I think maybe it's worse having three people in love with me. If I get a "such like" letter from Jimmy now it will be the last straw. I'm certainly not going to write to him even if I have owed him a letter for so long. That's the best way to make that die out completely, but how to manage all this other is rather beyond me. I can't bear to hurt Joe, but he wants to come all the way here to see me again, so I've got to write soon. Never rains but it pours you know.

I think the worst thing of all is that it was partly because of me, I guess, that Betty and Carleton broke up. Oh, I'm so bewildered. Please pray that I'll have wisdom, and most of all that I'll know God's will for me, and that if I've made mistakes in the past that somehow things will work so that no one will suffer for it too much.

In a letter to Margaret dated November 13, 1940, Bob endeavored to explain his reaction to her doubts about their relationship. In part he wrote:

As for the occasional difficulties with your heart, darling, I am not very worried. The nearest thing that I can compare it to is the faith we have in the Lord. There are many times when we have less faith than at other times. There used to be in me during the first two years of my seeking to live a more consecrated life a rather frequent recurrence of doubt about whether there was even a God or not. My doubts now have largely been dispelled and I never have that complete feeling that God is not living & real. Doubts now are to me much more momentary. And, sweetheart, the more I live with the Lord, the less I have of bothering doubts. Perhaps it is that way with our love. Yes, I have had such feelings several times—but very short-lived ones. Doubts seem to be a normal experience where emotional things are concerned. When we are together more, I think we will find our love getting more and more happily confused with feelings of allegiance and devotion to one another. You know, sweetheart, it always helped me when doubts came on me concerning the Lord to think of what I knew definitely He had done in my life. So I have thought sometimes concerning whether you were the girl or not. I return to those first hours with you—to all the things that have gone to show us that His hand is in it all. Perhaps that will help.

Let us never forget, sweetheart, that love at first generally has more of the infatuation which is largely sexual and that love depends partly on our bodily feelings and desires. That does not make it unreal but simply shows that it is not in itself able to make a complete love. The admiration or spiritual love must be coupled with it. Nor do I think that the infatuation need die down—even after marriage. It certainly should be present even if it is partial and wavering at times.

We shall talk all this over some more, darling, when we see each other. There are so many things we can talk about. I want to show you some things around here too—especially our married folks' quarters. Darling, it is still the greatest miracle I know of—the way we met, we who were so far apart, we who had calls that prepared us at the right moment, we who had to have an earthquake to make things perfect, we who continue to grow more nearly alike in our desires day by day. Sweetheart, I'll let you have those little "relapses" once in a while but I will certainly do my part to keep them from lasting long. I think few people could long for another more than I do for you.

My precious—only really a week till I take you in my arms. I don't believe all that stuff about "expectation's being more than realization." I think it will be a lot more fun to have one squirrel in the arms, than a half-dozen 700 miles away. At least I hope—if you think expectation is greater than realization—you'll not forget to turn your little lips up my way at the right moment if only for my sake. And I think you will kiss me—at least 2,000 times.
Love,X X X X X X X X X
Bob
P.S. Darling, I am meeting you at 9:45. We won't forget, will we?

In late November, she visited Bob in Louisville and they shared dinner with friends on Thanksgiving Day.

Meanwhile, as the likelihood of war between Korea and Japan increased daily, Margaret's mother and sisters, along with many other foreign women and children, left Korea. The Lutzes arrived in Leonia, New Jersey a little before Christmas in 1940, so Margaret spent the Christmas holiday with her family. It was a difficult time, their being separated from Margaret's father, Dexter. Bob, on the other hand, spent Christmas at home in Norman. It wasn't the most enjoyable holiday for him either. Not only did he miss Margaret terribly, but he also had surgical repair of an inguinal hernia. As was customary at that time, under doctor's orders he was restricted to bed rest for two weeks following surgery before being permitted to walk.

With their romance progressing, the young couple spent their holiday between semesters with Margaret's family in New Jersey. The first evening there, Bob suggested they go for a walk. There remained a few inches of snow on the ground and the night air was crisp as they walked arm in arm, yet they felt strangely warm as they strolled in silence. There was no one else out that night—or perhaps there were people everywhere. They had eyes only for each other, lost in that heady intoxication of true love's deep emotional connection. Pausing a little distance from a street lamp, Bob drew Margaret around until they were facing. Gazing lovingly into her upturned face, his eyes spoke volumes. Without a word, he slipped a diamond engagement ring on her finger. As she held her hand before her face, the diamond sparkled in the light from the street lamp. Even though she had dared to hope she might get a ring soon, now that she was looking at the ring on her finger, it seemed almost too good to be true. They returned to the house and announced their engagement. Plans were made to marry on July 12.

Yes, that's the way it should have happened—or at least the way Margaret had dreamed it would happen. But in reality, she received no ring because Bob had not yet managed to save enough money to buy one. Later, however, during the spring holiday from classes when she was visiting her family, she was surprised to receive a small package from Bob in the mail. Her family excitedly gathered around her as she sat at the dining table and unwrapped the package with trembling fingers. When she opened the small velvet covered box she found inside, she gasped as the light sparkled from the facets of a diamond engagement ring. As she slipped the ring on her finger, she could hardly believe that she was actually officially engaged! Her sisters were jumping up and down and screaming and the rest of the family was hugging her and everyone was talking at the same time! No, it wasn't the romantic scene that she had envisioned, but with the ring securely on her finger, a sense of joy and contentment welled up from deep within her being. It didn't matter that Bob had not been able to save enough money to give her the ring when they had been together between semesters. It didn't matter that even now he had not had enough money to both purchase the ring and to travel to New Jersey to present it to her personally. And it wouldn't even matter when she later learned that he had purchased the ring at Lucky Morris's Pawn Shop in Louisville. All that mattered was that she was engaged to be married to the most wonderful man on earth—and she now had the ring to prove it!

Even before he gave Margaret the engagement ring, however, Bob was thinking of practical matters. With a wedding on the horizon, he wrote in a letter dated February 15, 1941:

> I think we should work out a budget, honey, as soon as possible, especially of expenses connected with the wedding. I do not know what to say about the honeymoon business. Personally, I would rather not do much traveling. A real nice, quiet, spot—a little cabin in the woods if such is possible would be the thing, I think. We could probably get one for four or five dollars for a couple of weeks somewhere out in the country. I am not sure what we would do for eats; maybe you could get along all right with a wood fire. We could take hikes out along the river—if there was one. Really, darling, that is the kind of thing I would like.

In the same letter, he wrote of a possibility for earning some additional income:

> One of my friends who is taking first year Hebrew got to talking with me and asked me what I thought of teaching a course in practical Hebrew. He said there would probably be a number who would be interested in such a thing. Well, I spoke to several boys to get their reactions on the subject. Seems as if quite a bunch might be interested. I would teach a sort of adult-primer that I began learning Hebrew from when I first went to Palestine. We would meet twice a week and I could charge the boys a dollar a month apiece. That is pretty cheap, really, and I think they would be willing to pay

that much. Now, darling, I think this may be the Lord's will. I have been wanting to do something like this but had no idea anyone would be interested in it. I don't want to expect too much but I might get as many as 10 or 15 in the class which would mean that many dollars a month. Anyhow, it is an interesting possibility and I ask you to pray definitely, will you, honey?

Although reared in the Presbyterian tradition, after much thought and prayer, considering her imminent marriage to Bob, Margaret decided to embrace the Baptist tradition. On Easter Sunday 1941 she was baptized in the Baptist Temple in Philadelphia by a family friend, Dr. Daniel Poling, the editor of *The Christian Herald*. Bob's mother's prediction was coming true—although it was not quite what she had expected. Bob did go to seminary and he was going to marry "a nice Baptist girl." Margaret graduated from Beaver College in May, 1941. In July, Bob's parents and sister drove to Louisville where they met Bob and then drove on to New Jersey together.

The ceremony took place at five o'clock on Saturday afternoon, July 12, 1941, in Leonia, at the picturesque Methodist Church of Margaret's Uncle Frederick and Aunt Rosetta Croxton. The bride wore a white gown, made by a college friend. It was fashioned with a sweetheart neck and bouffant skirt. A long veil was attached to her hair with flowers and white gladioli formed the bridal bouquet. A friend from Korea, Kay Clark (Margaret's birthday twin), was maid of honor. Margaret's sister Betty and Bob's sister Mary Virginia, both wearing pale blue, served as bridesmaids. Bob's father, J. L., served as best man.

A longtime friend of the Lutz family, Dr. Walter Erdman, assisted by Dr. Donald Miller, performed the double-ring ceremony. Both had served in Korea with the Lutzes; Dr. Miller had been one of Margaret's favorite high-school teachers.

In the absence of her father who was still in Korea, Dr. Frederick Croxton gave his niece in marriage. Margaret's mother, Lenore, sang two songs, and after the bride reached the altar, the guests joined in singing *The Marriage Hymn*, an old custom observed in Korea.

As her mother finished singing "I Love Thee" by Grieg, the last words hung like bells in the air: "I love but thee through all eternity."

It would soon be time to repeat the vows that they had memorized when suddenly, she sensed the enormity of what she was doing with remarkable clarity: "for richer or for poorer, for better or for worse, in sickness and in health." Her life, culminating in meeting Bob, passed before her in an instant. She realized that she was marrying not a man, but she was also marrying a vision, an obsession, a call. In marrying Bob, it also would become her vision, her obsession, her call. As the past flashed before her, she experienced an overwhelming sense of God's plan for her life. She realized that she not only was facing the unknown of marriage, but she also was facing the unknown of strange places she could not even imagine—perhaps danger, hunger, sickness, poverty. She thought of encountering unfamiliar people—Arabs and Jews—in a strange land, people without much resemblance to her beloved Jewish college friends who were present to witness her exchanging of vows with Bob. But in that instant, with a clarity of purpose and conviction, she knew that when she uttered the words, "With this ring, I thee wed," that she truly would become one with Bob. She knew in the depths of her being that whatever challenges they might face, they would always face them together.

Following a reception in the home of Margaret's uncle and aunt, Bob and Margaret traveled by car with Bob's family to the Blue Ridge Mountains where they spent some time on the way to Louisville. They would begin their married life together as seminary students at Southern where Bob had completed his first year.

As they settled into the busy life of work and study, there was little time to wonder what challenges lay ahead. They both were aware, however, of an overwhelming sense of rightness that the life they were forging together was meant to be.

Two decades and half a world away, Margaret was jarred from her reverie by five-year-old Debbie's insistent, "Mommy! Mommy!"

"What is it, Debbie?"

"Where is Daddy and when can we see him?"

"He's in the hospital," she responded slowly. "I'm not sure when we can see him, but it will be soon—I pray—very soon."

Chapter 9
How the Journey Began

As the days passed while she waited for permission to cross into Jordan, Margaret lovingly caressed the memories of the man with whom she had shared more than two decades of adventure. Meanwhile, during these days of waiting, Bob was plumbing the depths of his memory as well.

When he had been brought to the hospital following his encounter with the antipersonnel mine, a surgeon had tried unsuccessfully to restore circulation to his mangled left foot during an eight-hour operation. Without a blood supply to his foot, the only option, therefore, was amputation.

As he faded in and out of consciousness following the surgery, he was pleased to learn that Edward was in the same room with him along with other patients. He also took comfort in learning that Edward's eye wounds were healing and that the prognosis was not as grim as the doctors had feared initially. Bob was unaware that his foot had been amputated above the ankle—he only knew that his lower left leg felt numb. Later, as the severed nerves began to grow randomly and push against the tender end of the stump, he would learn what a blessing the numbness had been. He would experience phantom pain interspersed with itching where the foot should be—itching that could not be relieved by scratching—because there was no foot to scratch.

Through the open door he could see a Jordanian policeman smoking a cigarette while standing guard. This re minded him of the dire circumstances in which his recent attempt to return Edward to the farm had placed them. As the medication induced fog began to clear a little, he pondered his fate and that of his family and colleagues. At this lowest of low points in his life, his mind searched clumsily through the fog for some lifeline of faith or conviction that would interrupt his headlong plunge into the dark abyss of hopelessness and depression.

When one's day to day routine is shattered by some traumatic event and one's frantic rush through life is abruptly halted, that which is truly important in life comes into sharper focus. It is at times like this that one eventually ponders how the journey began—and so it was with Bob Lindsey. Waking from a fitful sleep, he desperately strained to focus his thoughts. At first the images swirled wildly in and out of focus in a panorama that reached all the way back to his childhood in Norman, Oklahoma: parents, sister, school, Preacher Hallock, close friends, Boy Scouts, Oklahoma University, Classical Greek, preaching in one-room country churches, Palestine, Jerusalem, Hebrew University, Hebrew language study, war in Europe, Yokahama, Margaret Lutz, earthquake in Nikko, shipboard romance, seminary, marriage, children, return to Palestine, the new State of Israel, pastoring the church in Jerusalem, the farm and all the home kids, biblical research, Edward trapped and so unhappy, must get him back where he belongs, oh no—the world is exploding!

And then he slept again.

With the passage of time, however, the images began to appear more slowly. Bob began to focus on those people and events in his life that had influenced his becoming the person he became and on the events that had culminated in his lying in a Jordanian hospital bed under police guard.

Even in his pain, Bob couldn't help but smile inwardly as he remembered the carefree days of summer as a young boy growing up in Norman, Oklahoma. In those days, most young boys of Norman went barefoot (even at school) from April or May until it was cold in late autumn. When Bob entered the first grade at McKinley Elementary School on Flood Street, he saw children in the fourth grade wearing shoes in early September. When he came home from school, he expressed to his parents the concern that when he got to be in the fourth grade he would have to wear shoes all the time!

Bob's curiosity and adventurous spirit were evident at an early age. On the way to school on one occasion, he stopped to explore the newly dug basement of a house under construction and couldn't get out. Finally, after what seemed to be a very long time, he got a toehold and climbed out, barely getting to school on time. Should he have gotten a spanking at school for being tardy—he could have expected another at home from his mother, probably with a kitchen utensil known as a pancake turner!

Bob loved the outdoors. Many happy hours were spent fishing for trout in Colorado with his father on family vacations. Boy Scouts provided further opportunities to enjoy the outdoors through camping. He worked on most of the merit badges and one year won a bugling contest with a free trip to scout camp.

When Bob was about five years of age, Dr. E. F. Hallock became pastor of the First Baptist Church of Norman. Dr. Hallock was known as "Preacher Hallock" or "Preacher" and served as a primary role model in Bob's life. Bob and Edgar Junior, who was a year older than he, became lifelong friends.

The year he was eleven, Bob publicly acknowledged before the church his faith in Jesus as Savior and Lord. Although his faith was strong, he was somewhat sensitive at this age. During prayers in his church at a meeting of a boys' organization known as Royal Ambassadors (RAs), he prayed something that caused the boys to laugh. He was so embarrassed that he never returned to RAs. However, he did attend church services regularly with his parents.

Growing up in a University town, Bob was exposed to high academic standards early in life. He attended public school through the sixth grade, but attended grades seven through twelve at University High School on the campus of the University of Oklahoma. A close friend from church named O.T. McCall was the same age as Bob and they spent a lot of time together even though O.T. attended public school at Norman High. Remembering their childhood and youth, O.T. recalled,

> The students who attended University High were primarily children of the faculty and administration of the university. By reputation they supposedly considered themselves to be more elite than the "commoners" at the public school, but Bob Lindsey was certainly unpretentious. People always noticed him, however, even though he didn't try to attract

attention. Oblivious to convention, he was happy-go-lucky and seemed not to care what was expected of him. He was spontaneous, refreshingly different, uniquely himself.

Bob also was an excellent student and musician. One summer while he was still in high school, he was asked to play two solos on his trumpet at a University of Oklahoma band concert.

Writing of his religious experience in the years following his conversion, Bob admitted:

> Religiously, I was not much during those years. I remember thinking how dull a life must be that of a preacher who lives with a bunch of dry, old, dusty theological volumes. What a waste of time! I got a little interested in the Bible, however, when I tried for a while to read two chapters a day. I found the Old Testament had some rather interesting stories.
>
> Preachers were a bit of a puzzle to me then. My first remembrance of one in my home was when one of the yearly evangelists came with the pastor for dinner. He was a huge fellow and rather scared me. My dad offered him a cigar but he refused. My mother always said she had felt a prejudice against preachers ever since she was a little girl. In those days, they usually served fried chicken when the preacher came and the children all ate at the "second table" after the adults had eaten. She used to say that she never knew a chicken had anything but a back and wings until she was grown!
>
> I was about sixteen when I remember the first strong religious feelings—not that I had not tried to pray often, nearly every night after my conversion—but this was different. I was playing in a jazz band, a high school extracurricular activity, and I wanted to write a popular song. But, for some reason, I could not do it. I kept thinking, "I must write a hymn first!" To this day I do not understand that conviction but there it was. I did not do either, as it turned out, but within a few months I was

debating with myself why I should not be a preacher. It was a tough battle and all mixed up with other ambitions, but the Lord won. My final decision came that summer, while attending Youth Week at the Falls Creek Baptist Assembly.

During that week Bob served as a reporter for the daily camp newspaper. He felt quite privileged to interview Dr. B. B. McKinney, the renowned song writer and music professor at Southwestern Baptist Theological Seminary in Ft. Worth, Texas, and was deeply moved by the experience. He also was profoundly affected when he heard Dr. R. G. Lee, the silver-tongued orator from Memphis, preach his judgment sermon, "Payday Someday." After the sermon, Bob climbed to a designated place on a nearby hill where he played a few hymns on his cornet. Later, at bedtime, he was to play taps. While he was sitting there on the side of the hill, with the night sounds around him and countless stars overhead seeming close enough to touch, he thought of a matter he had been praying about for the past year. Once again, in prayer, he asked the Lord if He were calling him to preach the gospel. As he quietly prayed, he felt God's Spirit confirming in his own spirit that the call was real. There on the hillside, at sixteen years of age, he made his decision: "I must preach." That same night he threw away the old felt mute he used with his trumpet when he played in the jazz band.

He soon shared his decision with Preacher Hallock, his family, and a few close friends. His decision to become a preacher was not well received by his parents, who wanted him to become a doctor. When he remained firmly resolved for several years, however, they finally accepted his decision.

While attending the University of Oklahoma, Bob was active in a religious organization known as the Baptist Student Union (BSU). During his freshman year, at a joint BSU meeting with the BSU from Oklahoma State University in Stillwater, he met a freshman named Uel James. The two became lifelong friends and on numerous occasions Bob and Uel would spend the weekend together in Norman or in Stillwater. Uel appreciated Bob's parents and enjoyed the meals and a place to sleep at their house. In fact, it was not uncommon for Bob to have guests sleeping all over his room. On

Sunday mornings, in order to know for how many to prepare dinner, Mrs. Lindsey would slip into the bedroom and "count heads." Uel observed that Bob's mother, Elsie, was a somewhat domineering person. Once, while discussing his mother with Uel, Bob confided that his mother "gives me fits," but then philosophically added, "I think the Lord may be putting me through this to develop patience."

CHAPTER 10

PREACHER BOY

In August of 1935, the year he graduated from high school, Bob began preaching Sunday evenings for a newly formed congregation that met in a school house in the rural community of Willow Valley near Lexington, Oklahoma. It was common in those days for the schools to be used for religious services, as well as other civic activities. The first time he preached, Bob's sister Mary Virginia and his friend O.T. McCall drove there with him. It was too hot to be inside, so the benches were moved outside for the thirty or so people present. Bob wrote of the experience:

> I was eighteen when I preached my first sermon down in Willow Valley schoolhouse. I could not help preaching. It had to be. I made a lot of mistakes that first night out under the gas lanterns, asked the folks to stand up when they should have sat down and vice versa. But my sister was there and her eyes were full of tears when I finished and gave the invitation.

The Willow Valley church soon was having both Sunday morning and Sunday evening services. After preaching there several months, Bob began holding services on Sunday morning and evening in a schoolhouse at Lindsey Ridge, eight miles south of Norman. Recalling the experience he wrote:

> I found a little schoolhouse district called Lindsey Ridge (not after me) out across the river where there were no services and I started going every Sunday. I preached twice and sometimes three times including a service in

another schoolhouse down the road. It was mostly zeal without knowledge but the young people came and the house was filled at night, lots of times with young folks of "courtin' age." I had to do all the praying, piano thumping and preaching as well, although a couple of the little boys took up the offering. Offerings as I remember ran around thirty-five cents a Sunday with a half-dozen mils thrown in.

In the summer of 1937, after his sophomore year, Bob Lindsey and Edgar Hallock, Jr., along with director Susan Daniel and others from the Norman student group, went to BSU Week at Ridgecrest, North Carolina, the Southern Baptists' main conference center. When the program concluded, Bob and Edgar hitchhiked to New York City, hoping to work for passage on a ship to Europe where they hoped to attend the Baptist World Youth Encampment. They visited a number of foreign ships, trying to get work on one that would take them to Europe, but failed. Consequently, they worked and preached at the Eighth Avenue Mission in Manhattan every night, and then at 11 P.M., they would go to Times Square where they shared the testimony of their faith with anyone who would listen.

At the mission, Bob and Edgar met Mr. Aspenoll, an older lay preacher of Welsh Brethren affiliation, who taught them how to share their faith on the streets. For example, Bob and Edgar would accompany the Welshman to a public park where Bob would play his trumpet and Edgar his clarinet. Aspenoll had six cards with "SIN" written on them and another card with the cross on it. As Bob and Edgar played their instruments, he would stand where people were passing and he would put a sin card on the sidewalk and quietly start talking to it about sin. People would begin to gather to see what this fellow was up to. Then he would put a sin card behind him, and others on his right and left, on his head and heart, while talking about sin as being all around in what you do, what you think, and what you have in your heart. Next he would put all the sin cards on the sidewalk and cover them with the card with the cross. He thus clearly made the point that Jesus' sacrificial death on the cross will cover all one's sins. Then he would give an invitation, asking that they receive God's provision for the sin problem and pray for forgiveness right then and there. (He also had other cards for other object lessons.)

At times Bob and Edgar would stand in a public place some fifteen feet apart from each other and have a lively argument. By shouting back and forth questions and answers about sin, God, Jesus, and Christian matters, they would soon attract a crowd. When a number of people would stop to listen, they would quiet down and gather them together for their "object lesson" preaching.

That summer Bob and Edgar really learned to live by faith. They slept at the YMCA until their money ran out and then they began to sleep on benches at Penn Station. This continued until one night a policeman woke them, told them it was not legal for them to be sleeping there, and then took them downstairs to a room where they were permitted to spend the rest of the night. The policeman was there at 5 A.M., however, to get them up and out. That morning they had only eleven cents between them, so they spent ten cents for a loaf of bread, which was their breakfast, and one cent for a Tootsie Roll, which they divided. Some Metropolitan Life personnel took them to lunch that day and a Christian "brother" gave them two dollars the next night. Another day the American Mission gave Bob two dollars and Edgar one dollar. Increasingly, Christians who admired their ministry gave them money, enabling them to sleep inside at the YMCA for the rest of the summer. They learned that a day-old loaf of bread cost only a nickel so breakfast often was only bread. At one mealtime they had only sixteen cents with which they bought sixteen bananas, and so that was their lunch—but there was always a sandwich offered at the Eighth Avenue Mission in the evening. When they left New York City for Norman they were rich in experience but had gained no weight that summer!

In preparing for future ministry, Preacher Hallock encouraged Bob to concentrate on Greek and Hebrew so that he could interpret the Bible effectively. In response to this advice, he elected to major in Classical Greek at the University of Oklahoma and to minor in English since Hebrew was not offered. Another minister, J. Wash Watts, who had served in Palestine from 1922 to 1929, advised him, that after graduating from OU, he should go to Palestine to learn Hebrew before attending seminary. Later, Leo Eddleman, who had been serving in Palestine since 1935, wrote Bob the same suggestion.

Bob arrived in Palestine on February 4, 1939 with a study tour of forty-six people. After completing the two month tour, he then made arrangements to live with Zeb and Ruth Weinstock in Jerusalem and to study Hebrew at Hebrew University. Thus began Bob's lifelong love affair with the land of the Bible and with its diverse peoples.

CHAPTER 11

FAMILY MAN

The sleeping city was roused from its slumber by the sound of the *muezzin* in the mineret of a nearby mosque as he called the Muslim faithful to first morning prayer. He soon was joined by a cacophony of voices as the call sounded from other mosques across the city. With considerable effort, Bob Lindsey opened his eyes. The room appeared a dreary grey with the only illumination coming from a single high window admitting little light at this early hour. At first, he couldn't understand where he was or the reason for the intense pain in his left leg. At the sound of voices, he laboriously turned his head toward the door. An involuntary chill ran through his body at the sight of two Jordanian policemen talking in low tones outside the room. The events of the past few days were a hazy blur—but now he realized all too well where he was and why he was there.

As the last words of the call to prayer faded, Bob remembered the first time he was awakened by the *muezzin's* call more than two decades earlier. He had come to Palestine on a two month study tour, and then remained to study Hebrew. He had made many friends— Jews, Arabs and expatriates. A strong bond was formed between Bob, the land, and its people.

His thoughts then turned to Yokahama and meeting Margaret Lutz, the earthquake in Nikko, and the shipboard romance. Even in his pain, he couldn't keep from smiling weakly when he thought of his family's faces when they first had seen Margaret standing at the rail beside him—his sister with her smug smile, his mother looking sternly over the top of her glasses, and his father with a knowing grin. His mother had been determined to see that he didn't get distracted with a girl he had just met, but in the end she had acquiesced and had accepted Margaret as a daughter when she and Bob were married.

As he drifted again into merciful sleep, he was thinking of Margaret walking down the aisle toward him in her white gown, carrying white gladioli, and more flowers holding the long veil in her hair. "With this ring, I thee wed" — and then he slept.

He was awakened by the sound of dishes clattering on the breakfast cart. A short man with a gold front tooth entered carrying plates of *humous* (chick pea and sesame dip), *lebani* (yogurt), flat loaves of bread, and glasses of hot, sweet tea. The first two days following surgery, he had been able to eat only chicken broth, fighting waves of nausea. This morning he felt his appetite returning a bit.

As he slowly dipped the bread into the *humous*, he remembered other simple meals when first he and Margaret were married. Both were seminary students and he was working at a variety of part time jobs. One of the most memorable was his encounter with a "Red Antenna" while selling shoes from door to door in a poor section of Louisville. In one particular home, he was showing some sample shoes to a middle-aged woman while a young woman looked on with interest. Bob noticed that she never took her eyes off him and that she seemed to possess an exceptionally large smile. As the older customer pondered Bob's merchandise, he turned to the young woman and attempted to engage her in conversation. "And what do you do?" he asked. She giggled as she responded while displaying an even larger smile, "Oh, Ahse a Red Antenna!" Bob had not the slightest idea what that was, but followed his instinct not to pursue the matter further. Later, he learned that the term "red antenna" referred to the practice of pimps painting their car radio antennas red in an attempt to facilitate attracting customers for prostitution!

In addition to his part time jobs, he pastored a small country church as well. Ah — how he had bonded with those good folks in the little frame church with the hand sawn benches! Their letters to him through the years indicated that they were still praying for him and Margaret and their work in Israel. Margaret also had worked part time in a department store until their first child was born. In retrospect, they had managed to stretch money and food pretty well so that they always seemed to have enough. They both were content to be together as they prepared for the work to which they believed that God had called them.

As careful as they were with their food budget, he recalled one occasion when they had "splurged" in order to prepare a special meal. The occasion was a visit from Margaret's parents in September of 1942. The visit was a time of great excitement for two reasons: first, Margaret had not seen her father in over twenty-five months; and second, Bob and his father-in-law were meeting for the first time.

When the Japanese troops had arrived in Pyongyang in early December 1941 (corresponding with the bombing of Pearl Harbor), all foreigners had been arrested and imprisoned. The foreign Protestant preachers subsequently were expelled, but Dexter, an agronomist, was interned along with a Presbyterian physician, Dr. Bigger, and eighteen Catholic priests. They were placed under guard and lived in Dr. Bigger's house on the Pyongyang Foreign School compound from January through June, 1942. The conditions could have been much more difficult, and were so for many, but Dexter was permitted to keep a cow and to grow vegetables in the yard, so they had milk and something to eat. In July Dexter was sent on a Japanese ship to South Africa where he and others were exchanged for Japanese being held as prisoners of war. He then was sent to Brazil on a Swedish liner being used as a diplomatic exchange ship, the *S. S. Gripsholm*. After seemingly endless bureaucratic delay, he sailed on the same ship to New York, landing there in September. Now the Lutzes were anxious to visit their daughter and son-in-law before settling in Washington, D.C. where Dexter would be employed by the federal government in a wartime capacity.

In the early spring of 1943, following an uncomplicated pregnancy, the Lindsey's first child, David Lisle, was born on March 25 in a local hospital in Louisville. Margaret recovered rapidly and David was healthy. He did seem to cry a lot and Margaret worried that she wasn't producing enough milk. The usual concerns of first time parents were addressed, however, and so Bob Lindsey, family man, along with his wife was initiated into the "Order of Interrupted Sleep." In spite of work, studies, and sleepless nights, Bob enjoyed his son a great deal. He delighted in tossing him playfully into the air as David squealed with delight and Margaret tensed and protested protectively.

Bob received his Master of Theology Degree in May of that year and started working on a doctorate in theology, hoping to make considerable progress while waiting for the door of service in Palestine to open. Throughout the school year of 1943-44, Bob and Margaret corresponded with officials of the Southern Baptist Convention in Richmond, Virginia regarding appointment to serve in Palestine. The board studied their life stories including their "call from the Lord to a field of service," checked references, looked over their school transcripts, and scheduled Bob and Margaret for physical exams. Following the notification of their acceptance, they traveled with their one-year-old son by train to Richmond for the April 18 appointment service. As the fifteen candidates were presented to the board, they were challenged to consecration and dedication to a lifetime of service overseas. Bob and Margaret were the only ones appointed to Palestine.

In anticipation of the end of the war, a primary concern of the board at that time was how to meet the needs of humanity in the coming postwar era. As they surveyed the actual physical conditions of the peoples of the world at large and compared them to conditions in Europe following World War I, it became painfully clear that there were very few young appointees relative to the tremendous need. Therefore, the Southern Baptist Convention issued a "call to service," asking for hundreds or thousands to respond. While a considerable number of people responded to the call, then, as now, the need far exceeded the response. The month following their appointment, the Lindseys received their first salary check in the amount of $207.

As World War II continued to rage, in the summer of 1944 Bob enrolled in a nine-week Arabic course at a Seventh Day Adventist school in Takoma Park, Maryland, outside Washington, D.C. During the 1944-45 school year, they both studied at Princeton Theological Seminary in Princeton, New Jersey, where Bob received another Th.M. Degree. It was during this time that their second child, Margaret Lenore, was born on April 2, 1945. (She was named Margaret after her mother and Lenore after her maternal grandmother.) After the baby was home several days and still of novel interest to big brother David, he asked his mother, "Where's my baby?" He couldn't see her since she was out of sight in a bassinet on a table. Margaret replied, "She's up high." Two year old David thought his mother had said, "She's a pie," so he started calling his sister "Pie" (also spelled Py or Payh in subsequent correspondence). The nickname stuck, and throughout childhood, either "Pie," Margaret Lenore, or "Little Margaret" was what the family and friends called her. Later, as a teenager, she opted to be called Lenore.)

Bob wrote the board requesting reimbursement for expenses relating to childbirth. Since there was no precedent for such a request, there was no allowance available. He learned, however, that there was a two hundred dollar outfit allowance provided to assist in purchasing items to take overseas. The Lindseys used the allowance to purchase clothing, shoes, a refrigerator, a washing machine and other supplies that they would need to take to Palestine.

Bob and Margaret secured passports for the family and applied to the British for visas to enter Palestine, and after months of delay, the necessary visas finally were issued. (The British had governed Palestine since the end of World War I under a mandate from the League of Nations.) Because the shipping industry had been ravaged by the war, it was difficult to book passage to the Middle East. While working out these details, Bob bought a camera and took a course at the Institute of Photography in New York City.

At last, passage was booked on a Swedish liner, the *S.S. Gripsholm*, which sailed from New York City on October 16, 1945. The ship was the very same one on which Margaret's father, Dexter Lutz, had sailed some three years earlier when he was repatriated. As they sailed out of New York Harbor, even while busily settling into their cabin and attending to the needs of their children, they both were conscious of a sense of destiny. They were filled with awe as they pondered the divine influence that had directed their lives and placed them on this path. Whatever the future held, they knew that they would face it together—as a family.

CHAPTER 12
RETURN TO PALESTINE

The accommodations aboard the *S.S. Gripsholm* were excellent. The family had a private cabin with hot and cold running water, fresh towels each day, and wonderful meals. A few decks below the cabins there was a gymnasium and Swedish steam bath. The weather was ideal, and none of the family was sick on the voyage.

There were among the passengers on the ship over a hundred people who were bound for service in various countries sent out by many different American churches. The entire group joined in prayer meetings each morning and two meetings on Sunday. The Lindseys took their turn with Bob leading the singing and Margaret playing the piano.

While passing through the Straits of Gibraltar and entering the Mediterranean, Bob met a young American Jewish man, Bruce Jacobson. One quiet night on deck, Bob asked him how the Jews understand the Kingdom of God or Kingdom of Heaven. (Some religious Jews since Bible times have used "Heaven" and other words in place of the word "God" so as not to violate the commandment prohibiting uttering God's name in vain. Kingdom of Heaven and Kingdom of God are generally used interchangeably by Christians.) Bruce replied, "Christians basically have a wrong idea about what Jews mean when they talk about the Kingdom of Heaven. What the rabbis meant—and what we Jews believe today—is that to get into the Kingdom of Heaven a person has to decide to do what God wants him to do, and that is all laid down in the Torah and the Mishnah. Anybody who keeps the commandments as laid down in these books has let God start ruling him—he is in God's Kingdom! Somehow Christians have gotten the idea that when all the Jews get back to

Israel or Israel's army takes more and more of the Middle East to incorporate it into Israel—they think of it as 'setting up' the Kingdom of Heaven. This simply is not true. Why, we can have the Kingdom of Heaven wherever we are, when we keep the commandments God gave us!" The spiritual insight of his new Jewish friend had a deep impact on Bob's understanding. His friendship with Bruce was to continue to the end of Bob's life. A traumatic incident in the future would bind the two together in a way that neither could have imagined at this time.

When the *S.S. Gripsholm* docked in Naples, the passengers were advised that the ship had a broken engine block. After waiting four days on board, the Lindsey family, with their luggage and freight, was transferred to a U.S. Navy troop ship, on which they sailed to Port Said, Egypt. Once they arrived in Port Said, Bob was exuberant! He enjoyed everything about the place—the *souk* (market), street cafes, dusty streets, and even the odors characteristic of the Middle East. He sent a telegram to the Baptists serving in Jerusalem stating when they expected to arrive.

That evening they boarded a train bound for Lydda, Palestine. The next morning they looked out the window of their compartment as the first rays of sunrise illuminated the landscape. They saw a Bedouin encampment in the desert near Gaza with their black camel hair tents surrounded by donkeys, camels, goats, and sheep. Even at this early hour, the encampment was bustling with activity. Small children chased each other in and out among the legs of the camels. Women cooked over open fires as the men and older children busied themselves with the flocks and herds.

They soon began to see scattered Arab villages, then Jewish settlements and towns. At Lydda, Palestine, they changed to a smaller narrow-gauge train for the climb up through *waddies* (ravines that are dry except during the rainy season) and mountains toward Jerusalem. Passing by quaint villages with flat-topped houses, they arrived in Jerusalem on Wednesday afternoon, November 7, 1945. Bob was *back home* after a four and one half year absence!

When the Lindseys arrived in Jerusalem, they discovered that, in spite of Bob's telegram, no one was at the station to meet them. Consequently, they hailed a taxi that took them to the Baptist compound at 4 Henrietta Szold Street. The afternoon sun cast a golden hue on the buff colored cut limestone houses and shops lining the cobbled stone streets. The red tile roofs interspersed among flat roofed buildings added a charming Mediterranean flair that belied the political unrest that might explode at any moment.

Henry and Julia Hagood, and Kate Ellen Gruver were very surprised when the Lindseys arrived. They had received no communication from the Baptist board that the Lindseys had left New York on October 16 nor had they received Bob's telegram sent the day before from Port Said. The Hagoods were new colleagues who had been in Palestine only a few months themselves. Bob knew Kate Ellen from his previous stay in Palestine.

The ability to be flexible and adaptable is essential for one to cope successfully with the unexpected situations of life. This was particularly true in post-World War II Palestine. The Baptists had planned for the Hagoods to move to Nazareth before the Lindseys arrived, so that the Lindseys could occupy the main living quarters on the property in Jerusalem. The house that the Hagoods were to occupy in Nazareth was not yet available, however, so in the meantime the Lindseys settled into a nearby guest house. They occupied a large room with three east windows which let in the morning sunshine and they took their meals in the guest house dining room. Bob bought a small hot plate on which to heat water to boil the baby bottles; it also took the chill off the room at night. David and Margaret Lenore quickly made friends with the Hagood's son Jimmy and with Rhadia, an Arab girl in the care of the Hagoods.

The next afternoon, Bob met the train to claim his trunks, refrigerator and washing machine—but one trunk was missing. The baggage master sent telegrams to Lydda and Port Said trying to locate the trunk but to no avail. Bob was especially anxious about that particular trunk since it contained sheets, shoes, and his Hebrew typewriter. He was much relieved when it finally was located and delivered to them—four months later!

The first few days were spent getting settled as much as possible under the circumstances. On their first Sunday in Jerusalem, Bob preached at an English language service held in the Baptist Chapel. In the afternoon they were invited to tea by new friends, and those who were serving in Jerusalem with other church groups stopped by to welcome them. During the week, Bob delighted in showing Margaret the sights around Jerusalem and visiting favorite restaurants and shops. Margaret loved the city and its people from the beginning.

Soon Bob began a systematic study of Hebrew. Margaret, however, was unable to begin language study at that time since they were unable to find anyone to care for the children. (She later studied with a tutor who came to the house for her lessons.) David was two years and eight months and Margaret Lenore was only seven months—and Margaret was five months pregnant! She and the children suffered the common intestinal ailments people usually experience in a new country when they encounter new strains of microorganisms, but Bob remained relatively healthy.

On December 1, 1945, Bob wrote his first letter to his parents in Oklahoma after having arrived in the Holy City. Regarding the economics there, he told them that everything in Jerusalem—food, clothing, cars, tires—were sky high! Attempting to reassure his parents, he wrote:

> The political situation is still unsettled in Palestine, but there have been no Arab-Jewish shootings for a long time. What little skiffs there have been were between Jews and British soldiers. There are at least 60,000 troops in Palestine so the situation is pretty much under control. Anyone who carries firearms without a government permit is liable to the death penalty and anyone caught in possession of such is liable to life imprisonment. So the British mean to keep the place in hand.

While still living in the guest house, Bob traveled to the coast to visit a Russian Christian farm where he met Samuel Anishka, a Russian Baptist farmer who had immigrated to Palestine in 1925. While there he also visited the Weinstocks and spent a night with them. It was a happy reunion, being with the family with whom he had lived when he had studied Hebrew in Jerusalem.

Bob was assigned to be pastor of the Baptist Chapel, which had maintained services on the property since 1927. The congregation had scattered during World War II so he began the task of rebuilding. The church really never had been constituted in the traditional Baptist way and did not have a formal membership. Rather, they had welcomed as members any who came, whether for a short time or for an extended period, a tradition Bob Lindsey was to continue as pastor.

December 1945 was an extremely difficult time as hundreds of thousand of homeless European Jews who had survived the Holocaust now faced the winter. The majority languished in Displaced Person (D.P.) Camps set up by the Allies because they had nowhere else to go after they were liberated from the Nazi death camps. Immigration of Jews to most countries of the world was reduced to a trickle, and perhaps most troubling, the British restricted them from entering Palestine where efforts to set up a "Jewish National Homeland" continued. On December 15, at the Nuremberg War Crime Trials, a communiqué written by Dr. Wilhelm Hoettl was read in court. Hoettl had written it in August 1944 in Budapest after he spoke with S.S. Col. Adolf Eichmann (who had visited Palestine briefly before the war). Eichmann told Hoettl at that time that his records indicated that four million Jews had been killed in various extermination camps, while an additional two million had met death in other ways. While many died of starvation, exposure, and disease, the majority of the two million had been shot by the Security Police. Hoettl's communiqué addressed his concern over less "reputable" methods of extermination:

> To lock men, women and children into barns and set fire to the structures does not appear to be a suitable method of combating these bands, even if it is desired to exterminate the population. This method is unworthy of the German cause and hurts our reputation.

When the Jerusalem Post released this sickening news the next day, December 16, the population was shocked! The bereavement caused by a holocaust of such magnitude was unfathomable. It was against this agonizingly tragic backdrop that the Twenty-second Congress of the World Zionist Organization convened in Basil, Switzerland that December. It was certainly one of the saddest Jewish gatherings ever.

As the Lindseys adapted to life in Jerusalem amidst the uncertainty and unrest, Bob began to look for ways to assist those in need. He was concerned not only with the needs of his congregation, but also with the needs of others as well. The process of change was at work all around him, and Bob began his service by making some changes of his own.

Chapter 13

Baptist House

One of the first tasks that Bob assigned himself was to change the sign at the entrance to the Baptist property reading "Baptist Mission" and replace it with one reading "Baptist House." After two world wars and with the British troops still so plainly visible, he felt the term *mission* was not suitable since it had a somewhat militaristic connotation in Hebrew. In addition, *mission* suggested *missionary*, and nearly two thousand years of persecution and forced or coerced conversion to Christianity at the hands of Christendom had resulted in a stereotypic Jewish view of the term. A missionary was typically viewed, not as one who serves, but as one who attempts to manipulate others through fear or deceit to change one's religion against one's will—even going so far as to buy children in order to raise them as Christians.

During his previous time in Palestine as a student Bob was motivated through his living with the Weinstocks to return to Palestine to serve them and other Jews who had accepted Jesus as their Messiah. He firmly believed that more Jews would have recognized Jesus as Messiah had Christianity not presented them with a distorted view of Him. The view was so distorted that few Jews (or Christians for that matter) even recognized that Jesus was Jewish, lived an observant Jewish lifestyle, and spent his whole ministry preaching and teaching among his fellow Jews. All his original followers were Jewish and it was only after his resurrection that his followers were instructed to carry his message to the non-Jewish world as well. Bob firmly believed that one's religious faith is valid only if one freely makes a conscious choice to follow a particular faith. This stood in marked contrast to the prevailing *millet* system of the Middle East in which one is born into a particular religion and one's

74

culture and civil rights are inseparably linked to one's religion.

The day after Christmas the Hagoods were finally able to move to the house in Nazareth, so the Lindseys gratefully moved into Baptist House (where Kate Ellen Gruver also lived). It was built of Jerusalem stone with colorful Italian tile floors and included a comfortable living room, dining room, kitchen, three bedrooms, and a basement. A four-room addition at the back of the house provided two bedrooms upstairs and two rooms at ground level, one of which was used for storage and the other became Bob's study. The house was well protected with iron bars on all the windows and with heavy steel doors and locks—standard practice in the Middle East. In back of the house was a garage.

On the front southwest corner of the property stood the Baptist chapel, built of stone and stucco in 1932 for $1,000. The chapel accommodated about forty people and contained a limestone baptistery behind the pulpit with two dressing rooms. Beside the chapel was a building used for children's activities and was known as "the club house." (Some years later when the street was widened the club house building was reduced to less than half its original size.) Near the chapel was a very large cistern that gathered rain water from all the buildings on the property. On the back of the property was a tennis court, a play area with a sandbox, swings, a seesaw, and a slide. There were many trees and bushes all over the compound along with some grass.

Wilbur and Evelyn Skaggs had come from Egypt to spend a few days with the Lindseys. Two days after Christmas, however, Bob was away on an overnight trip, when the holiday quiet was shattered by a great blast. Margaret described the event in a letter to Bob's parents:

> I was so glad the Skaggs were here that Thursday night because Bob wasn't and it was then that the police headquarters were blown up. I don't know how much it was played up in the papers back there but it was a pretty thorough piece of work. Our lights were out anyway; they always are out on Thursday night. It was about 7 P.M. and the children were in bed. After two explosions they seemed to be getting closer and the rifle fire and street fighting sounded as if it were in the next street.

When an explosion shook the windows we got the kids, wrapped them in blankets and carried them down to the basement. Of course none of it was as close as it seemed. It was several blocks away, but I was very, very glad I was not alone.

The next day we were under very strict curfew and couldn't go out of the house except to buy bread when a big truck came up with it. Evelyn went out to get bread and said she felt very funny buying bread with a British soldier having her carefully covered [with his rifle] along with the rest. Being right smack in the Jewish section, when a curfew hits, it really hits us hard. For a week after that we had curfew every day from 4 p.m. to 8 a.m. and had to be strictly in the house.

On Friday January 4, 1946, Bob Lindsey, Kate Ellen Gruver, and Merrel Callaway were in Nazareth for an executive committee meeting with Henry Hagood. Merrel was a Baptist assigned to Arabia but was in Jerusalem studying Arabic. Henry was quite ill but managed to participate in the meeting. His health had been deteriorating over the past couple of months as he battled severe diarrhea along with a sinus infection while his weight had plummeted fifty pounds. Friday night Henry sat propped up in bed due to difficulty breathing. As his condition continued to deteriorate, he was taken to the local Edinburgh Medical Mission Society (EMMS) Hospital where he began receiving penicillin injections every four hours.

On Sunday morning friends phoned Bob with the shocking news that Henry had died at 11:00 Saturday night; he was only 29 years of age. He had worked and studied for ten years in preparing to serve in Palestine. Arriving in Palestine June 1, 1945, he, his wife Julia, and baby son Jimmy had been on the field only seven months. Bob and Merrel sadly returned to Nazareth where they conducted the funeral. Henry then was interred in the Protestant Cemetery for Foreigners on the northern edge of Tiberias, on a hillside overlooking the Sea of Galilee.

Following Henry's death, Julia prayerfully considered what course her life should take. She still had a deep desire to remain in the country and serve the people in some capacity. She had always wanted a large family so she thought perhaps she might be able to care for some of the growing number of orphans in the country. She already had been caring for young Rhadia whose mother had died. She received permission from the Board to begin a children's home and Kate Ellen Gruver came from Jerusalem to work with her.

As the work in Jerusalem continued, Bob preached regularly in the Jerusalem Baptist Chapel—in Hebrew on Friday evening and Saturday morning and in English for two services on Sunday. A children's Sunday School class was taught in English. The congregation was a cosmopolitan mix of Arabs, Jews, and expatriates—of Russian, Polish, Austrian, German, Dutch, American and other nationalities.

On the seventh of March, 1946, at 2 A.M., Margaret was awakened with labor pains and Bob took her immediately to the British Hospital. The Jewish, Arab, and British sisters (nurses) were quite nice, but the weather was cold and damp and there was no heat in the hospital. At 6 A.M., Dr. Oppenheimer delivered the Lindsey's first *sabra*, Barbara Ann. Margaret did well with no drugs or anesthesia. Later, a British consul came in and gave her some flowers. Although she appreciated the flowers, she suspected he had intended to give them to someone else since she was not British. After seven days Margaret was permitted to get up and walk around, and she made several new friends who were also patients there. On the tenth day the doctor released her and Barbara to go home. The joy of having a new baby was briefly tested when they received a letter from Bob's parents indicating that they were disgusted with them for having three children when it was quite enough to have two. Margaret was determined that her in-laws not prevent them through intimidation from having more children. In response to the letter, she remarked to Bob, "It's the best thing in the world—having babies. I love it. She is so sweet and soft and pretty. What we would have missed if we hadn't had her!" Margaret and Bob further proved their determination not to be intimidated—three more times!

Margaret's love of children was matched by Bob's fondness of and desire for children. Even before they were engaged, he wrote to her in February of 1941:

Sweetheart, did you ever think I did not like babies? The last thing I hollered at the Eddlemans [Leo and Sarah] as I boarded the Arab bus in Nazareth to go to Tiberias was, "I'm going to get me one of those too" [talking about their baby whom Sarah was holding on the porch upstairs]. Darling, I don't think you could love children more than I do. I have not had to change any diapers yet or anything quite that bad. I may change my mind after that but I really don't think so. Children are a heritage from the Lord and how I do believe that. I really can't understand the person or persons who do not want children. To think of all the couples that could have and don't want them. Of course, dearest, I don't think we should have any quite the first year. Still, whenever you want one, I'll do all I know—even try to save a little for hospital bills.

One of the adjustments that Bob and Margaret made to living in the Middle East was adjusting their expectation of effort needed to complete tasks relative to time. They learned to be flexible and adaptable because they believed that the "good things of life" as well as the "bad things" are either ordered or permitted by the Lord. This attitude helped the Lindseys when they or the children were ill, when an Arab shepherd would let his sheep graze and make a big mess in their backyard, or when a little neighbor girl would come and stay all day and not go home. It helped when it was impossible to buy milk that wasn't sour, when they could not buy the food they wanted, when necessary telephone calls or telegrams couldn't be completed. It even helped when Bob discovered that his only winter coat had been feeding the moths during the warm months.

In the spring Bob planted a large vegetable garden on the back side of the Baptist property. Gardening was not his favorite activity, but he did it so they would have a better variety of food on the table during these difficult times.

Always looking for suitable ways to enlarge the work in Palestine, and because of Bob's contacts with some Russian Baptist farmers, he started investigating the possibility of starting a Baptist *moshav* (cooperative farm).

Meanwhile, as he continued to pastor the church in Jerusalem, it soon became evident to Bob that the available New Testaments in Hebrew too often left the readers wondering what the text actually was teaching. One translation in common use was that of Franz Delitsch, and another was by Isaac Salkinson. Both men produced their works between 1870 and 1890—before Hebrew was revived as a spoken language. Consequently, the language of the translations was archaic and artificial, giving some readers an aversion to them. Bob met with several interested Hebrew-speaking men and they decided to do a translation into Modern Hebrew. In the first phase, they each worked alone, translating from modern English and French texts. Meeting regularly around a large table at Bob's house they discussed their findings late into the night. The next phase would be to translate the New Testament into Hebrew from the Greek text.

On July 22, 1946, Margaret Lindsey was sitting in her home with her Hebrew tutor when a large explosion shook the city. They soon learned that the target was the King David Hotel with the British High Commission offices in particular. The whole south wing of the hotel was destroyed by the blast, which proved to be the most deadly of the violent acts perpetrated in Palestine during the British Mandate. Ninety-one people were killed, including Britons, Arabs, and Jews. For the first time the Jewish community demanded the capture and delivery to the authorities of those responsible for the killing—thought to be the *Irgun*. This group was one of two radical Jewish groups who had given up on diplomacy and sought to drive the British out by force in order to set up a Jewish state that would open immigration to Holocaust survivors that the British had essentially locked out. (Telephone calls warning of the bomb and urging evacuation of the building were made shortly before the blast but were ignored, perhaps because of a number of previous "false alarms.")

Due to a severe housing shortage and unsettled conditions in Jerusalem, the Lindseys and another appointee, Violet Long, opened a youth hostel on the Baptist property. Soon they had eighteen young men and women in residence, mostly Jewish but including a few international students as well. The hostel occupied the two dressing-rooms in the chapel, the club house, the basement and two rooms on the ground floor of the Lindsey's residence. It operated throughout the major hostilities, providing morning and evening meals for the residents.

Another significant event that touched Bob's life involved his Baptist colleague Julia Haygood. In April 1947 Julia took little Jimmy with her to Jerusalem for three months of Arabic language study. She continued to return to Nazareth on week ends to assist with the orphanage, however. At the language school Julia met a young bachelor from Scotland, Finlay M. Graham. He had served six years in the Middle East as a navigator in the British Royal Air Force and after completion of his service he had returned to serve as an evangelist and church developer. He was known to professors and students as an unusual scholar with a special gift of mastering Arabic. A romance developed and Finlay and Julia were married September 11, 1947, at the Baptist Church in Nazareth with Bob Lindsey officiating. The wedding was a memorable occasion and is recalled with some humor by Julia:

> The church was filled to "standing room only" with guests as "Hakimi" Wilson began playing the pump organ in the Baptist Church signaling the beginning of the wedding. (*Hakimi* is the feminine form of *doctor* in Arabic.) I stood on the balcony of our adjacent house searching for any sign of Bob's car. Finley waited at the altar with John Bone, his best man. Dr. Bathgate, who was to escort me, paced nervously outside the church door. Finally, after what seemed an eternity, Bob's car appeared up the road in a cloud of dust. As the car came to a halt beneath the balcony, Margaret guided their children into the church and Bob came bounding up the stairs. "Sorry we're late, Julia," apologized Bob. "Do you happen to know if Henry had a pastor's manual?" Not only was Bob Lindsey late but he was totally unprepared to officiate! While in America or England the delay in the ceremony might have been disturbing, in Nazareth it was nothing out of the ordinary.
>
> Miraculously, I was able to quickly find Henry's pastor's manual and Bob immediately set about selecting

portions of several different ceremonies. Consequently, he was continually flipping back and forth in the manual during our ceremony. After Dr. Bathgate and I reached the altar, the guests joined in singing a hymn. Bob forgot to have the guests sit at the close of the hymn so everyone continued standing as he began speaking.

The best man added to the spontaneity of the ceremony as well. Being a proper Anglican, John Bone noticed that their were no pillows upon which the bride and groom could kneel to receive holy communion, so he stepped back and sent one of the children to my house next door to get two pillows from the bed. With everyone still standing, he slipped the pillows in front of Finlay and me. I immediately grabbed the pillows and tossed them to one side since I had no intention of kneeling!

Bob also had forgotten to ask, "Who gives this woman in marriage?" so as the ceremony progressed, Dr. Bathgate decided to leave the altar. At that point, Bob remembered and asked that Dr. Bathgate return to the altar for the question and that the guests be seated.

At the close of the ceremony, as Finlay and I started down the aisle, little Jimmy (who was almost three) broke away from his grandmother and pushed his way in between us and walked down the aisle with us holding our hands.

After the reception, the newlyweds left for their honeymoon that included a Bible conference in the small Lebanese village of Kefr Mishky and then on to Damascus for one night. On their wedding day, Finlay was appointed to service by the Southern Baptist Convention *en absentia* although the Grahams did not learn of the appointment until they returned from their trip. Finlay earlier had traveled to Denmark to interview with Southern Baptist officials who were attending a meeting of the Baptist World Alliance there. When the Grahams returned to Nazareth they were greeted with *"Mabruk! Mabruk!"* by everyone they met. (*Mabruk* means literally "blessing" but it is the English equivalent of "congratulations.") Evidently everyone knew something they didn't. When they arrived at the post office, they discovered that Finlay had received a telegram informing him of his appointment to service by the Southern Baptists. The news had been too good for the postmaster to keep and the news had traveled throughout Nazareth.

In March of 1948 they moved to Taibe for service in Transjordan and then in October of that year they moved to Lebanon. They would prove vital to Southern Baptist work in Arabic speaking Middle East countries for decades to come.

And so, once again Bob Lindsey intimately experienced the cycle of life—with sadness he had officiated at the funeral for Julia's first husband, Henry Haygood, and with joy he had officiated at her wedding to Finlay Graham. In much the same way, he was experiencing the death of one political era and the birth of another—and both death and birth are commonly accomplished through pain.

CHAPTER 14

THE PARTITION OF PALESTINE

Since its inception in October of 1945, the United Nations had been working on the extremely difficult Arab-Jewish-British problem concerning Palestine. On Saturday November 29, 1947, the U.N. was scheduled to vote on the partition of the country. The plan called for Palestine to be divided into some six main areas, three of them Arab and three Jewish. The Arab areas would become an Arab state and the Jewish areas a Jewish state, yet both states were to share an economic union. By means of a common currency, road system, and import customs system, the country would be kept as one unit economically. The vote was concluded Saturday evening in New York, but Palestine is seven time zones ahead, so word was received there in the early morning hours of November 30. Later that day Bob Lindsey wrote of the remarkable events.

This has been a historic day. So many things have been happening during it that I sit down to write before I forget any of them.

The excitement began early this morning at one-thirty. The hundreds of people had sat all night waiting for returns by shortwave concerning the voting on the question of the partition of Palestine at the UN Assembly. Finally the news came! Thirty-three voted for partition, thirteen against! At last after nearly 2,000 years of wandering, Jews have a state.

We live in a Jewish section of Jerusalem with thousands of inhabitants within a literal stone's throw. Some of the young people in our hostel are Jewish. By one-thirty this morning several had thrown coats around their pajamas and dashed out to the street to join other pajama-clothed young people and to run together to the Jewish Agency building some two blocks from us. Shouts rang out in the street in front of our window:

Yesh khaluka! Yesh khaluka! Yesh medina ivrit! Yesh aliyah khofshit! (There is partition! There is partition! We have a Jewish State! We have free immigration!)

In the spirit of the occasion, British policemen and soldiers stopped their lorries and trucks and loaded on the pajama-clad youngsters. As they rode they sang and clapped:

David, melech Yisrael, khai, khai vekayam! (David, king of Israel, lives, lives and is alive! lit., is established.)

It was an amazing sight! Only a few days ago police and soldiers had been in disfavor with the Jewish population. Now they were singing and dancing the national "Hora" with the people.

I was so sleepy I couldn't get properly awake until four o'clock. By that time the rising noise of increasing hundreds of people on the streets kept me from sleeping. I got up and joined some of the young people who had come in to get properly dressed and run back to see the fun.

When we got to the Jewish Agency building, big circles of people had formed in the streets and were dancing and singing. Trucks loaded with young people and children rolled slowly by shouting and clapping. Youngsters had commandeered the khaki buses and were crammed into them, on them, around them till you wondered how they stayed on. Two or three impromptu speeches were made from a balcony. There were old men and women. There were whole families. I recognized the bearded proprietor of our neighborhood hardware store and told him "mazal tov" which is a congratulatory phrase for all such occasions. The horizon turned a deep red in the east and silhouetted the Russian Tower on the Mount of Olives, tinting us all and the Agency buildings a morning pink.

We walked down the main avenue of New Jerusalem, King George. Everywhere were people walking up and down. Near Jaffa Road, a great crowd had gathered and were singing and dancing. A British tank, the kind that the police use here, went by with at least thirty young people clinging to its iron sides and one holding a large national Jewish flag. (It has a white background with a light-blue-colored six-pointed star on it.)

On the way home, I met several of our neighbors. One, our cleaner, a man who lost much of his family in Hungary during the war and who has managed to get his brother into the country, grabbed my hand and pulled me into his shop. "Here," he said, pouring out a tiny glass of something strong, "take this. It is healthy for today. Ach, Adon Lindsey, it is all because of the Americans. All because of your President. I really cannot believe it is true."

Many said things like that to me. People here have doubted for so long that anything would come of all the official commissions they can hardly believe it. Politics has colored issues so frequently that most people doubted whether even the United States was serious about Palestine. And the last few days have been nerve-wracking—waiting for what finally the UN would say. There have been so many delays, so many uncertainties.

The day has not been without its tragedies either. Arab gangs have attacked Jewish buses at three different spots along the main roads. At least five Jewish people are reported killed, a number of others injured. A British policeman of long experience in Palestine told me this evening that in three or four days there would probably be organized trouble from Arabs. That, however, is to be expected and it may be sometime before we see real peace.

Nevertheless, there is great relief. Now the 18,000 people in Cyprus will, it is hoped, be let into Palestine. The thousands who come in leaky boats each month may be able to land in Palestine immediately. Shulamit's mother (Shulamit lives in our hostel; she is a Jewish Hungarian refugee) may come from Cyprus sooner than the expected year. Mrs. Friedman's brother will be coming from the D.P. camp in Germany.

The violence that followed the UN vote for the partition of Palestine continued to escalate, signaling the beginning of the Arab-Jewish War. Within days, five Arab nations began to attack the Jewish sectors of Palestine. At the same time, radical Jewish groups continued their violence toward the British occupation forces. Bob wrote of the continuing violence following the vote for partition:

The next day other Jewish buses were attacked and other passengers wounded and killed. Within a few days Jews had begun putting armor plate on the buses, taking any road possible around Arab towns and villages. An Arab strike was called in Jerusalem.With Arab stores closed, an Arab mob began to attack Jewish wholesale stores in an Arab area; they burned, pillaged and looted the whole Jewish wholesale district. Jews were killed on their way to the Wailing Wall in the old city. British soldiers,commanded to use no force for several days in the mistaken hope that the mood for violence would cease, soon realized that things were out of hand. Arab irregulars from the various countries round about crossed in increasing numbers into Palestine with any kind of gun they could obtain, and began nightly attacks on the Jewish quarters. Jews, of course, quickly organized for self-protection and the war was on!

As in every war, however, the majority did not want to fight. Most Palestine Arabs stood to lose everything in a fight with the Jews and they knew it. Most Jewish people had had enough fighting for six long years before and they did not want it. Some of our Arab members continued to meet in the church with the Jewish Christian brethren for a month after the troubles began and in places, Arab and Jewish children played together for several weeks after November 29. Vicky, a fine little Christian Arab girl, who took care of our children in the afternoons, continued to come to work until the middle of February but at last the tension was too great and the communities separated completely, pillboxes at every border.

Many have asked what is actually the truth about the Arab-Jewish conflict. Whose country is it anyway? I cannot answer that question absolutely, of course. Only God can. But it does seem to me that both Arab and Jewish claims have much validity. Arabs claim Palestine because they have formed the majority of the population for many hundreds of years. Jews claim it on the grounds of a historical connection of many hundreds of years and the pressing need for a solution to the Jewish problem the world around. I think both peoples are right. That means, naturally, that only a compromise will give a measure of each group's desires. The UN plan was such a compromise and perhaps not as bad a one as some have thought. It gave both Arabs and Jews the political rights of sovereign nations, yet the economic possibilities of a single country. The political leaders of the Arabs rejected the plan,however, and history has again changed to some extent "our best-laid plans."

It should be noted that partition was also strenuously rejected by the leaders of some of the Jewish factions as well—perhaps most notable was future Prime Minister Menachem Begin who envisioned a Jewish state of different composition. However, regardless of the opposition of many, the birth pangs of a nation had already beg

CHAPTER 15
BIRTH PANGS OF A NATION

On February 1, 1948, the offices of the English language Zionist newspaper, *The Palestine Post* (which would become *The Jerusalem Post*), were devastated by an explosion. Witnesses reported that a police car was involved in the attack (later determined to be driven by British deserters wearing police uniforms, working as mercenaries). Three weeks later, Jewish West Jerusalem was shaken again—by an even worse catastrophe.

At 6:30 in the morning of February 22, 1948, young David Lindsey climbed into bed with his parents, telling them he wanted "peoples in bed with me." Suddenly, an enormous explosion shook the city. Bob and Margaret rushed into the children's bedroom where Margaret Lenore and Barbara were still in bed. Glass and plaster covered David's bed, but miraculously, the girls were unharmed. While Margaret comforted the children, and cleaned up the broken glass and debris, Bob quickly dressed and rushed outside to locate the source of the explosion and to help the injured. He later wrote of the incident:

> As I ran down Henrietta Szold Street toward the downtown area, broken glass from shattered windows crunched under my shoes. Turning onto King George, the air was so thick with dust from the explosion that I paused to tie my handkerchief over my nose and mouth. When I reached Ben Yehudah Street, only a couple of blocks from our house, a site of massive destruction loomed before me. The first thing I noticed was that a whole five-story building had been completely demolished. Broken glass, stone, and concrete were every-

where. Steel doors had been ripped from their hinges as if made of cardboard. Bodies lay among the debris in grotesque positions alongside body parts torn from other victims. As I stopped in shocked disbelief, the eerie silence was punctuated only by the groans and cries of the injured and dying. As a few people gathered, we began to help the living out of the wrecks of their homes. I worked for eight hours in the rescue operations and finally went home when it seemed apparent that all the living must have been taken out. I later learned that three British Army lorries, loaded with explosives (which British deserters had parked on Ben Yehudah Street) had exploded, bringing down three tall buildings and damaging a number of others. Fifty-four people were killed and more than one hundred fifty were injured. Viewing the devastation, it seems miraculous that more people were not killed.

Shortly after this, one of Bob Lindsey's Hebrew language teachers was killed by gunfire in the street.

Baptist House lost any semblance of privacy as more and more people were invited into the hostel. The Lindsey's had only two rooms that were "private" — their bedroom (where the children also now slept), and Bob's office (although a young man slept on the couch in there too). The whole Jewish section of Jerusalem was similarly crowded.

The increasing civil unrest ultimately made it expedient for the women and children of those serving in Palestine to leave the country. As soon as possible, Bob and Margaret with their children and their colleague Eunice Fenderson traveled by armed, armored bus in a convoy to Haifa. Bob arranged passage for them on a ship going to the United States and then returned to Jerusalem in another armed convoy. The trip to and from Jerusalem was especially dangerous since the Arabs were attempting a blockade of the main road from the coast through the hills to Jerusalem.

Bob planned to stay for the duration of the conflict because he wanted to be with his congregation and with those in the hostel during the difficult days ahead. In a letter dated 24th March, 1948, he wrote:

> I plan to stay and help to keep things together in these difficult days. Our Jewish friends appreciate any help that we can give at this time. They have suffered many years at the hand of people who call themselves Christians, and I feel that if we can help, we should do so.

Writing of her decision to evacuate with the children, Margaret explained:

> Tragedy and horror mounted as the days passed and seemed for us to culminate in the Ben Yehuda Street disaster. Bob and others from our place worked all day helping with rescue operations. They came at intervals for something to eat—dirty, tired, unable to speak of the tragic sights they had been witnessing. The next day, Bob said that he felt that I should take the children and leave with Miss Fendersen, who was planning to leave the following week. At first I protested strongly, until I realized that having the children there was only adding to the anxiety and responsibilities for my husband, which seemed to be increasing daily. Although we had found through experience that God wonderfully protected our children, it seemed clear that at that particular time it was my responsibility to take them to a place of safety.
>
> It was as clearly my husband's responsibility to stay, and Miss Violet Long felt that it was also of great importance to continue her hostel work, especially during this time of stress. Our hostel was providing housing for a number of Jewish people at a time when they were having to leave their homes or were being bombed out and were desperate for rooms. Besides our regular group of hostel young people, we had made room for numbers of refugees from border sections from which they were obliged to leave. The food and kerosene shortage made it necessary for someone to spend a great deal of time with officials, trying to get ration cards, and

still more time standing in lines for supplies. Through great patience, plus her natural attractiveness, Violet was able to register our hostel with the Jewish authorities and secure food and fuel rations for all in the house.

Good-byes were difficult because of a certain feeling of finality, as if we had come to the end of an epoch or period of some kind. One could not help wondering, with so much death and the prospect of worse things to come, which of the familiar faces one would see again. We made one false start, with early farewells and a hurried breakfast, only to find that the convoy of armored busses in which we would travel, had been attacked and was unable to get through the day before. The following day we left Jerusalem. The morning air was crisp and cool but the sun was warm and the sky blue. Spring was in the air, but we could not enjoy it from the dark inside of an armored Jewish bus. Bob traveled with us to Haifa. He, Miss Fenderson and I each held a child on our laps. We were crowded into a bus on long, low seats. There were small slits in the top of the bus, which had armor plate shutters, to be opened or shut as circumstances dictated. There was an air of tension inside as we waited for the convoy to start. Everyone was quite conscious of the fact that the convoy could very easily be attacked on the stretch of road that ran through Arab controlled territory. We were tightly squeezed in but were asked to move closer to make room for another person. Our only back rests were the knees of the people behind us! At last we started rolling through the Jerusalem streets and out of the strife-torn city. Praying all the way, we rejoiced when the convoy reached Haifa without incident.

Bob's plans were altered, however, when it became necessary to evacuate Violet Long from Jerusalem. She had served in Palestine as a Southern Baptist representative since January of 1946 and planned to stay in Jerusalem in spite of the increasing violence. With the May 15 deadline for completion of the British pullout from Palestine drawing near, the violence further escalated. Consequently, it was decided that Violet Long should go to Egypt where she could stay for a couple of months with the hope that conditions would improve in Palestine. Because of the effectiveness of the Arab blockade of the road going north and west to the coast, however, the only way Bob could get her out was through the east. He later wrote of their April 21, 1948 departure from the besieged city:

> One of the good things about an American white shirt is the fact that it can be reversed, buttoned in the back, and, when accompanied by a vest treated similarly and covered by an ordinary coat, looks like a clerical collar. Thanks to that fact I was able to leave besieged Jerusalem last April via the only safe road out.
>
> We live in the new part of Jerusalem in the midst of one of the nicest Jewish sections. There, in the little chapel which is used by Jerusalem Baptist Church, it is my duty to hold four services weekly, two in English and two in Hebrew. Our section, the largest Jewish section in Jerusalem, was already long since disconnected from the Arab areas of town by rock barriers in the streets and pillboxes in the balconies of the houses on the borders. However, two barbed-wire areas, remnants of an attempt to protect British soldiers from Jewish terrorists, separated the main Jewish area from the Arab sectors. It was still possible to cross from a Jewish sector through a British zone into an Arab area but, of course, Jewish persons did not dare go further than the British zone. And to get out of Jerusalem, only one road was really safe, the road running east to Jericho and up to Amman, Transjordan. On all the other roads there was fighting. It would be necessary to leave our area, pass through a neutral British zone and get a seat in an Arab taxi going to Amman. We would have to go only as American Christians but, wearing the usual European dress, we would be taken for Jewish as readily as Americans by Arabs. And there were some of the Arab fighters who would shoot first, ask questions later! That is where the reversal of the shirt came in.
>
> Saying good bye to our Jewish neighbors we

shouldered our lightly-packed suitcases. (I intended to return alone to Jerusalem) crossed into the neutral zone where I changed my shirt and vest to the required position and went into the Arab sector. Fortunately, many Arabs in Jerusalem are nominal Christians and all Jerusalem Arabs are acquainted with the clerical collar. Although looked over carefully by some of the Arab irregular guards, we were in a few minutes safely "on the Jericho road" riding away from the tragic city, which a few weeks later became the scene of the bloodiest battle Palestine has seen in many years.

On April 23, 1948, Bob wrote Margaret from the village of Taibe, Transjordan:

Believe it or not here I am in Taibe, the new village where Finlay and Julia have come to make their home. Violet and I came from Jerusalem two days ago to Amman hoping to get Egyptian visas. We were able to get the Egyptian visas but unable to get plane passage to Egypt. Whom should we see on the street on Thursday morning, however, but Finlay and Julia. They invited us to go out to Taibe, which is in the direction of Syria, and then they would take us to Beirut where air passage would be more easily obtainable.

Taibe is strictly an Arab village but it is in some of the most beautiful country I have ever seen in Palestine or Transjordan. The hills roll down towards the Jordan. There are some 25 villages in a radius of 15 miles from here and any of them you can see from the village itself. The land is rich and fertile as we saw this afternoon on a hike outside the village.

Their house has five rooms. Mrs. Saccar lives in one with little Jimmy. The floors are of concrete but terribly roughly made. Part of the walls are of mud and straw but I must say that I like it a great deal, especially their living room which has a bamboo ceiling, which with their new Persian rug, gives the place an air of a sort of den. They

> have no electricity of course, but the gas lamps are good.
> Water is brought each day in tannikis and Finlay is trying
> to rig up a can so one spigot at least will have water.

After four days in Taibe, circumstances resulted in Finlay and Julia Graham taking them to Damascus rather than to Beirut. From there Bob and Violet flew to Cairo where she was welcomed at the American Mission, a girls' school, and Bob went to stay with some acquaintances. After a week in Cairo, with conditions in Palestine continuing to deteriorate, Violet decided to go on to Alexandria where she booked passage on a ship due to sail for America on May 22. To get back to Palestine, it was necessary for Bob first to fly to Cyprus. He wrote from Cyprus to his Area Secretary of the Southern Baptist Convention Foreign Mission Board on May 9:

> I am in Cyprus on my way to Haifa. I am to leave
> tomorrow by plane for Haifa. It is a chartered plane on
> which I was able to get a seat. The British apparently still
> maintain control of the airport in Haifa though the Jews
> have taken Haifa over completely—Arabs had been
> shooting for months there before they did so. I am still
> uncertain whether it will be possible to make the trip to
> Jerusalem but understand that the roads from Haifa to
> Tel Aviv and one of the main roads from Tel Aviv to
> Jerusalem is completely in Jewish hands.

Bob landed in Haifa on May 10 and proceeded on to Tel Aviv, but was unable to go to Jerusalem because of fighting. On May 14, 1948, sixty-two year old David Ben Gurion announced the establishment of the State of Israel and was named its first Prime Minister. The next day the United States recognized Israel as a sovereign nation. Immediately upon the declaration of Israel's statehood, soldiers from seven Arab countries attacked the new nation with an avowed purpose of pushing the Jews into the sea. Thousands of Arab residents left their homes and fled to the surrounding areas under Arab control to escape the war.

On May 22, Bob wrote Margaret from Tel Aviv:

> Darling,

Well, here I am sitting in a cafe in Tel Aviv not so far from Yedida's place. I have really met a lot of people since last week. [I] have been invited to several homes and today even went swimming with a man and his 20-year-old daughter, rather a nice looking girl with long black hair. She reminds me a lot of you. This afternoon I went to see a boy named Popkiss who was near the bus station the other day when a couple of bombs fell. Lots of people were killed near him but he got off with only a few bad shrapnel wounds. The bombs killed some 41 people but if the public had not been so negligent, no one would have been killed. The trouble was that few people went to the bomb shelter. Everyone in the shelter was alright. People are much more careful now when the alarm goes off.

The Egyptians keep coming three or four times a day. Seems they think they have easy picking. Actually they do very little actual damage. Their bombs are only 25 kilos. I am wondering about Jerusalem these days. Yesterday the paper said Jews have gotten to the old city but the Arab Legion has been shelling Jerusalem. 3 shells fell at Ratisbonne. I wonder if any fell near us. We have absolutely no connections you know. I have written a long letter to Shreckinger and Miss Tierstein, asking them to go ahead as best they can until I get back.

Yesterday I sent a telegram to you asking about 400 dollars I had cabled the Board for. I cannot get at any of the funds I have in Jerusalem. My plan is to come back via Switzerland and France and Holland. I should arrive sometime the latter part of June.

I wonder if you realize how much I still miss you. I wonder too if I will ever be able to kiss you enough to make up for all these weeks without you. Life seems almost too short to miss out on any one of those precious moments with the one you love more than anyone else in the world.

Perhaps, on the other hand, our separations bring out the love one really has—or as perhaps some are—don't have. I only know that this separation has only resulted in my dreaming more of you than ever before if that is possible.

Ernest Schreckinger and Miss Tierstein, who were residents in the hostel, agreed to be in charge of the Baptist property in Jerusalem. After three weeks in Tel Aviv with no way to get to Jerusalem, Bob reluctantly boarded a ship sailing for France. He finished the letter begun in Tel Aviv in Marceilles, France:

> This letter I started so long ago that I am ashamed to send it now but actually there was no way to send mail until we arrived at Messina and then I had no stamps, it being a holiday and all there. We arrived in Marceilles June 6 and I have been so busy getting things settled, helping people with bags, etc. that I have only dropped you this note and will write you another today.
>
> All my love, darling,
> Bob

After he received funds in France, he sailed on to America. Bob was reunited with Margaret and the children at her aunt's house in Leonia, New Jersey. They continued to Oklahoma where they would spend their furlough.

Since the November 1947 United Nations vote to partition Palestine, attacks on Jews and Jewish settlements had been constant. The Jews had known for many years that their increasing presence and growth would ultimately result in increasing Arab-Jewish conflict. Although during World War II Jews fought with the Allies and gained their sympathy, under the British Mandate they were not permitted to import tanks, cannons, and guns needed to prepare for a war. Consequently, when the actual war finally erupted, the Israelis' armaments consisted primarily of light weaponry that they had smuggled in, stolen from the British, or manufactured in clandestine factories. Subsequently, during the fighting they also were able to capture some enemy arms. Once independence was declared and the fledgling nation was officially recognized by other nations, however, they were able to purchase needed armaments and equipment openly.

For the Israelis, their greatest asset was courage and determination—the alternative was annihilation. There simply was nowhere else on earth they could go—the doors were either closed or very slightly open to immigration. The Arabs, on the other hand, had their own aspirations for independent statehood—but those plans included all of Palestine. Further complicating the matter, the plans of the more radical Jewish elements also included all of Palestine.

It is interesting to note that at the same time Jews were immigrating to Palestine, Arabs also were immigrating, drawn in part by increasing economic prosperity brought about by Jewish settlement. For example, their draining the malaria infested northern swamps opened the region to agricultural and urban development. Differences in religion and national aspirations, however, made peaceful coexistence a seemingly unattainable goal. In religious and ethnic disputes, emotion rather than logic is generally the rule—the Arab-Jewish conflict is no exception.

In June and July of 1948, the fighting was at its height in and around Jerusalem. The Jewish quarter of the walled Old City fell to the Arabs and for forty-two days the Jewish section of the New City outside the walls was shelled at random by the Arabs. Around 700 people, mostly civilians, were killed—thousands more were wounded. During those days and nights more than twenty people lived, slept, and ate in the basement of Baptist House. They stacked stones and bags full of dirt around the basement windows and ventured outside to cook what food they had over a wood fire, since no other source of fuel was available other than what wood could be scavenged. The fighting had disrupted all essentials—in addition to no fuel, there was no electricity, food was extremely scarce and the only water available was from cisterns. Indoor toilets were no longer functional.

By the first of the year, after a series of cease fire declarations, the fighting had subsided somewhat so that conditions were beginning to normalize. In January of 1949 the *Knesset*, the unicameral legislature of Israel, moved from Tel Aviv to Jerusalem and proclaimed Jerusalem the capital of Israel. Chaim Weizmann was elected to serve as Israel's first president.

It was out of this cauldron of unrest and suffering that the nations of Israel and Jordan were born and took their places upon the world stage.

CHAPTER 16
LIFE IN THE
NEW STATE OF ISRAEL

Bob's parents were much relieved when he finally arrived in the United States. In a letter to Bob, Margaret and the family dated June 27, 1948, Elsie Lindsey wrote:

> I think the sweetest voice that I have heard since Bob spoke his first words thirty years ago to his mother and dad was when Bob called Friday night. I was simply thrilled beyond measure. You will never know how I have worried the past three years since you all left the American shores for Palestine. I know that you wanted to go, but it was so hard for Dad and I to think it the thing for you to do, and I do hope and pray that you will not return in our lifetime. There are so many things in America for you, and I know you are going to find them.

With the U.N. peacekeepers in place, however, Bob and Margaret were anxious to return to the Middle East. Following their furlough in Oklahoma, they traveled to New Jersey for a brief visit with relatives. Then, on March 27, 1949, the Lindseys boarded a commercial airliner for an all-night flight to Europe, with stops in Iceland and Ireland and then on to Paris. That was the first time Margaret and the three children ever had flown. The family spent a week sight-seeing in Paris, then flew on to Athens and finally to Lydda, Israel.

Bob had been out of the country for nine months—the rest of the family for over a year. As the Lindseys excitedly disembarked from the plane, they looked up and, for the first time, saw the Israeli flag flying over the terminal. The flag had two horizontal blue stripes on a white field with a blue six-pointed star between the stripes. The star is called the *magen David* (literally, Shield of David).

The hexagram or six-pointed star is formed by two equilateral triangles which have the same center and are placed in opposite directions. It was used as early as the Bronze Age, possibly as an ornament or a magical symbol, in many diverse cultures from Mesopotamia to Britain, with its use spreading in the Iron Age. According to G. Scholem:

> The prime motive behind the wide diffusion of the sign in the 19th century was the desire to imitate Christianity. The Jews looked for a striking and simple sign which would "symbolize" Judaism in the same way as the cross symbolizes Christianity. This led to the ascendancy of the *magen David* in official use, on ritual objects and in many other ways....When the Nazis used it as a badge of shame which was to accompany millions on their way to death it took on a new dimension of depth, uniting suffering and hope. While the State of Israel, in its search for Jewish authenticity, chose as its emblem the *menorah* (a seven branched lamp stand), a much older Jewish symbol, the *magen David* was maintained on the national (formerly Zionist) flag, and is widely used in Jewish life. (*Encyclopedia Judaica*, vol. 11, p. 696-697).

Because Bob was in Tel Aviv on the day that independence was declared, he, Margaret, and all their children were given "permanent resident" status. This had the advantage, among other things, of their not being required to request visas to enter the country. (In the future, however, the status had the disadvantage of requiring the Lindsey children—both boys and girls—to petition for release from military duty when they were ready to pursue university studies in America.) Bob wrote of their arrival:

> At the airfield in Lydda where we landed things seemed normal enough. Almost too normal—it took us

over an hour and a half to pass customs, produce medical examinations, have letters looked through, etc. and we could not help noting that the whole system was the one left by the British when they left this country. Even the simple desks and the typical paper files were the same we have always known in this land. There was one difference: the officials spoke Hebrew or English with a non-English accent and seemed at great pains to put us at our ease. Politeness was the motto—a virtue not always considered important here. And we have found most of our relationships with the already smoothly-running machinery of the State accompanied with this courtesy ever since returning.

The trip to Jerusalem was an expensive one as well as a bumpy one. As it was late in the afternoon by the time we got away from the airport, we were obliged to hire a special taxi. Fortunately, an American gentleman anxious to get to Jerusalem was glad to share expenses so we felt justified in getting the taxi. The road to Jerusalem is now approximately twice as long as it used to be due to the fact that a small part of the older road is still held by the Transjordan Arab Legion. The new road is sometimes called "the Burma Road" because (like its namesake) of the speed and difficulty with which the road was built last year by the Israelis in order to preserve connections between Jerusalem and the rest of the Jewish section of Palestine. It was asphalted in such a hurry that by now the majority of it is full of "chug-holes" caused by heavy traffic and the winter rains. A few weeks ago, I might add, repair on the road was begun and by the end of summer it will undoubtedly be in good shape.

Along the way they saw buildings that had been bombed and burned while others bore distinctive pock marks left by bullets. When they reached Baptist House, they were greeted with a heartwarming homecoming. Neighbors rushed over to welcome them back. The grocer, Mr. Suber (whom the children called "Superman"), hearing that they were home, closed his little shop and came running over to give Bob kisses on both cheeks—but Margaret got only a handshake!

The Lindseys knew shells fired from the Arab-occupied Old City had landed on their house and compound and were eager to learn how much damage had been done. They were amazed to discover that the place looked much the same! Most of the Lindseys' friends, including the children, proudly told of having been wounded at least once, and showed their scars to prove it. Fortunately, all the wounds of people on the compound from shell fragments had been relatively minor. This was in spite of the fact that on one occasion several large fragments had pierced the basement windows and buried themselves in the door and wall on the opposite side of the room. Upstairs, one shell had hit above Bob and Margaret's bedroom and had penetrated the tiles but not the ceiling. Three or four shells fell into the back yard and made sizeable craters. The workshop and garage had many holes in them caused by shrapnel. Every window in the house had been broken, but the Schreckingers had installed new glass as soon as possible.

A young man who once had stayed with the Lindseys for a month, had been killed by a direct hit from a 25-pounder. The survivors readily related details about conditions during the forty-two days of shelling.

"During the shelling we had only about one *pita* a day to eat," volunteered one of the hostel residents. (*Pita* is the Hebrew name for the flat loaves of bread, weighing about 4 ounces.)

"Yes, we are looking all right now," said a neighbor, "but you should have seen us during and after the shelling."

"That's for sure," said another. "I lost twenty-five kilos and Amos lost thirty."

"Look at the holes where the shells hit," excitedly remarked another pointing to the holes still in the yard and where holes in the streets had been repaired.

Four months after their arrival Bob wrote of the destruction he observed outside the Baptist compound:

> There are sections of the city, especially in and around the Old City, where the destruction has been much worse. Not a few buildings we have known and admired are mere hulls now, roof and windows long since blown

off. I have managed to get to the Bible Society building. It is gutted and the kindly shop we used to know is littered with pages of Bibles and broken furniture. It stands very near the Old City wall and was one of the buildings fought over by both sides.

Today at least 85% of the city of Jerusalem is in the hands of the Israeli army. With the signing of an armistice with Syria in Galilee two weeks ago, the last of the Arab countries to make an armistice, we cannot help believing that it will not be long before normal relations with the neighboring states is again resumed. As it now looks, there will be no formal peace treaty with any of the Arab states—merely a proclamation on the part of the United Nations that peace has come to the Middle East.

Two things are impressive about the people of Jerusalem as we see them today. One is the oft-repeated word "miracle." I have personally talked to no one who does not say that it really was a miracle that the Jews of Jerusalem were spared the wrath of the Arab armies. We now know how little ammunition, guns and materiel were actually in the hands of the Israelis. In the middle of May they seem to have had only two real tanks and a very limited number of rifles and small guns, yet with homemade hand grenades and superhuman courage they stopped a well-equipped Arab army with much greater resources in materiel and supplies. The great majority of Jerusalemites seem to believe deeply that only God saved them.

The other impressive thing is the spirit of the people. With victory has come a new stability, a new hope for the future. At least three people I know who talked formerly of leaving Israel for greener fields in some other country now say they cannot even consider leaving. The common struggle has brought about a strengthened morale.

With all this has come a new tolerance I believe. Christian workers are being welcomed and treated with the greatest courtesy. Moreover, I have seen no instance of maltreatment or disrespect of a Jewish Christian as yet.

Today he is an Israeli whatever his faith. Not that there is still no prejudice against Christians and Christianity as represented by people, who in the past erroneously called themselves Christians and who persecuted Jews, but security and a homeland has definitely increased tolerance.

Upon their return, the Lindseys' main tasks were first, to gather their scattered congregation; and second, to make plans to extend their service for the Lord. All the Arabic-speaking members of their church had fled the country before or during the war and did not return. Two of their Jewish members had immigrated to England. Bob went to Haifa and Petah Tikva to look up their Russian members. He also started a weekly Bible study with a small group of acquaintances in Tel Aviv. Around 300,000 refugees had entered Israel in the previous fifteen months, some of whom were Baptists of Jewish background. A number of these found their way to the existing Baptist churches. The Baptist Convention in Israel (or BCI, made up of Southern Baptist representatives serving in Israel) advertised in the newspapers that they were seeking contact with all the new Baptist immigrants. They met many and helped some of them as they established a new life in Israel. For example, they helped some Russian Jewish Baptists to buy a Caterpillar tractor with which they could increase their food production.

Increasing food production was a top priority during these days of persistent food shortages. As a result of the shortages, Bob and Margaret spent many hours standing in lines trying to buy food when there was so much other work to do. Consequently, because of the scarcity, they were forced to make do with whatever was available. For example, for days at a time beets were the only vegetable available in the market so Margaret invented various ways to serve them. It was a special treat when occasionally onions were for sale. On April 13, 1949, during the food shortage, Bob wrote:

> Today is Erev Pesach, the day on which all the house must be cleaned of anything connected with leaven. In former days and still today in places, Jews are in the habit of having a mock sale of all their property to a Gentile in

order to avoid making the mistake of leaving even a crumb of leaven in the house. The Gentile would buy it all and then sell it all back eight days later to his Jewish neighbor — and in return get a little pocket money for his trouble.

Today I walked into our grocery and suggested with a smile that Mr. Suber might have something he wanted to sell an interested Gentile. "You," he said with a grin. "Believe me, you are no Gentile for me. You are one hundred percent, no, one hundred and ten percent a Jew." And then, so I would not think his words were a joke, he added, "I am not joking now, Lindsey. I am telling you straight. For me you are a Jew. Anyhow, what does it matter? I like anyone who loves people."

In 1947, the United Nations had proposed that Jerusalem become an international city, being neither part of Israel nor of a Palestinian state. When the war was over, however, Israel occupied the largest part of Jerusalem and the Palestinians, a smaller part that included the ancient walled city. By a U.N. agreement, a strip of land about seventy-five yards wide running roughly from north to south through Jerusalem was a demilitarized, unoccupied, buffer zone, or "no man's land." While the area east of the buffer zone was occupied by Arabs, the area did not become a separate Palestinian state. Transjordan took control of the Arab territory in Jerusalem and a large swath of land on the so-called West Bank, the area west of much of the Jordan River and part of the Dead Sea. This area, together with the former Transjordan became known simply as the state of Jordan. Both Jews and Arabs living in Palestine prior to Israel's 1948 declaration of statehood were called "Palestinians." The state of Jordan with its Palestianian Arab majority became a defacto Palestianian state although this fact was never acknowledged by Jordan or the other Arab states.

The only crossing point between Jordanian East Jerusalem and Israeli West Jerusalem was Mandelbaum Gate, situated at the edge of the Musrara neighborhood at the junction of Shmuel Hanavi (Samuel the Prophet), St, George, and Shivtei Yisrael (Tribes of Israel) Streets. It was part of a house on the Israeli side (rather than a "gate") that once had belonged to a Dr. Mandelbaum from whom it derived its name. A corresponding building on the Jordanian side was connected by a paved street across the buffer zone or "no man's land." It was used primarily by diplomats and tourists and was monitored on the Israeli side by Jewish and United Nations officials and on the Jordanian side by Jordanian and United Nations officials. The Mandelbaum Gate could be compared to Checkpoint Charley that existed in the Berlin Wall. In both cases it was difficult for everyone and impossible for some to cross over either way. Whoever crossed had to be "released" by one side, and "received" by the other. The requirements about who could leave and enter either side changed from time to time on both sides of the border. There was neither regular mail service between the east and the west in Berlin or Jerusalem, nor telephone service!

Christmas of 1949 was a memorable experience for the Lindseys and their church in spite of the fact that Jerusalem was a divided city. Before the war many Christians would visit the Church of the Nativity in Bethlehem on Christmas Eve. Now most of the people of the Baptist congregation could not get a permit to cross from Jerusalem, Israel, to Jerusalem, Jordan, and the few miles on to Bethlehem. On Christmas Eve more than seventy people attended a special service at the Baptist Chapel. After the service several cars, filled with adults and children, drove out to Kibbutz Ramat Rachel on the border, four miles from Bethlehem. They stood in an open field and sang Christmas carols while looking across the fields to the distant lights of the city where Jesus was born. Standing quietly, they could hear the church bells ringing in Bethlehem, primarily a Christian Arab city at that time. Bob, Margaret, and their children, as well as many of the church members, continued this tradition for the next eighteen years, until the border between Israel and the West Bank was opened in 1967.

David, Margaret Lenore, and Barbara Lindsey attended a Hebrew elementary school in Jerusalem. Not only did they get an education in Hebrew, but they learned the customs as well. Their teachers explained the meaning of each religious holiday, and the children participated in all the fanfare. The Lindsey children especially liked *Purim*, the Feast of Lots, commemorating the deliverance of the Jews by Queen Esther from a general massacre plotted by the evil Haman.

They had a school carnival in which the children wore costumes, often of traditional national or tribal dress from their countries of origin. One Purim, in the spirit of their family traditions, Barbara and Margaret Lenore dressed like Korean girls (their mother having been reared in Korea) and David like a cowboy (representing Bob's Oklahoma heritage).

A general spirit of tolerance of all Christian churches prevailed in Israel. However, some Christians and Jewish Christians (most of whom insisted that they were still Jews and preferred the term "Messianic Jews") experienced persecution from time to time at the hands of Jewish extremists. It was in this atmosphere of tolerance that, in June of 1950, the Minister of Religion of Israel asked the Jerusalem Baptist Church to present regular radio broadcasts each third Sunday. The forty-five minute programs in Hebrew, designed for Christians, were broadcast on Sunday afternoons over Radio *Kol Yisrael*, (Voice of Israel). Other Protestant groups had their opportunity on the air on the second Sunday of each month.

On the beginning of *Shabbat* (Sabbath), Friday evening March 16, 1951, Margaret delivered her fourth child in Sharei Zedek, the Jewish Orthodox Hospital in Jerusalem. He was a healthy boy that they named Daniel Norman, but whom they called "Danny." The planned birth of a fourth child was evidence that Bob and Margaret's love for children enabled them to resist efforts both by Bob's parents and by their Board to discourage them from having more children.

Ingenuity and creativity were hallmarks of Bob Lindsey's service in Israel. A motorcycle had been their mode of transportation, but with the birth of their fourth child in 1951, the Lindseys faced the growing need for a car. There were very few cars for sale, however, and importing one was not an option. So Bob went to several salvage yards and bought the chassis of a Fiat—an undercarriage, an engine, transmission, wheels, tires, and lights. He assembled the parts—and it worked! He then built a body of plywood, installed used car seats and a windshield, and painted it gray. He neatly painted the car's name in Hebrew on the front, *"TZENA,"* meaning "AUSTERITY." Needless to say, it attracted considerable attention around Jerusalem. A reporter snapped a photo of the family riding in the car and, with an article, published it in the *Jerusalem Post*. However, the reporter renamed the car "Jerusalem Model, 1951."

After nearly two years of translating the New Testament into Modern Hebrew from English and French texts, Bob and his Israeli friends finished the task. The translation was done in handwritten Hebrew and was the first step in producing a New Testament in Modern Hebrew. It was a fertile learning experience and Bob and his friends were anxious to move on to the next step of producing a translation from the Greek text into Modern Hebrew. All the members of the team, however, were under too much pressure from other work to pursue the task at that time—nor was the team ever free to work together again. It would be eight years before Bob would be able to resume the translation in earnest.

After three years of work by the Lindseys and others, the church in Jerusalem was stronger and more vibrant. Bob, however, was anxious to return to the United States to finish his doctorate within the seminary's allotted time. The approaching birth of another child (evidence of their continued resistance to reproductive intimidation) added a sense of urgency to their plans in the spring of 1952.

The Lindseys felt an even stronger bond with the people of the land after having experienced such difficult times with them, but there was also a sense of rightness in Bob's completing his doctorate. The skills gained would provide additional tools that would prove invaluable in his future work. Thus, it was with mixed emotions that the family prepared for its return to America.

CHAPTER 17
A DOCTOR IN THE HOUSE

Margaret's sister Betty Friedericks and her physician husband Carl, who had been serving in Nepal, were returning to the United States with their children for furlough and stopped for a visit in Israel on the way. The Friedericks family then sailed with Margaret (who was almost seven months pregnant) and the four Lindsey children on the *S.S. Independence* from Haifa on May 21, 1952. Bob opted to stay for another six weeks in order to complete preparations relating to the church and other work for the time that he would be away on furlough. He then flew to California where he joined Margaret and the children, who were staying temporarily with Margaret's sister Rachel and Lee Chamness and their family while awaiting the arrival of child number five.

The birth of Robert Lutz Lindsey on August 7 was an exciting time for the Lindsey family except for seventeen-month-old Danny, who wasn't quite ready to permit the new arrival to usurp any of the attention he had previously enjoyed. Following Margaret's recovery, the family drove to Oklahoma to visit Bob's parents as well as the First Baptist Church of Norman, which provided financial and interpersonal support for the Lindseys throughout their service in Israel.

The Lindseys settled near Southern Baptist Seminary in Louisville, Kentucky. Bob and Margaret found the stores, churches, and the city in general much the same as when they had completed their studies there eight years earlier. In retrospect, it was a good experience for the whole family. While Bob spent most of his time in the library, researching and writing his dissertation, the children were learning new skills and experiencing new things. Margaret kept the two younger boys at home but the three older children attended public school. It seemed quite strange to them at first to be taught in English, for although the Lindseys spoke English at home, instruction at their school in Israel was in Hebrew.

By the middle of October the family had accomplished the major tasks associated with relocation to Louisville. Margaret wrote her parents in a letter dated October 16, 1952:

We are finally more or less settled although there's a lot to do in the house and yard, neither which can be done very fast because Bob has to put in so many study hours. It will mean 50 hours a week if he is to be allowed to take his orals in March as he wants to do, so that he can then work on his thesis until the deadline of September. Everyone who has done or is doing it gasps when he says he is trying to get that much done, so I would not be entirely surprised if he doesn't make it. Bob is squeezing in as much speaking as he can on weekends but trying to keep the week free for study.

We've got the living room quite livable now. We sanded the floors and found they were nice under all the dark paint. I painted the woodwork and one wall...We got a good rug which was about half price because it had been used in a booth which a furniture store had at the county fair...We found a baby grand piano for $150 which has a nice tone. New couch and chairs, and tables that Bob made out of new doors finish the room. Still have to get drapes but they'll have to wait until we get a little out of debt!

The children seem to be very happy in school and church activities and are making the adjustment satisfactorily I think. The complaint about them in school is the same as in Israel—too quiet. I was surprised to hear it about Barbara as she is anything but that at home. She's doing very well with her work and loves learning to read.

Danny is a darling, trying to talk more, and lives for going "bye-bye" in the car. I do have trouble with him hitting and poking little Robert. I hope he will get used to him some day so that I will dare leave them alone together.

The children enjoyed playing in the park, watching the squirrels, learning to ride a bicycle, and experiencing four distinct seasons. In Israel they had become accustomed to basically two seasons: one is hot and dry from May to September in which no rain usually falls, and the other is a cold and wet, beginning with the autumn rains in October and usually extends until the first part of May.

Bob's dissertation, entitled *The Philosophy of a Christian Approach to Jews* was accepted and he was granted the Doctor of Theology Degree. He later exchanged it for the Doctor of Philosophy in Theology when that degree replaced the earlier one offered by the seminary. Although it had taken him a little longer than he had hoped to complete the degree and consequently had required an extension of their furlough, preparations to return to Israel were in place by March of 1954.

The Lindseys sailed from Leonardo, New Jersey, on an American freighter for Israel on March 4. The passenger list consisted only of the seven Lindseys and one other man. The accommodations were pleasant and they ate with the officers. When the crew members were not busy, the Lindsey children kept them entertained. The three older children also worked on their lessons from their Calvert Correspondence Courses in order to complete the unfinished school year.

While passing the Azore Islands, the Lindseys were astonished to see millions of birds. They learned that when early Portuguese explorers first visited the islands, they were uninhabited and had scarcely any animals except birds, particularly hawks, called in Portuguese *açores*, to which the islands owe their name.

Their first port of call was Zadar, Yugoslavia. Always alert for any opportunity to experience a new place, Bob traveled with the family by bus to Rijeka. A few days later, they boarded the ship again when it called there. When the ship arrived at Trieste, Italy, the Lindseys rented a car and toured the area. Later, when the ship called at Bari, they rented another car and toured the countryside where they were impressed by the friendliness as well as the poverty of the people. (This was only nine years after the end of World War II. Recovery was slow in many areas following the war.) After a final stop in Brindisi, Italy, they sailed for Tel Aviv, arriving in the shallow water port three and one half weeks after leaving New Jersey.

Since large ships could not reach the wharf at Tel Aviv, they anchored some distance out and passengers and freight were taken ashore in shallow-draft tenders. When the Lindseys stepped onto the wharf, their waiting colleagues broke into loud cheers and clapping. Margaret felt a little embarrassed by the loud welcome in front of the Israeli officials and longshoremen, but Bob was too busy greeting everyone to give it a thought. A forty mile drive to Jerusalem brought them home again to Baptist House. Describing the occasion, Margaret wrote:

> All our colleagues were at the boat to meet us and they gave us a tremendous welcome with a sheaf of gladiolas and many heartwarming words and smiles. We now have six couples and Miss Fenderson, so it looked like quite a group when the rocky little motor boat that took us from ship to shore in Tel Aviv drew up to the dock. The Nazareth group went back home, but then came to Jerusalem the next day and we all had a big dinner together.

While Bob and Margaret unpacked and got settled again, the older Lindsey children looked up friends in the neighborhood. Both they and their friends were surprised to see each other "two years taller." Eleven year old David had not forgotten his Hebrew, but nine year old Margaret Lenore and eight year old Barbara had difficulty conversing at first. Before long, however, they were happily chattering away in Hebrew with their friends. The children enjoyed riding the bicycles brought back from America for the older children along with a tricycle and a dump truck with pedals for the two younger ones. Due to the strong U.S. dollar exchange rate with the Israeli currency, the Lindseys were able to hire a lady to help with house cleaning and another to take care of the little boys in the afternoon five days a week. This permitted Margaret to be free to do the family shopping, to make visits, and to be involved in other activities.

Bob assumed pastoral responsibility for the church again where he led three weekly services. Although he had returned to Baptist House as Doctor Robert L. Lindsey, he was still plain "Bob" or "Pastor

Lindsey" to almost everyone, still unpretentious as ever. A few people, however, always insisted on referring to him more respectfully as "Doctor Lindsey."

His office was a large room located at the rear of Baptist House. Here he spent his time counseling with visitors, answering the questions of inquirers and church members, preparing translations of books and articles, preparing sermons, and attempting to keep pace with the constant flow of correspondence that resulted from his serving as secretary of the Baptist Convention in Israel (BCI). When the BCI decided to make Jerusalem the center for its literature work, Bob's office served as a clearing house for the preparation of manuscripts, printing arrangements, and proofreading demanded of such work. (The BCI would later relocate its publishing work to Tel Aviv.) During the time he was not involved with other responsibilities, which was usually late at night, Bob edited the translation into Modern Hebrew of C. S. Lewis' book *Miracles* and Ronald Bainton's *Church of Our Fathers*. While others did the actual translation, it was Bob's responsibility to insure that the Hebrew was faithful to the original English text. He also helped translate and edit a new hymnal for Hebrew-speaking people, which was printed in 1956 with the title *Shir Hadasha*, (*A New Song*). Although it included many traditional hymns translated from English into Hebrew, it also included many hymns and choruses originally written in Hebrew. The new hymn book proved to greatly enhance the worship experience of Hebrew-speaking Christians.

By the time the Lindseys had returned to Israel, plans were well underway to erect buildings at the farm where the George W. Truett Children's Home would be relocated. The home kids (as they were affectionately known) and nearly everyone concerned with Baptist work in Israel gathered on September 25, 1954, for the ground-breaking ceremony for the buildings at the farm in the beautiful Sharon Valley. Three of the children, Dalal, Ali, and Raufi together turned the first spade of soil.

Milton and Marty Murphey were in charge of the children's home in Nazareth at this time, and it fell mainly to Milton to keep abreast of the new construction at the farm. He set up camp on the property in order to be on hand to try to keep things moving. Periodically, the children of the orphanage were brought to the farm to view the progress of the construction. By early summer the buildings were completed and furnished.

During that summer there were separate week-long camps for boys, girls, and men at Baptist Village. Then Bob directed an all-Israel Baptist encampment at the facility for a week. Each room was full of happy, talkative youth, both Arabs and Jews, enjoying fellowship. Together they discussed the claims of the Gospel as the solution to many of Israel's problems, especially the bitterness and hatred that many Arabs and Jews feel for each other. However, it was readily apparent to these Arabs and Jews who had acknowledged Jesus as Lord of their life that they truly could experience forgiveness and love for each other.

Ever since the Baptists had bought the land, it had been referred to simply as "the farm." Now, in addition to being a farm, it was to become the new location for the children's home. In the future, facilities for a Baptist retreat and conference center would be built, as well as a place of meeting and worship for a local Baptist congregation. The sign near the road appropriately read "Baptist Center," in English, Hebrew, and Arabic (literally, Village of the Baptists or Baptist Village in Hebrew and Arabic—the name by which it later would be known). Everyone concerned experienced a great sense of excitement as well as a little apprehension as they anticipated the first event that would mark the official opening of the Baptist Center—moving day for the children's home.

Chapter 18
A Quiver Full of Arrows

Like arrows in the hand of a warrior,
So are the children of one's youth.
How blessed is the man whose quiver is full of them...

—Psalm 127:4, 5a

Few people have ever experienced anything like moving day from Nazareth to the farm near Petah Tikva for Milton and Marty Murphey, their sons David and Mark, the Arab workers, and the nineteen children: Adnan, Affaf, Aida, Ali, Amira, Ann, Bacilla, Dalal, Damianous, Easa, Edward, Hadiya, Katrina, Lorice, Milady, Raufe, Rema, Rhadia, and Therese. As they arrived at the farm and viewed the completed buildings and grounds that would be their new home, the children and workers were struck with the contrast to the cramped facilities they had vacated in Nazareth.

The main building was in the form of an "H". A large multipurpose room, affectionately called "the playroom," was located in the middle of the "H", while the two wings included offices, school rooms, bedrooms, dining room, kitchen, utility rooms, and quarters for the workers. In addition to functioning as an informal place of gathering and play, the playroom served as an assembly room for school on weekdays and was used for church on Saturdays. One of the wings had a second story that contained an apartment where the Murpheys would live.

The bedrooms were painted colorful shades of pink, green, and yellow. Now, only three or four children would occupy the same room, rather than six or seven as in Nazareth. Each bedroom had its own sink and there was a large bathroom on each wing. No longer would all nineteen children have to share one bathroom.

The yard was carpeted with grass, rather than bare rock and gray dirt as their previous residence. The swimming pool, the play room with a large stone fireplace, and the light, attractive class rooms seemed almost too good to be true. As if that weren't enough, there also were wide covered porches and corridors where they could run and play during bad weather.

The curriculum of the school followed that of the Israeli schools so that the students could pursue further studies at the university level. Originally, except for Hebrew language study, classes were taught in Arabic by local Arab teachers. The home children grew up speaking both Arabic and English, and because they studied Hebrew in school, they soon became fluent in Hebrew as well. In fact, they spoke a mixture of the three languages, moving from one to another to find a word to express what they wanted to say.

As the home children grew older, high school classes were added. Some subjects in addition to language study were then taught in Hebrew because of the availability of a Hebrew speaking teacher and other classes were taught in English. Although the establishment of the school at the farm grew out of the home children's need for education, boarding students were later accepted. Children of Baptist colleagues and others came to the school from Jerusalem, Haifa, Tel Aviv or elsewhere.

Ironically, even though most of the home children were Arabs, they all learned and sang the Israeli National Anthem, *Hatikva, (The Hope)*. *Hatikva* is a song of yearning and hope for a homeland that became the anthem of the Zionist movement in 1897. The Hebrew words mean:

> *As long as deep in the heart*
> *The soul of a Jew yearns,*
> *And towards the East*
> *An eye looks to Zion,*
> *Our hope is not yet lost—*
> *The hope of two thousand years*
> *To be a free people in our land,*
> *The land of Zion and Jerusalem.*

When the Murpheys were assigned to a year of Hebrew language study in Haifa, the Lindseys were assigned to serve as directors of the children's home and the farm. In addition, Margaret would serve as principal of the school. In the spring prior to the move, Bob wrote in a letter dated April 12, 1956:

> In a kind of general fruit-basket-upside-down action, about three or four of our five couples on the field are changing places this year. The main reason is the need of the younger fellows to get language study.

Margaret also wrote of the move in an April 28 letter:

> Bob says he wrote you about all the "fruit basket upset" we had at the meeting. The whole business was a complete surprise to me, and I guess to everybody. I certainly hadn't contemplated taking over the orphanage responsibility, but in many ways I am enjoying the prospect and hope to be able to do a good job. Of course, this puts Bob a whole lot closer to his Tel Aviv office as well as freeing the Murpheys for language study which they've never had a minute for, having taken over the Home the minute they arrived in the country. I must confess that when we learned that the Scoggins would not return, I rather hoped that we would be "forced" to stay in Jerusalem! Of course, I have no business being this much attached to any one place, perhaps that is reason enough that we should move.
>
> We plan to move about the end of August. Last week when in Tel Aviv we went to see the Headmaster of the Scottish School and talked to him about the possibility of entering the children there next fall. They could live there in the dormitory and go home each Friday till Monday, or they could come in each day (about a forty-five minute trip). Probably we will do the latter as the children are not at all in favor of living away from home. At least we'll try it. Another possibility is to have them part of our own school there at the farm, which I will be supervising, and

have them in a special class of their own. They can't fit with the others whose main language is Arabic, and we want them to have good English and good Hebrew. At present I am rather in favor of sending them to Tabitha (the Scottish School) because they will have wider contacts there. There are about 300 and some students in that school, which goes through high school. About 30 or 40 of them are Americans from the Embassy, UN and business people. I think I will keep Danny and Robert at the farm and perhaps use the Calvert course with them, although Miss Clark says Danny is ready for first grade. He seems to be the brain of the family, is fascinated with numbers and does with ease what would seem to be second grade arithmetic.

Perhaps you saw Bob's telegram published in "Time" magazine some weeks ago in which he said that actually the problems here are ideological but that no ideological solutions are possible without real security for all.

The Lindsey family moved from Jerusalem to Baptist Village on August 21, 1956, to assume their responsibilities at the farm. They came with all their furniture and possessions, including Mack the dog. Mack was a stray Cocker Spaniel that they had adopted in Jerusalem. He soon earned a special place in the hearts of all the children at the farm as well as the workers. The Lindseys occupied the second floor apartment where the Murpheys had lived and became parents to the nineteen home kids as well as their own five. Their quiver was full indeed—but was about to get a little fuller!

Margaret was eight months pregnant with their sixth and final child when the Lindseys moved to the farm. Subsequently, on September 29, 1956, Deborah Kay was delivered in the Scottish Hospital in Tiberias. Because of their love for children, they had resisted all efforts of "intimidation" and had chosen to follow the biblical admonition to "be fruitful and replenish the earth" as Margaret had jokingly commented in a letter.

Danny and Robert Lindsey attended Hebrew kindergarten in the nearby town of Petah Tikva. Much to their chagrin, David, Lenore, and Barbara were enrolled in the Scottish School in Jaffa (*Yafo* in

Hebrew, an Arab city beside—now surrounded by—primarily Jewish Tel Aviv). Not only did it mean leaving the home kids, with whom they were very close, but it meant walking half a mile to the main road at sunrise to catch a bus to Tel Aviv. At the main bus station, they took another bus to Jaffa and then walked to the school. The reverse trip put them back home about sunset. The school was very strict and they hated the whole arrangement. The unpleasantness, however, only lasted a couple of months. When hostilities broke out with Egypt in what would be known as the Sinai Campaign, all the Lindsey children stayed at home for their safety. When the war ended, the three older children did not return to the school in Jaffa but attended school at the farm. The younger boys returned to kindergarten in Petah Tikva.

December is a beautiful month for Christmas in Israel. The Christmas of 1957 was typical of their years at the Baptist Center as described in a letter Bob and Margaret sent to friends and supporters:

> Baptist Center
> Petah Tikva, Israel
>
> December 3, 1957
>
> Dear Friends:
>   As Christmas approaches we are thinking of each one of you and we want you to know it. We wish you might drop in and join us in preparation for our second Christmas at the farm. You would find our roses in gorgeous bloom but the weather turning chilly enough in the evenings to make a bright fire in the huge stone fireplace a welcome sight. The red poinsettias blooming in the yard look Christmassy and the children will soon be bringing in loads of evergreen for decorating.
>   The nineteen children of the Home and our own six are counting the days until December 25th, so although we are not reminded by newspaper, radio, or shop displays that Christmas is coming, nevertheless we are not allowed for one moment to forget it! Rehearsals for the Christmas play and choir vie with coming term tests for the time and attention of everyone--teachers, helpers, and children. This

year our play will be "on the road" for we are traveling to Nazareth to present it on the 22nd in the Baptist Church there. Members of the church will entertain the children in their homes and the boys and girls are wild with excitement. King Herod (usually known as Adnan) is having trouble with his lines, but if he follows the precedent he set for himself last year, he will bring down the house!

People from the surrounding area have already been asking if they may come and see what we do on Christmas. This season has great attraction for the local populace. If they have come from Europe, they are nostalgic for Christmas sights and sounds. If they were born here, they are very curious about it all. We plan to present our play on Christmas Eve for friends from Petah Tikva, Tel Aviv and nearby colonies. Our buildings can be seen from the busy highway, once again we will light a gigantic tree on the roof and play carols over the loud speaker, which can be heard far and wide. All during the year we have people turning in to our road, having been attracted by the "Baptist Center" sign, and coming to ask questions. We know that this opportunity for witness will be multiplied at Christmas time.

After the play we will have Open House and refreshments. The children are busy making decorations for their rooms: cutting, pasting, painting eggshells, stringing popcorn, collecting pine cones, each hoping his or her room will rate the most "oohs" and "ahs" from visiting Jewish children. They've been saving their allowances, too, for gifts for each other and for needy ones. They are showing more and more unselfishness in their plans, which makes us happy.

If you could step in and see the children gathered around their bright tree in the playroom, their faces pink from the blazing fire, you would find a special "Merry Christmas" shining in their eyes. All of us wish you a year rich with God's blessings.

With our love and prayers,

Bob and Margaret

As parents at the children's home, the Lindseys tried to treat all the children the same without showing partiality. All of the children, including the older Lindsey children, worked two hours a day in the fields under the supervision of the men who lived in workers' cottages and farmed the Baptist acreage. Much of the vegetables, dairy products, and meat used at the center was produced right on the farm. In addition to the garden and field work, they all took turns with other chores every day. They took care of the cows and chickens, cleaned classrooms and bathrooms, set the tables, washed dishes, and sorted clothing and ironed. Each child got a weekly allowance that was deposited in his or her in-house bank account, which the Murpheys had set up. Each child had his or her own checkbook, and each wrote a check to draw out money. They also were required to balance their records with a bank statement they received every month.

When a child did not obey the rules, Bob and Margaret never spanked them. They would reason with the child, and if that didn't work, they denied him or her some privilege such as going on the next picnic. Once the children understood the expectations of the directors, they usually lived up to them.

During a meat shortage, Bob and Margaret went out to eat with several Baptist colleagues who were visiting at the farm. They heard about a certain restaurant that was serving liver, so they drove there and enjoyed a nice meal. When it was time to pay, the cashier went to the cash register to accept their money. Walking out, Bob noticed that someone had left a piece of liver on a plate, and seeing an opportunity for Mack to eat some meat, he wrapped the liver in a paper napkin and put it in his pocket. Arriving back at the farm he told his friends that he had found some liver at the restaurant that someone left, and that he'd brought it back for the dog. When one of the women in their party asked where the table was located where he had gotten the liver, Bob replied that it was a certain table near the door. She then told him that was where the cashier had been eating before he had gotten up to accept payment!

The teachers and students at the farm started printing their own newspaper and named it *The Catfish Line*. (Considering Bob Lindsey's enjoyment of taking the children to fish for catfish in the Yarkon River that ran along the back side of the farm, the name chosen for the newspaper is not surprising.) It included articles written by all the children as well as the directors and teachers. The paper, as many as ten pages, was typed by the students, mimeographed on legal-size paper and mailed to nearly everyone they knew. It included news, poetry, fiction, jokes, birthdays, and a sick list. *The Catfish Line* continued for many years, and the following titles and excerpts of articles from the issues show what most interested the children.

Bible Verses I Learned in November.
    In November we bought some baby chicks to raise, but the chicken house burned down and killed them all. We had 17 sheep but two of them died from snake bite so we now have 15. We have so many geese that we can't count them. We have 17 head of cattle. Six are heifers, six bulls and five are cows.

The police took our dog Alexis for rabies tests since he bit someone.
    Our New Choir Robes and Blue Uniforms.

Alexa gave birth to a new calf. She's a girl.
Ali and Johann took our mares, Marcha and Tova, to be bread [sic] by a stallion that belongs to the government.

Our horse Marcha died...ate something that she should not have.

We now have three intramural basketball teams, the Tigers, Bears, and Eagles.

Corrie Ten Boom spoke of her experiences with God in the concentration camp, and she stayed all night with us.

On Dec. 28th our Farm Choir sang for Art Linkletter's TV program that will be shown in the States next Christmas.

We all went to the French Circus. The magician could make things disappear.

On our trip to Ein Gedi, we swam in the Dead Sea, then swam in fresh water at Ein Gedi. A group of soldiers came and sat down with us. We sang some songs for them, and they sang to us. Then we taught them, "Is your Mother at Home, Molly Malleny?" and they taught us "We are Going by Foot."

Dr. Edgar Hallock, a Baptist serving in Brazil, was in Europe for a meeting of the Baptist World Alliance and also made his first trip to Israel to visit the Lindseys and us. During that visit Israel had her first International Bible Contest; Edgar was really impressed that Bob was one of the five judges. The others were rabbis.

Every year Bob had several special events for the seniors in the high school. He would lead them in a seminar about an important place, and then after the academic work, he would take the youth there for a visit. They traveled as far away as the Negev, Eilat, and Massada.

On other occasions, he and Margaret would take all the children to Ashkelon or Caesarea and stay all night on the beach in two big tents. Their favorite games were football (soccer) and the "war game." In the mornings Bob had prayers with them, and encouraged the children to memorize key Bible verses—the prize was usually one piece of candy per verse. There was more scripture memory and fun at the end of each school year when a "Vacation Bible School" would be held. Daughter Barbara remembers memorizing the first ten chapters of Acts during one contest.

When the Murpheys returned to the Baptist Center to assume responsibility for the children's home after a year of language study followed by a year of furlough, the Lindseys were enabled to expand their horizon with regard to other work. A special family bond had been established between the Lindseys and the home kids, however, that would last forever. In the not too distant future, that bond would influence Bob Lindsey to risk all for the happiness of one of those children.

CHAPTER 19

THE EXPANDING HORIZON

Even though responsibilities at the farm occupied the major portion of Bob's time, he was involved in other endeavors as well. For years the Lindseys had enjoyed good friends among Israeli artists. Bob conceived the idea of a Baptist art gallery that would increase opportunities for Christian interaction with the Jewish people. He located suitable property in Tel Aviv and led in opening the art gallery in 1957, named *Dugith* (later transliterated *Dugit*), a Hebrew word meaning "little fishing boat." An Israeli director was hired who was keenly aware of trends in art, and had discernment in choosing good exhibits. *Dugith* promoted the work of a number of budding Israeli artists, several of whom later became well known. The exhibits always drew an appreciative crowd. The popular gallery sold art, books, and Christian literature. *Dugith* also was chosen as the name of the Baptist publishing endeavor when it was relocated to Tel Aviv from Jerusalem.

In a letter to friends and supporters dated December 8, 1958, Bob and Margaret reflected on the past year and shared a glimpse of their evolving ministry.

> Once again loving thoughts are coming your way from Israel at Christmas time. Hanukkah, the Feast of Lights, is being celebrated this week, with parties, lighted-torch parades, and a new candle lit each evening in every home until eight candles will be burning on the last day of the feast. The festivities remind us that the Light of the World has come, and we rejoice in His coming.

Bob as a four-year-old in Norman, Oklahoma with parents J.L. and Elsie Lindsey and sister Mary.

Bob Lindsey and Margaret Lutz relax aboard the Japanese ocean liner *S.S. Heian Maru* en route to U.S.A., August 1940.

Bob Lindsey on motorcycle with Margaret, David, Lenore, and Barbara in Bob's plywood car *Tzena*, Jerusalem 1950.

Lindsey family prior to furlough in 1957, from left to right—
Barbara, Lenore, Robert, Debbie, David, Margaret, Bob and Danny.

Bob Lindsey in center translating for Billy Graham on left and Israeli official on right, March 1960.

Lindsey at work in his study in Tiberias near the time (February 14, 1962) that he discovered that the Gospel of Luke was composed before Mark's Gospel.

Congregants gathered outside Baptist Chapel in Jerusalem, 1962.

Lindsey chats with David Ben Gurion, former Israeli Prime Minister and founding father of the modern state of Israel, during a break at an event in Jerusalem, 1971. (Photo: Shlomo Lavie)

Martha Murphey leads the Baptist Village Youth Choir, composed primarily of the "Home Kids" as they perform at the Baptist Church in Jerusalem. Edward "Eddie" Zoumout, the Arab youh that Lindsey attempted to assist in returning to Israel from Jordan, is on the far left of the back row.

U.S. President Jimmy Carter and Bob Lindsey pose on the steps of St. Andrews Church in Jerusalem under the watchful gaze of the Secret Service following the Sunday morning service in which Lindsey preached, 1981.

Bob Lindsey and Hebrew University professors David Flusser and Shmuel Safrai discuss a text. (Photo: David Harris)

Jerusalem Baptist Church following the arson, October 1982.

Service on Shabbat following the arson. Many Jewish neighbors and friends attended the service in a show of solidarity with the Christian congregation.

Jerusalem MayorTeddy Kollek presents the Mayor's Medal of Appreciation to Lindsey as wife Margaret looks on, December 1986.

Lindsey leading Shabbat service in the "Tent" while awaiting
building permit to rebuild fire bombed church building, a permit that was
years in coming.

As we look back on the past year we feel deep gratitude for the evidences of God's working. The Murpheys returned from furlough in August to reassume the duties of directing the Children's Home. Although we had enjoyed the activities of the past two years, we were very happy to see them back, for we keenly feel that the witness in this area can be greatly strengthened as we have the time and personnel to pursue the opportunities before us.

Margaret has continued as school principal here at the farm and we have enlarged the school by accepting boarding students. We have a fine teaching staff with one teacher from Nazareth who takes care of the Arabic part of our curriculum, one from Jerusalem who teaches Hebrew and a young American couple who are part of a student program which has proven most interesting and helpful. Every Monday afternoon a number of our national workers from Nazareth, some from Jerusalem, and of our local staff here, meet for a seminar under Bob's direction. This year we are having an intensive Old Testament study with special emphasis on place names and identification. One of the most interesting features is the field trips we make from time to time. Next weekend we will have a trip to Eilat and through the Negev.

Last February we began to use two cars we had available to collect the people in the surrounding area who were believers and had no opportunity for meeting for worship. As the year progressed, the group expressed the desire to organize into a real congregation. We had Baptists from East and West Europe, America, and a number of "Sabras" (locally born young people), both Jews and Arabs. We were so happy that a spirit of love and tolerance overcame all the differences and we were able to organize on November 17th. It was a service never-to-be-forgotten by the charter members who came forward one by one to sign the "Book of the Congregation" and then celebrated the Lord's Supper for the first time together.

In August we moved into a lovely new home which was nearly finished, located in a grove of Eucalyptus trees a few yards away from the other buildings of the Center. It is right for us and we are enjoying family life again after being part of an institution. David and Margaret Lenore were part of our first eighth grade graduation last June. Margaret Lenore and Barbara especially enjoy their piano lessons and choir. Danny and Robert go to the local Israeli school in Petah Tikva since we don't have classes here to fit them. Debbie (age 2) helps her mother very much in the work both at home and in school!

Margaret's parents, Dexter and Lenore Lutz, visited the family at the Baptist Center in January, 1959. On the way there from Korea, they had visited their daughter in Nepal, and had done some work in India. Always looking for something special to do, Lenore Lutz directed the home kids in a musical drama, *Amal and the Night Visitor*. Her namesake, granddaughter Margaret Lenore Lindsey accompanied the performance on the piano.

By June of 1959, the Lindseys had been working in Israel for five years since their last furlough, and it was time for them to return to America for a year. The family was excited about the furlough for two reasons: 1) they planned to spend two months camping through Europe on the way, and 2) Bob planned to work on translating the synoptic gospels from Greek into Modern Hebrew with Dr. Elmo Scoggin at Southeastern Baptist Theological Seminary in Wake Forest, North Carolina.

On June 16, 1959, Bob, Margaret, and their six children, ranging in age from sixteen to a little less than three years, embarked on their grand adventure. While on a book buying trip to England in 1958, Bob had purchased a van and had shipped it to Cyprus, where he left it for the use of Baptist colleagues for the year. Prior to the family's departure, he shipped a travel trailer he had designed to Cyprus. It was large enough to carry all their luggage, tent, and camping equipment. When they arrived in Larnaca, Cyprus by ship from Tel Aviv, they picked up the van and trailer before taking a ferry to Beirut, Lebanon where they visited the Baptist Seminary and did some sight-seeing. Then they sailed to Egypt where they spent several days before proceeding to Greece by ship.

Camping out in Europe for two months with six children demanded the cooperation of each family member in order to maintain civility and sanity. It wasn't long before they had developed a routine. Upon arriving at a campsite, each family member had a task: putting up the tent, inflating air mattresses, cooking supper, or arranging a lot of paraphernalia where it could be located when needed. Even little Debbie did her part.

Since campsites did not always have a place to do laundry, Bob came up with a creative solution to the problem of doing the daily wash. He mounted a large plastic bucket that held about six gallons of water on the tongue of the trailer. In the morning they would put in all the dirty clothes, add water and soap, and then put the lid on tightly. All day this improvised washing-machine sloshed as they drove along the bumpy roads. Arriving at the next campsite the clothes would be clean. All that was required was simply to rinse them and hang them up to dry.

Such a trip was difficult but financially feasible, and proved very educational for the entire family. They found that the European campsites were well-kept. They had showers and, usually, clean toilet facilities. The cold shower was free, but for a hot shower they put coins into the timer and hurried to finish bathing before the time ran out or before their coins ran out. Most meals were eaten in the camp or picnic style along the road. Sometimes, however, they ate in restaurants. Bob always sought out a place where the local people ate. Not only was it less expensive than the places catering to tourists, but it enabled the Lindseys to gain more of an appreciation of what the local people normally ate. Particularly memorable to the children was one evening when they had arrived in a town after dark. The entire family went to a small local cafe where their entire meal consisted of a huge platter of sliced fresh tomatoes drenched in fresh olive oil, sprinkled with basil and eaten with fresh, hot bread.

From Greece their journey took them through Yugoslavia and Italy. While visiting the Vatican, six-year-old Robert got lost from the family and it seemed ages before he was found. They continued on to Austria, Switzerland, and Germany. Along the Rhine River they celebrated Robert's seventh birthday. After traveling across France, they crossed the English Channel on a ferry and then toured England and Scotland. Arriving back in London, Bob sold the van, trailer, tent and other items. Then it was on to New York City by air where they arrived on August 26. The expedition had taken ten days longer than the two months they had planned, but the experience had given them a greater appreciation of the natural beauty and cultural diversity of the countries they had visited. Their horizons were continuing to expand.

As mentioned earlier, the Lindseys had opted to spend their furlough in Wake Forest, North Carolina near the Southeastern Baptist Theological Seminary in order for Bob to work with his friend, Elmo Scoggin, a Hebrew professor. After serving five years in Israel, Dr. Scoggin had taught at the seminary during the family's furlough. At the end of the furlough year the seminary had prevailed upon him to stay on. Bob and Elmo already had spent many hours studying together in Israel, exploring the problems of translating the Greek New Testament into Modern Hebrew. Here at the seminary Bob also would have opportunities for interaction with the Greek professors. He planned to dedicate the year to the translation of the gospels from Greek to Modern Hebrew.

Bob had yearned to resume the translation project since he and a group of friends in Jerusalem had completed their preliminary translation some eight years earlier. Ever since he had embarked on the task of New Testament translation, the practical needs of those he served, as well as the needs of colleagues serving with him, had always taken precedence over the more scholarly pursuit of biblical research needed for translation. At last he had been blessed with a block of time in which he hoped to make considerable progress toward his goal of providing an accurate and easily understandable New Testament text for those reading it in Modern Hebrew. The tension between time demands for biblical research and the demands of practical ministry, however, was something that this scholar with a pastor's heart was to experience throughout his remaining years of service.

CHAPTER 20
SYNOPTIC PROBLEM

In consultation with Greek scholars at the seminary, Bob decided to use the Nestle and Kilpatrick texts of the Greek New Testament. He first began translating the Gospel of Mark, the shortest of the synoptic gospels and considered by many scholars to be the oldest Gospel. *Synoptic* means "same view," and refers to the three gospels of Matthew, Mark, and Luke because they contain much common material. The Gospel of John, on the other hand, is dissimilar to the Synoptics in both content and style. The similarity of the first three gospels has resulted in the practice of their texts being arranged in parallel columns to form a "synopsis" so that they can be viewed together. The so-called "synoptic problem" relates to the problem of accounting for their parallel relationships as well as for their divergences. Bob's ultimate solution of the synoptic problem was not the focus of his efforts, but rather was a product of the process. The goal of his endeavor was to make his translation from Greek into Modern Hebrew one that would be fully understood by present-day Israelis, but written in the style of Mishnaic Hebrew — the Hebrew in use in the Holy Land around the time of Jesus.

In the introduction to his *A Hebrew Translation of the Gospel of Mark* (Tel Aviv: Dugith, 1969), Bob describes his motivation for the translation and his initial findings that set the course for his future research:

> Some years ago I came to the conclusion that a new Hebrew translation of the New Testament was badly needed, especially by the young Hebrew-speaking Christian congregations in the State of Israel. In 1951,

with the aid of a couple of Israeli translators who worked from English and French texts, I completed a preliminary trial translation. This work was mainly intended to indicate the difficulties to be expected in a more serious translation which I felt must later be made from the Greek text.

It was, however, not until 1959 that I was able to begin the necessary research for this later stage. I chose the Gospel of Mark under the impression that it was the first of our gospels and contained the kind of simple Greek text which would make translating relatively easy. According to the widely-held theory of Markan Priority, which I had no reason to doubt, this Gospel first appeared around 70 A.D. and although not necessarily written by the person we know from the New Testament as "John" Mark, it was apparently used as a principal source in the composition of the gospels of Matthew and Luke. According to the same theory, the writers of these later works wrote independently of each other and not only used the Gospel of Mark but a second common source usually called "Q." It is also generally held that the author of the Markan Gospel must have derived much of his information from Aramaic oral sources, yet wrote his book in Greek.

Rather, to my surprise, the preliminary study of the Greek text of Mark turned up the conclusion that the Greek word order and idiom was more like Hebrew than literary Greek. This gave me the frightening feeling that I was as much in the process of "restoring" an original Hebrew work as in that of creating a new one. Like many a Semitics student before me, as I later realized, I wondered if the Gospel might not be a literal translation from some Semitic original.

Hebrew syntax (word order) is unlike that of either Greek or the Romance languages. Bob observed the same phenomenon in Matthew and Luke that he had in Mark: very often, a literal translation of Greek verses word by word resulted in good Hebrew.

These Greek sentences or phrases with Hebrew word order are known to scholars as *Hebraisms*. A modern analogy that Bob liked to use to illustrate this phenomenon was taken from his boyhood. It sounded strange to him when he heard a German immigrant acquaintance tell his son, "Throw the cows over the fence some hay!" It is perfectly good German syntax but sounds strange in English, even though the intent of the speaker is understood. Thus, the Hebraisms preserved in the gospels provide solid evidence for portions of the material being literally translated by the authors into Greek from a written Hebrew source.

This is diametrically opposed to the theory that the gospels finally were written late in the first century after the material was passed orally for forty years or more and had been shaped by a Greek speaking church. Today, in many academic circles, there is the idea that what Jesus really said was essentially lost during the years of oral transmission. This theory came about in an attempt to explain why the synoptic gospels do not all have the same stories and when one or more do include the same stories, they are not always in the same sequence. Bob concluded that it makes no sense, however, for an oral tradition in Greek to preserve awkward Hebrew syntax. There is a precedent for the literal translation of Hebrew into Greek in the case of the Septuagint—a Greek translation of the Hebrew Scriptures— which was also the Bible of first century Christians as well as Jews living outside the holy land. Long before modern scholars invented the oral tradition theory, however, there was evidence that the sources our gospel writers used were written documents. Around 130 A.D., Papias, the Bishop of Hierapolis in Phrygia, wrote a book entitled *An Interpretation of the Sayings of the Lord*. In it he stated that Matthew had drawn up his record of Jesus' sayings in the "Hebrew language, and everyone translated them as he was best able" (quoted in Eusebius, *Ecclesiastical History* III 39, 16). The Apostle Matthew, as one of the first eye-witnesses, wrote down what the Lord said and did, thus providing a written resource for later Greek Gospel writers. (To date, copies of the actual Hebrew text that Matthew is said to have written have not been found.) Papias also commented on the Gospel of Mark, saying that Mark, as Peter's interpreter, wrote down what he heard Peter say that Jesus said and did, but "not in their order." Evidently, Peter's teaching did not attempt to follow the chronology of Jesus' life and deeds. Here, again, there is no long oral tradition—according to Papias, Peter spoke and Mark wrote down what he heard.

The existence of written manuscripts of Jesus' sayings and deeds from an early Jewish source or sources written in Hebrew predating our oldest known copies of the gospels is of great significance. This places the sources before the writings of Paul and the influence of large numbers of Gentile Christians and lends support to the authenticity of the sayings attributed to Jesus.

Bob knew that most scholars from the nineteenth century onward had assumed that Jesus and the Jewish population in Palestine spoke Aramaic. It is a Semitic language (as is Hebrew) and was spoken and written widely in Persia and Babylon from at least 1000 B.C. It was the primary language spoken by the Jews in exile in Assyria, Babylon, and Egypt. It was assumed that after the Jews returned to Palestine, they continued to speak Aramaic as their primary language. With the discovery of the Dead Sea Scrolls, however, there emerged considerable evidence that from around 164 B.C. and onward to the time of Jesus, spoken Hebrew experienced a revival in Palestine. Accumulating textual and other archaeological evidence has indicated that Hebrew was also a colloquial language, not merely a theological language of the priests and scribes. It is probable that many also knew Aramaic and Greek as well. Even today in the Middle East (and much of the rest of the world), being multilingual is the norm. Indeed, commerce and culture necessitated that a large portion of the population be multilingual. (The United States is one of the few countries where being monolingual is usual.) Thus, Bob Lindsey and most scholars in Israel came to believe that Hebrew was the primary spoken and written language at the time of Jesus. The Hebrew of this time (the so-called Second Temple Period) is termed Mishnaic Hebrew, to distinguish it from the older Biblical Hebrew.

During his furlough year, Bob spoke to civic groups, friends, and churches about his Gospel research for his translation project. Some of his discoveries proved troubling to ultraconservative Christians who insisted upon a "literal" translation of the text. What they may have failed to realize, however, is that any translation, of necessity, incorporates a certain amount of interpretation—even the most literal so-called interlinear translations. This is particularly true when translating from a more concise language such as Biblical or Mishnaic Hebrew into a language with much more extensive vocabulary such as Greek or English. For example, it may be possible to translate a certain Hebrew word by eight or ten different English words, depending upon the context. The translator attempts to select the word that most accurately conveys what he or she believes is intended by the original text. He or she may be influenced in the choice, however, by a certain amount of bias that he or she brings into the process.

Many times a literal translation of a Greek sentence into a modern language makes no sense in the modern language, whether English, Hebrew, or whatever. When there is no clear meaning, it is often because in the original language the word or phrase involves a metaphor, parable, simile, or hyperbole. For example, in Jesus' parable of vineyard workers some worked all day, others worked nine hours, or six, or three or one hour. The landowner paid all of them the wage for a day's work. Those who worked the longest complained. The landowner said, "Is thine eye evil [bad], because I am good?" Matthew 20:15 AV. The statement is a literal Greek translation of an older Hebrew text. While the expressions "good eye" and "bad eye" have no meaning in Greek or English, they are well known Hebrew idioms. Having a "good eye" simply means that one is generous, while having a "bad eye" conversely means that he or she is stingy. (This is still a common Hebrew idiom in use in modern Israel today.) So what the landowner actually is saying is, "Are you stingy because I am generous?" Thus, the literal translation of the Greek text (as occurs in most English translations) does not convey the intent of the Hebrew idiom.

Bible translation is slow, tedious work. On many mornings Bob would go to his office at the seminary and begin translating a verse in Mark. After working all day and all evening, he might have translated only one verse from Greek to Modern Hebrew to his satisfaction—and even that might change with future insight. At other times, progress was somewhat more encouraging.

In the summer of 1960 the Lindseys flew to London where Bob sent the family on to Israel. He then discussed textual problems with Professor G.D. Kilpatrick of Queen's College in Oxford, before flying to Israel on the third of August. Since Bob had been granted assignment for full time biblical research and translation, the family settled in Tiberias in a house belonging to the Church of Scotland Mission. Tiberias is located about fifteen miles from Nazareth and about eighty miles from the Baptist Center.

The house was located on a hill, some one-hundred stone steps above the water, with an inspiring view of the Sea of Galilee. This black basalt stone dwelling was near the Church of Scotland's large hospital compound. One entered the house through a gate in the garden wall and climbed steps up to a veranda. The ground floor had two rooms at the front and a long kitchen and dining room at the back, all with tiled floors. Also, there was a bathroom with a large bathtub that had "feet." An outside stairway led up to the second floor consisting of a very large room and two smaller rooms, with verandas at the front and back.

Behind the house in back of the kitchen was a small plastered room that became Debbie's playhouse. It had a most unusual feature—she was probably the only little girl in Israel with a playhouse erected over an ancient mosaic floor! Behind the main house was a small, two-room caretaker's house of plastered cement blocks. One room served as Bob's study, while the other was used for storage.

The family moved to Tiberias on the seventh of September, 1960. When school started, the three older children boarded at the Baptist Center, and came home every two weeks by bus on Friday afternoons, returning on Sunday afternoons. The younger boys attended a local Hebrew school. Debbie attended an Orthodox Jewish kindergarten where she sang *Jesus Loves Me* for them the first day! Margaret helped the younger children with Calvert correspondence courses in English in the afternoon.

Every day Bob spent hours in his backyard study, praying, preparing sermons, reading, writing letters, and translating. He felt the need of training himself to read and think in Greek and translate it directly to Modern Hebrew without his mother tongue entering his mind. He believed that the English could obscure the meaning in some passages. It was very difficult to achieve this, but, with persistence, it became possible.

When Bob was studying in North Carolina he made up several sheets of paper with three columns. As he came across Hebraic syntax phrases or sentences, which he called Hebraisms in the Greek, he would copy them in the Matthew, Mark, or Luke column, noting the chapter and verse where found. After being in Tiberias a year, he completed the task of screening the synoptic gospels for Hebraisms. As far as Bob knew, no one had ever published a paper showing these Hebraic parallel passages in the synoptic gospels.

Soon Bob was holding services and Bible studies on Friday evenings—in the backyard when the weather permitted; otherwise they met inside the house. The Bible studies attracted a variety of people, including one man who was a fisherman that fished using a cast net as in Bible times.

That period in Tiberias was a great experience for the entire family. Bob made steady progress on the translation; Margaret loved the view of the lake and enjoyed new friends. The older children enjoyed week ends there during the school year and especially looked forward to summer break. David later recalled how meaningful it was to return home from boarding school on a Friday afternoon and to enjoy a big meal with the family at the beginning of the Jewish *Shabbat* (Sabbath). Bob and Margaret went swimming with the children in the Sea of Galilee, hiking, fishing, and on picnics at favorite places in the hills. Debbie often had her playhouse full of little girls from the neighborhood while the boys played soccer in the street outside their gate. But there was no way Bob and the family could know that an event was fast approaching that would shatter the tranquility they enjoyed—an event so devastating that it would threaten to uproot the family and to destroy the labor of the past twenty years.

During the summer of 1961, while the older children were home from boarding school at the farm, Margaret went to Natanya for Hebrew language study at *Ulpan Akiva*. Lenore (having dropped the Margaret) assumed her mother's responsibility in looking after the younger children, cooking and cleaning. She always tried to get the work done early in the day before it got too hot so all the children could go swimming in the lake. Barbara painted large murals on the outside walls of her father's office and store room. She also brought her father iced tea every afternoon.

That summer, while Margaret was studying Hebrew, Bob was studying German with a tutor. Tokho Kaufman also tutored the Lindsey children in science and math correspondences courses. In a letter to his parents, he remarked:

> ...I am working away at German. It is certainly a tough language to learn when you are almost 44 years old. I do not have to bone away in the way I used to in college since this girl Tohko Kaufman helps me every day but it does keep me busy every minute I'm in the office.

In a letter to Margaret, Bob tells her about celebrating his forty-fourth birthday with the children:

> My dearest and best,
>
> A note to let you know what a nice 44th birthday I had at 4 Hapalmach Street yesterday. At about 4:30 Barbara and Margaret Lenore corralled the gang—all except Danny and Robert who had gone fishing and were not to be found—and we gathered in our front room to celebrate.
>
> Fortunately, earlier in the morning we had all had great fun pulling clothes and radio tuners and records out of the big barrel [which they had shipped while on furlough]. Inside were not only wonderful clothes for Debbie, and even a couple of dresses for Barbara and Margaret Lenore, but also powders for drinks and several cake ready-mades, that is, ready-to-makes.
>
> So Margaret Lenore and Barbara had plenty of cake makings. They made a beauty, very Picasso, and they said I should not ask about its history. There seemed to have been a round lower layer, half of a round upper layer, and a couple of big lumps on top, all covered with white icing and sprinkled with candy tear-drops (or is that what you call them?) One of the small upper lumps had one of Tohko's faces on it, grinning like a chessy cat.
>
> There were eight candles in two rows and the afternoon wind was so strong Barbara had to relight them after she got into the room. I had to make a wish and then blew them out. Present were Drory and

Dahvid, Nava and Esther, as well as our four.

My first present was presented by a very sweet peck of a kiss from daughter Margaret Lenore (under orders from you, I understand) and I got three nice presents. One was a manicure set from Tohko, so I won't bite my nails, she says, another was a nice pen, a third was a pair of khaki shorts which turned out to be small but were exchanged for the largest the store carried. Am I that big?

Debbie failed to get my present—she had told me she was going to give me a ball, it was a secret, but that was what she was going to give me. Why? So I could play ball with her. She is so cute, and all the others too, that I can only wonder why the Lord has been so good to me....to us.

I must go and get some eggs now.

Lots of love,
Bob

"Bob? Bob! Oh, Bob!"

He was startled to hear a familiar voice calling his name as he turned to see his wife rushing toward his hospital bed with tears in her eyes. What was she doing here? She was supposed to be in Netanya at the *ulpan*. No, she was at the *ulpan* during the summer— she now was back in Tiberias. But when he saw the Jordanian policeman at the door, watching in a detached sort of way, he was once again reminded where he was and why he was there. But through the haze of painkilling medication, he wondered if Margaret was really there, or was this another dream?

CHAPTER 21
RETURN OF
A RELUCTANT HERO

It took two very tense days for Margaret to secure a pass into Jordanian East Jerusalem to visit Bob in the hospital. After crossing through Mandelbaum Gate, she proceeded directly to the American Consulate, which was located nearby. She introduced herself to the Consul who gave her directions to the hospital through Damascus Gate of the Old City. He did not offer to accompany her, however, so it was with some degree of apprehension that she made her way through the narrow, twisting streets. In the hospital, she found Bob, Edward, and several other men in a room guarded by a policeman.

When Bob saw her enter the room, he began to sob deeply. (It was one of the few occasions of their life together that she saw him cry.) As she fell into his outstretched arms, between sobs he moaned, "Look what I've done! Look what I've done! Causing everyone so much trouble, wounding Edward, embarrassing our Baptist colleagues in Jordan, getting arrested for trying to leave Jordan illegally—causing so much trouble for our Board!"

Margaret later recalled that Bob seemed totally unconcerned about his own physical condition but rather was consumed with regret for the problems he had caused others by his well intentioned actions gone awry.

"Aunt Margaret!" Edward shouted with joy as he scrambled out of bed and rushed to her side. As she turned to receive his enthusiastic embrace he continued excitedly, "At first I couldn't see much and they thought I might be blind, but my eyes are healing now and I can see." She was pleased to learn that healing was progressing without incident with a full recovery expected.

Margaret sat on the edge of Bob's bed, holding his hand in hers as he recounted what had happened. When he had arrived in Jerusalem, he had not contacted the Hoopers as planned but he had driven to the Musrara section and parked his car near Mandelbaum Gate. Having been like a father to Edward, he had decided to go get him, no matter what it took. Although having no clear plan, he simply had felt that this was something that he must do.

He had entered the U.N. section of Mandelbaum Gate and had walked confidently through to the East Jerusalem side as if this were something he were accustomed to do on a regular basis. Incredibly, no one had bothered to question his actions. He then had begun by going directly to the Friar's College to find Edward, but had discovered that he was not there. After having searched all day and into the evening, he finally had found Edward who was quite ready to go back to Israel with him. By this time, however, it was nearly midnight. Bob had made no effort to contact Edward's father since he previously had been adamant in his refusal to permit Edward to return to Israel.

Without proper passes, their only option was to cross through no man's land. Moving silently among the war-torn buildings lining the Jordanian side of the narrow strip, they had found a path not far from Mandelbaum Gate that looked promising. As they were carefully making their way along it, they were startled by the sound of the cocking of weapons nearby. Alarmed, Bob and Edward began retreating in the direction from which they had come, but in their haste they had gotten off the path and Bob had stepped on an antipersonnel mine. When they finally had crawled out of the mine field to the edge of no man's land, they had been arrested by Jordanian Legionnaires. They then had been loaded onto an army truck and had been taken to a nearby hospital where they had been treated and then placed under guard.

Bob later had learned that the surgeon, Dr. Rashid Nashashibi, had labored for eight hours in surgery in an attempt to save the mangled foot. Because he was unable to successfully restore circulation to the foot, however, he had no option but to amputate it and had done so above the ankle.

When the visiting time was up, Margaret gave Bob and Edward hugs and kisses, and then left the room crying. In the hall Dr.

Nashashibi attempted to comfort her saying sympathetically, "We understand, we understand. He was trying to help the boy." Margaret stayed at the East Jerusalem YMCA and had additional visits with Bob before returning to West Jerusalem on Sunday.

While she and Debbie stayed with the Hoopers, Margaret was able to visit Bob once more the following weekend. On her second visit she carried with her letters to Bob and Edward written by her older children, by the home kids, and by Baptist colleagues. Each in his or her unique way conveyed an expression of love and concern while attempting to encourage and reassure Bob. Most of the letters written by the children included quotations of scripture, not surprising since Bob had rewarded scripture memory with candy on campouts with the home kids during the Lindsey's tenure as parents at the farm.

An example of the deep emotion expressed in the children's letters to Bob and Edward are those written by Aida Marouf, the most prolific letter writer of the home children:

> Dear Uncle Bob,
> I am very sad for what I heard from every body what had happen to you. I am very sorry. But Uncle Bob, remember that this is the Lords purpose for all what had happen he has a purpose. Uncle Bob you don't know how much I think of you and Edward. You really meant a lot to me and all the other children and you will always mean a lot to me. I know how much you loved us children and I am sure you wanted to make it as a present for all of us children. I love you very much Uncle Bob, really I think you are such a nice father for all of us children and you have showed us all and me what a real believer you are in Christ. Everywhere, in Hifa, Nazareth, Petach Tikvah, we all are praying for you and Edward very much. I will always pray for you and everywhere where ever I go and will be. Please remember Aida and all the children and Uncle Murph and Aunt Marty and all around us, that we are praying for you and remember you always. I hope you have a bible and read it more,

I am sure you do. I really love you. I will never forget you, no never. May God be with both of you and help you get well completely. By[e]
I will always pray for you to come back to the farm.

Love,
Aida
P.S. Please read Edwards letter [to him that] I am going to write now. By[e] again from Aida.
May God bless the doctors to really help you.

My Dear Brother Edward,

I have heard all what happened to you and your father and our father Uncle Bob. Please tell Uncle Bob that all the people think he was a brave man and all the children too. You are very brave for you did not fuss about what happened but I know it hurts for what both of you got. I am very sorry. We are all praying for you and Uncle Bob. We all think of you very much. I hope you enjoyed Aunt Margaret coming to visit you. I heard she read you a lot of stories and from the Bible. Tell Uncle Bob to please not worry. We all love you both and do not think anything bad about you. All the people think good about you. Even the government want[s] you to come back. So please remember that we are praying for you and remember that the Lord has a purpose for all this. We all love you very much.
I will always pray for you to come back.

By[e].
Love,
Your sister Aida

In spite of the attempts of Aida and others to reassure Edward, he was plagued with feelings of personal responsibility for the loss of Bob's leg. So strong was his sense of guilt that he refused to speak of the incident for many years. Likewise, Bob's sense of embarrassment and regret made him extremely reluctant ever to discuss the incident.

After her second visit, in a letter dated September 29 to Bob's sister Mary, Margaret wrote in part:

> ...As it stands now, Bob still has not been released by the Jordanian military authorities and is in the hospital prison ward in the Old City of Jerusalem, in Jordan. We are never allowed over there except at Christmas and Easter, but the Consul was able to get me permission to visit Bob twice, both of the last two weekends. The last time he told me to make the most of the visit because I probably would not get another. The first time I saw him it was pretty shattering. He had lost a lot of blood & had had transfusions and was terribly weak but I could see an improvement the next day. It really seems miraculous to me that he lived through the ordeal, he was lying out in the field so long, conscious all the time, using his belt for a tourniquet, and the boy injured in the face, also conscious. I got him an electric razor and he looked much better after a shave and I think it helped him feel better. Edward couldn't see and at first they thought he would be blind but he's going to be all right. I got a transistor radio for him. They are rather relaxed in that hospital-prison in many ways, but I believe Bob has gotten excellent care surgically. The guards let me give him anything I wanted to after they examined it, except letters. I read them the letters though. Our children have been wonderful through it all. I think their letters along with letters from the home kids and colleagues helped more than anything to revive his spirits.
>
> We have been given every assurance that on this side they will consider it a special humane act and will not give him too much trouble from the military. I guess you understand what happened. This boy, Edward, had been in our Children's Home since he was a baby. We were tricked into taking him over last Christmas to see

his father in Jordan. Bob didn't go, but I was with the Murpheys and we took Edward. When our time was up on the other side and he was supposed to meet us he didn't turn up. The police were notified there but he wasn't found and since we had reached the deadline on our permits we had to go without him. Now when I look back on it I know I should have followed my instincts and refused to leave without him whatever trouble I'd have gotten into. Anyhow, we tried and have tried everything under the sun to get him back but in vain. Finally, a Catholic priest who has the privilege of going back and forth began bringing letters and we realized what a terrible time the boy was having. Edward's father tried to exploit him in the most horrible ways, beat him constantly and threatened his life. Finally, the Catholics took him into a school of theirs but he was miserable and kept writing these heartbreaking letters. Attempts were made through Consulate, UN—everything. Certainly the father had signed him over to us when he was a baby but Jordan recognized the father's right and gave him Jordanian citizenship. This school year was starting and the Catholics, not having any real responsibility for him, said he couldn't continue, so he had no refuge from his father in view. This is all the background leading up to Bob's attempt to rescue him in the only way that seemed possible. Of course, Bob didn't tell any of us that he was going to do it, but when a telegram came to me in Tiberias saying the car had been found near no-man's land, I felt immediately that he had made some such attempt. I feared the worse though, and I'm so thankful beyond words that he is alive. . . .

Loving you all,
Margaret

On October 1, 1961, the second International Bible Quiz was held in Jerusalem. Bob was supposed to be one of the judges, but everyone knew why he was not present. At the end of the recognition ceremony, the executive committee gave specially cast commemorative medallions to the judges. They also awarded Bob a medallion in spite of the fact that he was not able to serve. This unexpected and gracious act was seen as a significant honor and indicates the value the committee placed on Bob's unselfish though unsuccessful attempt to return Edward to the Children's Home. The medallion was later delivered to him in the hospital along with the following letter dated 10 October 1961:

Dear Dr. Lindsey:

It has now become possible for me to wish you a speedy and complete recovery from your injuries suffered in an exciting adventure. I hope there will be no serious aftereffects and that you will return to your work with your own great capacity for achievement.

Please allow me in the name of the Organizing Committee of the International Bible Contest, to present you with the medallion which was specially struck for the occasion. We do this because of your participation in the First International Bible Contest and because of your acceptance of our offer to act as a judge in the second contest.

With this medallion, go our best wishes,

Yours sincerely,
Harry Zinder
Director of the Organizing Committee
Second International Bible Contest

The news about Bob and the episode was widely published in Israel, Jordan and abroad. He became greatly admired in Israel, something of a folk hero. Feelings in Jordan were understandably different. Although his action was respected by some Jordanians such as the doctor who comforted Margaret, to others he was simply an enemy, a lawbreaker, a villain, a kidnapper who had failed.

One of the many who phoned Margaret to express condolences was Professor David Flusser of the Hebrew University. "Your husband is one of the finest scholars I have met," Flusser told her. Then, paraphrasing one of Jesus' teachings, Professor Flusser attempted to comfort Margaret with a bit of biblical wisdom and humor by stating, "It is better that the body should be whole, but better to enter paradise with one leg than to enter hell with two. This is good, because now he can give his whole effort to scholarship." Margaret knew who Professor Flusser was but she had never met him. Not realizing that he and Bob had discussed the fact that many of Jesus' sayings were spoken "tongue in cheek," she indignantly thought Flusser was mighty "cheeky" to say such a thing about Bob's misfortune.

Almost every day someone from the American Consulate, the Jordanian Army, the Israeli Army, the United Nations Border Control, or the Israel-Jordan Mixed Armistice Commission would visit Bob and interview him. Captain Joe Tiefenthal of the Israeli Army negotiated for his release from East Jerusalem. When he realized why Bob had ventured into no man's land, he was heard to exclaim, "Someday I would like to know the mother who had a son like Bob, who would risk his life for an Arab boy." Captain Tiefenthal and Bob became friends and saw each other many times in the years after the incident. His desire to meet Bob's mother became a reality some years later when he arranged to visit her in Norman, Oklahoma during a trip to the U.S.

A week after her second visit, Margaret wrote Bob's parents:

> The days seem to have sort of piled one on top of the other and I can't seem to keep track of what time has passed and to who I've written and when.
> I still wait every day, thinking, "Maybe today they'll send him back." I must say I've never had a better lesson in patience. Today the Consul was here. He had seen Bob this morning and said he is getting along all right, but still nothing definite on his release. He says it is not a matter of suspicion though, red tape, getting the thing done. They believe his story; there seems to be no problem there.

. . . I've been flooded with letters from here, Europe, England, the States. And phone calls, visits—endless. I must say your boy has a few friends!! I had no idea. I've been astounded.

I was with Bob the two weekends before this and did everything I could think of to make him more comfortable. He really can't concentrate enough to study, but I took him Time, Life, and some Saturday Eve. Posts, which he seemed to enjoy. Also fruit, candy, a can of corn and a can opener, because he felt his diet lacked roughage. They get meat quite often and a lot of rice and macaroni. They let him go with a wheelchair to the bathroom the last day I was there a week ago. . . .

Lots of love, keep up your courage,
Margaret

Friends and officials in both Israel and Jordan worked diligently to secure permission to move Bob back to Israel for further medical treatment where his family could have access to him. Almost three weeks after the accident, both sides agreed that Bob could be moved back to West Jerusalem. On October 5, 1961 a Jordanian Red Crescent ambulance took him to the Mandelbaum Gate. There, after Margaret had joined him, Bob was transferred to an Israeli Red Shield ambulance that took them directly to the new Hadassah Hospital. (Red Crescent in Muslim countries and Red Shield in Israel are the equivalents of Red Cross organizations elsewhere.) In a letter to Bob's parents, Margaret described the event:

We are so thankful that Bob is back in Israel. Truly God has answered the prayers of many, many people. Thursday afternoon the Consul called and said Bob would be returned at Mandlebaum Gate by the U.N. in half an hour. It was short notice but I checked with the hospital, got an ambulance and then a taxi and got there in plenty of time. (I've been staying here with the Hoopers all this time in the place where we used to live.) The tension the last week was dreadful because I expected every minute that he'd be released and sent back & couldn't understand why it was taking so long. The Hoopers had left for Haifa to meet some new Baptist colleagues 15 minutes before the call came. The transfer from the Jordan ambulance to the Israeli one was made in the middle section of land between the two "gates" in the presence of officials from both sides and the U.N. and our very kind Consul, Mr. Kinsolving. Oh, I have been thankful for him!

I rode in the ambulance with Bob to the beautiful New Hadassah Hospital in the hills out of Jerusalem. He seemed in pretty good spirits. Really he keeps remarkably cheerful in front of people. He has the best doctor in the country for this. He's an Englishman, Dr. Macklin, and our very dear friend Bruce Jacobson (an American) will do the artificial limb. Dr. Macklin says he will have to have another operation & make the amputation higher up in order to fit the prosthesis. Of course, that's a hard prospect after going through all this. There is some infection still to be cleaned up, so it will probably be about a week before they will operate again.

All the children were here yesterday to see their dad and I'm keeping Debbie with me. I think I am going to have to make a big move to Jerusalem because Bob has months of treatment and training ahead and I should be with him. Tiberias is no place for it.

I don't know if it makes it much easier for Bob. I'm sure it does, although it embarrasses him, but he is absolutely a hero here. All the papers write about his wonderful humane and courageous act and it has influenced so many for good. It's some comfort anyway. I wish you could see the flowers. He's had to distribute them all over his section of the hospital, there are so many. And letters, letters, from all over the world. To know so many people have been praying for his release and strength has been a comfort beyond words to me.

You should have seen Bob eat the first meal over here! I thought he'd never get enough. Though he's not hard to please, he's seen about enough rice and mutton, even though he likes it! At Hadassah he's certainly well fed and the hospital is the last word, a tremendous thing, every screw and pane of glass, American!

I'm trying to write to everyone but it's going to take a long time to get to all these hundreds of letters, so please tell people if they've written how much we appreciate it, and I'll eventually get them acknowledged . . . .

Lots of love,
Margaret

The relief and excitement of Bob's return was tempered by the sadness that Edward Zoumout still remained in East Jerusalem. In spite of the outpouring of expressions of love and concern from friends around the world, Bob still wrestled with two strong opponents. Although outwardly he appeared relatively cheerful, privately he was haunted by a sense of failure in his attempt to rescue Edward that was exacerbated by the loss of his foot. If only he had succeeded in bringing Edward home, he willingly would have given both feet. But he had failed—and that made it even more difficult to deal with his second opponent—fame. The news media had followed his story closely from the beginning. His daring, selfless attempt to bring Edward home had captured the imagination of much of the public. He was embarrassed by all the attention and was most uncomfortable with his new "larger than life" status.

In the quiet hours of the night, between periodic visits by nursing staff, Bob Lindsey prayed for strength as he wrestled with his formidable opponents. He was eager to put the notoriety behind him and to get on with life—even though it would be "life with a limp."

CHAPTER 22

LIFE WITH A LIMP

On October 16 the Jewish doctors amputated Bob's leg about eight inches below the knee in order to provide a firm base for a prosthesis. The surgery went well and on the last day of October, Bob was released from Hadassah Hospital.

The Lindseys did not return to Tiberias immediately but stayed in Jerusalem with the Hoopers at Baptist House. Bob needed medical supervision and physical therapy—and Margaret needed to learn to drive! In a letter to his parents on November 13 Bob commented:

> Margaret is busy learning to drive—takes two lessons every day from a driving school. She is doing very well but it is taking quite a long time.

Margaret's parents had come to Israel to be with her and the children during their ordeal. On November 1, Lenore Lutz wrote Bob's mother:

> Yesterday was a very special day for all of us here, because they brot Bob home from the hospital. I took Debbie and little Frank Hooper to kindergarten in the morning and she told the teacher, "My father is coming home today," and when she came home she brot a letter from the kindergarten children, written by their teacher. This morning she took back an answer from Bob. She is so happy to have her daddy home—She said, "When my father comes home I'm going to hug him; I'm going to hug him with my arms!" He had a big day with quite a

157

few callers and evening dinner with the Hoopers and his Hebrew friend Zelig who has done so much for Bob & Margaret all through this trouble.

Bob looks well, but of course has lost weight. He swings himself along quite easily on his crutches. He is so glad to be home again. Margie [Margaret Lindsey] and Mrs. Hooper shared the preparations for dinner last evening — Bob's favorite — fried chicken, mashed potatoes and milk gravy, salad, beans, biscuits, and chocolate cake.

Last week Dexter and I went to the Farm on Mon. On Tues. Margie came and we all went to Tiberias for two days. . . .Margie needed to get things from their home to use here. She brot some things in a wooden box which Debbie at once claimed as her refrigerator — so Dexter fixed it up with shelves for her. This morning Bob sat out on the patio and painted it. The only paint available was bright yellow but I'm sure Debbie will love it.

An elaborate reception held on November 14 at the farm was attended by some three hundred guests. It was a "welcome back" for Bob, and a "welcome to Israel" for new Baptist colleagues Lee and Sarah Bivins. When Bob came in on crutches, he was given a hero's applause. Bob spoke briefly saying that he did not regret having tried to fulfill a humanitarian obligation to Edward. He also praised the "devoted treatment" he had received at the hands of Jordanian physicians and nurses as well as his superb care by the Israeli staff of Hadassah Hospital. He praised the officials on both sides for his return to Israel and expressed how much the prayerful concern and love of all his friends and acquaintances meant to him.

By mid December, Bob began working in his study at home in Tiberias. He, Margaret and the children were greatly relieved when he received a letter from Oklahoma City pastor Dr. Herschel Hobbs, a member of the Executive Committee of their Board. He told of being at the Board meeting where Dr. Baker James Cauthen had reported on Bob's accident, saying that he was back in Israel and was doing well. Dr. Hobbs wrote, "Not one word of question was raised about what Bob did. I think that all of us understood."

On January 1, 1962, a telegram arrived stating that Bob's father, J. L.

Lindsey, had died. He was nearly eighty years of age. Bob did not fly back for the funeral. He had enjoyed a good visit with his father before he returned to Israel, and he still was recuperating from his accident three and a half months earlier. In a letter from Tiberias, Bob wrote to his mother on January 12:

> Last night I arrived home from the farm and from Jerusalem after waiting for nearly two weeks to get this artificial limb, and still I have not gotten it. Right now we are having such wet weather that they have been unable to finish the plastic parts of the leg. Maybe next week I will get it.
>
> Your telegram, or rather the telegram about Dad from the Board, came to Jerusalem and Mr. Hooper brought it to the farm. It was not clear when exactly the end came, but I understand from a later letter from Dr. Cauthen that it was on New Year's Day.
>
> Of course we were shocked...Naturally we had expected this kind of news for so long that we were, in a sense, prepared.
>
> I of course treasure every minute I got to be at home and with Dad during those 10 months we were in the states two years ago. And I am glad I can remember him as he was during those last years, as well as when he was so strong.

Bob was fitted with his new prosthetic leg by his longtime friend, Tel Aviv prosthetist Bruce Ya'akobi, who refused to accept payment for his services. He was motivated not only by his respect for Bob's attempted rescue that had resulted in the necessity of a prosthesis, but also by a bond he felt with this impulsive Christian pastor from Oklahoma that reached much further. He was the Jewish young man whom Bob had met on the ship in the Mediterranean when the Lindseys first came to Palestine in 1945. When Bruce had immigrated to Palestine he had adopted the name Ya'akobi, the Hebrew version of Jacobson. Their shipboard discussion of the concept of "the Kingdom of Heaven" and the spiritual insight his new Jewish friend had shared had resulted in a deep and lasting impact on Bob's understanding. Neither young man could have imagined the way in which this future traumatic incident would be woven into the fabric of their lives.

Bob Lindsey's resilience in adapting to life without his left foot and lower leg is chronicled in a series of letters he wrote to his mother:

Jan. 24, 1962

Tiberias is such a beautiful place in the springtime. After all our rains the hills around us are green. Yesterday I spaded a row along the upper terrace and we put in some kind of climbing plant. Our bougainvillea are in bloom and when they get full they will really make the garden pretty. . . I am trying to get used to my new leg—which I got last week. I think I will be able to get used to it but I can see it is going to take a few weeks. I wear it all the time when not sleeping already so I look pretty natural, even with the short crutches.

Feb. 7, 1962

Mary wrote last week and said it was snowing again in Claremore. The nearest snow we see is on Mt. Hermon but on nice days it surely is beautiful.

I spent 3 days this week in Jerusalem and Petach Tikva. They had to make some adjustments in my leg so it is a bit hard to walk again until the knee makes its place in the rubber supports. The doctor in Jerusalem— who operated—was very pleased with my progress, said he wanted to see me again in 3 months.

The man who made my leg insists he will not take anything but what the materials cost him. I will have to make another limb about next September, since you are always supposed to have an extra leg in case something happens to the one you are using.

I do appreciate Bob Rucker's telling you all about the limb business. I am still learning about the whole thing but I can see it will be okay soon.

April 9, 1962

Edward, the boy I tried to help, finally got over last week. Because of all the publicity about me some people on the other side went to work and managed to get him all the special permissions he needed to get home. So we are all very happy, and thankful to God.

My artificial foot is doing pretty well. I have learned to walk so it is not very noticeable, and think I will do better all along. The stump has been going down, shrinking, as usual, they say, and that has made difficulties about getting the leg repadded, etc. Last week I had a new cast of the stump made and tomorrow I hope to get the new insert, which should fit better. Right now I am wearing 3 special wool socks to make the stump fit, but when the new insert is fitted I should be able to wear only one sock.

Danny, as usual, is busy trying to figure out everything. The other day we were having a big discussion at the table about Jesus, God our Father, and so forth. We told him Jesus was God's Son, and the Bible says he is one with the Father. "Oh, I understand, I think," he said. "Jesus is sort of God Junior!"

May 25, 1962

I have sent off for the stump socks.

I am hunting an apartment in Jerusalem. We have been asked to leave Tiberias and take over the work in Jerusalem again. I am not very keen about it since it means more work besides the translation but there seems to be no other good alternative.

June 12, 1962

The stump socks have come through and I am happily wearing them as they are much shorter than the others I had. I am doing better on the limb all the time. Several weeks ago I took my first little hike in the mountains, was pretty tired when I got back but quite satisfied that there is little I cannot do now that I did before.

I am still looking for an apartment in Jerusalem. We have found one which is nice, in a new building, and with a fine view of the western hills of the city, but have been unable to finish the arrangements as yet.

July 8, 1962

We have been up to our hat bands in work, trying to find a place to live in Jerusalem, make plans for the work there, and take care of the kids since school was out. Now the little ones are finishing a week's camp at the farm, and in the week to come Margaret and I will have charge of the older camp of young people at the farm.

We have found a very nice and livable apartment in Jerusalem, but will not plan to move for a few weeks.

We are trying to prepare plans for a remodeling of the old building in which we lived in Jerusalem. We have to get ready for a lot of tourists next summer—and there are some coming by now.

Lots of Love,
Bob

One of the tourists visiting the Lindseys was W. M. Pratt, Jr., a Baptist pastor from Greenville, Texas. According to Rev. Pratt's account, he, along with several friends and their Israeli tour guide that he identifies only as Herman, had been dinner guests at the Lindsey's home in Tiberias. Their knowledgeable guide, with an earned Ph.D., had known Bob for years. He remarked, "You folks go back home and tell your President, Mr. Kennedy, that if he really wants to help our country, to forget about sending us one-thousand Peace Corps workers, and to send us fifty more Bob Lindseys!"

In Bob's letter of April 9 above he mentions that "Edward, the boy I tried to help, finally got over last week." After nearly a year and three months, Martha Murphey had received a call on Thursday, April 5, telling her that she could come and pick Edward up at the police station not far from Mandelbaum Gate. She recalls:

Murph had taken some photographers from the Board to Beersheva and wasn't here when I received the call from the police. Edward had come over into Israel through the Mandelbaum Gate with the assistance of the U.N. on Wednesday and had been released into the custody of the Israeli authorities. He was held overnight at the police station while his paperwork was being processed. I called our friend and lawyer, Dr. Joseph Alkahe, and he went with me to Jerusalem.

What a joy to see Edward and hug him! Edward also was very happy but was reluctant to speak about either the accident involving him and Uncle Bob or about his life while living in Jordan. I'm sure he felt badly that Uncle Bob had lost a leg while trying to bring him home. I don't think he talked with the other home kids about it either. Of course, everyone at the farm was very excited about his return. All the kids were waiting for us out by the main road and we were greeted wildly when we arrived about dark. I don't remember our celebrating his return with a party *per se*—it was enough for everyone to hug him and laugh and talk with him. With so many home kids and boarding students and workers—every day was kind of like a party in some ways! We tried very hard to facilitate getting things back to normal, now that Edward was back where he (and we) felt he belonged.

Bob Lindsey told me that he was proud of him when Edward was questioned by the Jordanian authorities while they were in custody. When asked why he wanted to return to Israel, he told them that he wanted to return to the home that had cared for him since he was a baby. That home was located on a farm by the Yarkon River where he and the rest of the children like himself worked and studied and played together. He showed no animosity toward the authorities and explained that he simply wanted to go home, home being the Baptist farm in Israel. And after so many months of concern, prayers, and efforts of numerous people, we all were extremely grateful that the family was together again.

Edward gratefully settled back into life at the farm. When he graduated from high school, he immigrated to Denmark where he married and settled in Kopenhagen. He made frequent trips back to Israel and maintained close ties with the other "farm kids" and the Murpheys until his death from a heart attack in 2000.

The quickening pace of life experienced by the Lindseys left little time to dwell upon the trauma of the previous autumn. In fact, the new responsibilities Bob assumed as the family returned to Jerusalem would prove both fulfilling and frustrating. Once again serving as pastor of the church on Narkis Street[1], along with other responsibilities, left little time to pursue what would prove to be the most significant discovery of his scholarly career.

CHAPTER 23

SOLVING THE PUZZLE

After two years in Tiberias where Bob had been able to focus primarily on his gospel translation research, August 1962 found the Lindsey family back in Jerusalem once again. Before they had left the Galilee they had purchased a small cottage in Poriah, a village located atop a hill overlooking the southern end of the Sea of Galilee (modern Lake Kinneret). In fact, one could walk to the crest of the hill a hundred or so yards away for a breathtaking view. The lake was bordered by towns and lush agricultural settlements, with the flat-topped hills of the Golan Heights rising above the eastern shore. Directly below, the Jordan River began its journey southward to the Salt Sea (Dead Sea).

The little cottage was a favorite family destination where the Lindsey family came for a day or two about once a month. They also invited Baptist colleagues, friends, university students, and the children from the farm to use the house as well. Once all the girls of the Baptist Children's Home came there for a retreat. Several of the children were finishing high school and leaving to study elsewhere, to work, or to establish their own homes. This was a very special time together before leaving the structured security of family, school, and work that life on the farm had provided. In fact, life was changing at the farm itself. As the number of residents of the children's home grew smaller, the student body of the secondary school grew larger due to the enrollment of the non-resident students.

The Lindseys settled into a small but adequate West Jerusalem apartment at 48 Harlap Street. It was about a ten-minute drive from Baptist House but bus transportation was also convenient and it was in walking distance as well. The second floor apartment had an open front balcony (good for storing bicycles) and a closed back balcony that they used for hanging laundry to dry. There were two bedrooms, a bath, and a half-bath (where the washing machine was installed). The living room doubled as the parents' bedroom while a walk-in closet became a bedroom for little Debbie. The view from the back balcony looked out over the Valley of the Cross where the Greek Orthodox monastery had been occupying its site since 800 A.D. On the corner was the Ohel Sarah Synagogue and around the corner was a green grocer (vegetable shop), a traditional grocery, a conditory (spice shop), and a dry cleaning shop. Close by were two well known landmarks—the Islamic Museum and the Jerusalem Theater.

The cramped apartment with the spectacular view was typical in size for that area. The Lindseys had chosen to live in an apartment nearby rather than to return to the spacious Baptist House because the facility was needed for other things. With renovation, the front rooms facing Narkis Street became a bookstore and offices. There was also space available for social gatherings as well as a meeting place for the developing Korean Baptist congregation and a Hebrew-speaking group.

While Bob realized a sense of fulfillment from his pastoral duties, he also experienced some degree of frustration in his lack of time to study and translate. There was no room for a study in the Lindsey apartment and Baptist House was much too public to expect to accomplish serious study without frequent interruption. Consequently, he rented a room on Al Fasi Street in Rehaviah near Jason's Tomb, halfway between their apartment and Baptist House. He called it his "hideout" and used this study for the next eight years. Only Margaret and a very few individuals were entrusted with its location in order to permit Bob to study undisturbed from time to time as duties permitted.

Soon after he acquired his "hideout" he began to meet on a regular basis with Professor David Flusser. An orthodox Jew born in Vienna in 1917, he and Bob were the same age. He had been a professor of classical Greek philology at the University of Vienna and he endeavored to study everything ever written in ancient Greek by Jewish authors, including the Greek New Testament. Subsequently, he immigrated to Israel as a young scholar and taught at Hebrew University in Jerusalem. He had been named Professor of Judaism of the Second Temple Period and Early Christianity at Hebrew University the year he and Bob began studying together. He had done extensive research into the Dead Sea Scrolls and the sect which produced them, particularly as the Scrolls relate to the New Testament.

The two scholars soon developed a deep and lasting friendship, referring fondly to each other simply as "Flusser" and "Lindsey." Bob eagerly looked forward to their discussions of the synoptic gospel texts. Both were comfortable enough with Greek and Hebrew that they could sense the appropriateness of a particular word or phrase of the Greek text. Consequently, a Hebrew under text containing perfectly acceptable idiomatic Hebrew emerged from a Greek text long considered to be somewhat poor grammatically when compared to classical Greek. He greatly valued Flusser's comments from a Jewish perspective as he offered insights into the customs and spiritual practice of the Jewish people in the land of Palestine during the time of Jesus. Flusser was particularly interested in a most radical conclusion that his Christian friend had reached in his research earlier that year while still living in Tiberias.

Bob had long concluded that the writers of the synoptic gospels of Matthew, Mark, and Luke had used one or more Greek manuscripts that were translations of Hebrew manuscripts telling what Jesus did and said. He sought to learn as much as possible about the nature and content of the original sources. As he studied the synoptics, a number of patterns emerged, both similar and dissimilar. As he pondered his voluminous notes, it was as if he were looking at a jigsaw puzzle, the likes of which he had never seen. The parts of the puzzle were pieces of a real picture, produced by authors who were working independently. Try as he might, he could not fit the pieces of the puzzle together in a way that would result in a clear picture.

Then, on the evening of February 14, 1962, Bob was studying a much used pattern in Mark, *kai elegen, elegon, and he was saying, they were saying*. Mark used it five times as often as Luke and nine times more than Matthew. Furthermore, Luke and Mark never used the expression in parallel verses except twice. When Matthew and Luke used it in the same passage, Mark didn't use it at all. As he pondered the puzzle, he concluded that one of the writers deliberately avoided the usages at points where he saw the other writer employing them.

Margaret and the three younger children living at home were already asleep in the upstairs bedrooms as Bob continued to wrestle with the puzzle. Because he had been fitted with his new prosthesis only about a month earlier, he was using the downstairs bedroom. Around midnight he slipped into a light sleep and had a fantastic dream in which "the synoptic problem opened up like a book." The dream was so real that he awoke with a start. With the dream fresh in his mind he looked over his notes and there it was—the clear picture for which he had been searching! Mark was not the first writer who was partially copied by Matthew and Luke. It was Luke who wrote first, and Mark was changing Luke! Matthew, in turn, was using Mark and knew Luke only through Mark!

By then it was probably around 2 A.M. as Bob hurried out into the cold night. Somehow he managed to climb the steps to the second floor where Margaret was sleeping in their bedroom. He turned on the light and shook Margaret awake while shouting, "Luke was first! Luke was first!"

"That's nice, dear," she replied sleepily as she struggled to grasp the significance of his discovery, trying to be enthusiastic since he obviously was extremely elated. "Margaret, it wasn't Mark who wrote first, it was Luke!" he explained. For the next half hour Bob excitedly explained how the puzzle now fit together perfectly. His euphoria lasted for days during which he wrote letters to several scholars in Europe sharing his discovery. A week after his monumental experience, the snow crowned Mount Herman as if to celebrate something wonderful!

In 1968, Professor David Flusser published his book entitled *Jesus* and expressed his indebtedness to Bob's work. He insisted that Bob's theory of a Hebrew origin for the basic gospel materials is correct. He also credited Bob with the first "really useful" clue to the interdependence of the gospels. "Lindsey's discoveries," said Flusser, "open roads to a far more positive portrayal of the figure of Jesus than most students and theologians hold today." Professor Flusser also mentioned Bob in his article on Jesus in the

1972 edition of *Encyclopedia Judaica.*

In 1969, Bob Lindsey and David Flusser called a press conference at Baptist House to announce the publication of Bob's book, *A Hebrew Translation of the Gospel of Mark,* by Dugith Publishers. It was published in hard back with an eight-page foreword written by David Flusser (in English). Bob's 75-page introduction in English deals with his discoveries and theories in detail. The Greek text of Mark parallels the Modern Hebrew translation on the opposite page. With regard to his translation project, Bob believed that "[t]he three most exciting conclusions reached due to the work of translating so far are 1) the proof of Hebraic literary sources behind our gospels, 2) the importance of this to the relationship of the gospels to each other, and 3) the delineation of the literary method of Mark."

Articles in Israeli newspapers and a number of American and other foreign publications resulted in the book and its translator becoming well known. At the time of the press conference, however, not all the reporters knew Bob. Interestingly, when one Israeli reporter heard Bob speaking Hebrew, he thought surely he must be an Israeli since he sounded like a native speaker rather than an American who had learned Hebrew in adulthood.

For various reasons in late April, 1970, Bob had to give up his one-room study known as his "hide-out" on Al Fasi Street. Leaving that room where he had studied for over eight years and where he had met with Professor Flusser and a number of bright university students was pure bereavement. The Baptist Convention in Israel had bought a large house on Nablus Road in East Jerusalem that was intended to serve as a student center, library, and center for many activities and meetings—and included office space for Bob. Thus, with the help of several friends, Bob packed his extensive collection of books and made the move to "Jerusalem House." But if there was one thing Bob Lindsey was used to, it was change and expecting the unexpected. Nothing seemed to remain unchanged for long—particularly here in Israel.

CHAPTER 24

WARS AND RUMORS OF WAR

On June 1, 1965, the Lindseys and their three younger children began their furlough by touring Spain on their way to the U.S. They were reunited with their three older children in Norman, Oklahoma, where they planned to spend the next year. In August of 1965 Bob officiated at the wedding of his eldest daughter Lenore to Ken Mullican, and in March of 1966 he officiated at the wedding of his daughter Barbara to Jim Lassiter. Before the Lindseys had left Israel for furlough, Bob and his colleagues had discussed their concern regarding the poor quality of many tours on which thousands of Baptists and other Christians visited the land of the Bible each year. They were especially disappointed when tour groups would visit Jordan and the West Bank first, with Arab guides who "mixed so much anti-Jewish propaganda into their commentary that tourists sometimes have hostile feelings toward Israel even before visiting it." Many tourists did not get to see their own denomination's work in Israel, and many left with a distorted view of the Christian work there. Often, tourists arrived in Israel exhausted because they had already spent most of their tour in Europe with only a short tour of Israel at the end. Moreover, thousands of the tourists were Baptists, and it was not possible for the Baptist workers in Israel to meet with all of them even though they felt a responsibility toward them.

Bob and several colleagues believed there should be an advisory board for students and tourists going to Israel. The idea was to advise those planning to take study groups and tourists to Israel in order to show them how to avoid problems and indicate the most significant sites for learning opportunities. He foresaw the day when thousands of medium and low income Christians could also visit and study in

Israel.

Once in Norman, Bob led in the incorporation of a non-profit organization called the *Bible Lands Study Association*. Its purpose was to be "an association of people from all walks of life who love and honor the Word of God and desire to promote the study of the Bible in the lands of the Bible for purposes of pilgrimage, fellowship, missions, and the peace of the nations." Bob believed that "the land of Israel and the language of Israel are the two most important factors needed in the training of Christian people for an intelligent and spiritual return to the Bible." He spoke about his endeavor with great conviction to any interested group or individual. He found, however, that it was not possible to achieve the objectives of the Association during their one year furlough. Consequently, the Lindseys took an additional one year leave of absence from their appointment in Israel in order to complete the task. The following year was a flurry of activity with Bob, typically, attempting more than the available time allowed—writing, studying, preaching, and endeavoring to build support for the Association. He planned the first study tour for the Easter season in the spring of 1967. The proposed tour did not generate sufficient interest due to the unsettled political situation in the Middle East. By May, disappointed in the little progress he had made with the Bible Lands Study Association, he made plans to return to Israel with his family.

As they prepared to return to Israel, Bob viewed developing events in the Middle East with growing concern. It was reminiscent of events preceding the Sinai Campaign of 1956. A letter dated January 9, 1956, that the Lindseys' Baptist colleague serving in Haifa, Marjorie Rowden, wrote to her parents illustrates the tension that was building prior to the initiation of that war.

> These are mighty tense times we are living in these days. Guess you have been following the papers about the Jordan riots.... About three weeks ago they had some bad anti-Western (particularly anti-American) riots, but things seem to have calmed down. So bright and early last Friday, Paul [husband], Becky [daughter] and I, Jim and Betty Smith, and Herman and David Petty all headed for Jerusalem....We got to Jerusalem about 10 am and

crossed the Mandelbaum Gate into Jordan. It was raining and we got a taxi straight to the National Hotel. We were practically the only guests in the hotel because everyone had been scared off by the troubles. We had a real good lunch and then took the whole afternoon walking through the walled-in area of the Old City....Early Saturday morning we got a taxi for Bethlehem. At 10 am we were back in Jerusalem (Jordan) and I got out of the taxi and decided to go shopping. All the rest took the taxi and drove to Jericho to be gone until 4 pm. I walked around the Old City....The Lindsey Family was all over there (in Jordan Jerusalem)so I was with them part of the time. Then at noon I went to the YMCA and had lunch with them (Lindseys). I rested in their rooms a while and then at 3 pm, Margaret and I decided to go out and shop some more. I was going to meet Paul and the others at 4 pm. Well, Margaret and I got two blocks down the street and saw a mob forming with sticks and stones. We watched for a minute and then retreated back to the YMCA, which is right next door to the American Consulate building. The mob grew larger and was around a thousand people headed straight up the road for the American Consulate. It was awfully scary. I did not have any of my papers (passport, visa) because they were with Paul. I kept praying that they would hurry back from Jericho. Also I was scared that they (Paul, Herman and the kids) had gotten stopped by other rioters on the highway. The whole country was rioting. Margaret and I took all 5 of her kids up on the roof of the YMCA for safety and for a good view, too. Bob was running around madly trying to get his car battery, which was being recharged, out of the garage not far away. He never did get the battery so he got some men to help him move the car off the street into the YMCA fenced-in yard. The American Consulate next door was crawling with American marines and Arab Legionnaires. The women and children of the consul had been driven over into Israel territory. Well, the Lord certainly was with us, because two minutes before the mob reached the YMCA the taxi drove up with Paul and all in it. We turned the taxi around in the face of the mob and I jumped in and he rushed us straight around the corner to the Mandelbaum gate. We got out and walked through the Arab check-post, through no-man's land and into the little wooden Israel check-post. As soon as we stepped into the Israel side the gun shots and tear gas bombs exploded all over the area. The mob tore down the American flag and broke all the windows in the American Consulate building. The wounded rioters were brought into the YMCA, although none were badly hurt. Margaret took her kids inside and Bob watched from the roof. The Lindseys stayed there until the next morning because they couldn't have gotten to Mandelbaum Gate....We called Jerusalem (from Haifa) last night and talked to Bob. He said that the next morning as soon as possible they got the car battery and crossed into Israel, but the rioters were still going strong....I surely hope and pray our people at Ajloun are O.K. The whole situation is Communist inspired and the people are too blind to see it. The mob was well organized and the anti-Western propaganda over there is terrific.

Following the election of Gamal Abdel Nasser as President of Egypt in 1953, the Arabs had blockaded Israel's Red Sea port of Eilat in the Gulf of Aqaba and closed the Suez Canal to Israeli shipping. In 1954, the Egyptians had launched some forty raids into Israel from Gaza. Seeking greater influence in the Middle East, the Soviet Union had supplied jet fighter planes and other weaponry to Egypt. Nasser then had escalated the conflict by publicly calling for the total annihilation of Israel. As a result, violence along Israel's borders was unremitting during the first six months of 1956 and Israel's rapid retaliations had proven no deterrent.

On July 26, 1956, Egypt nationalized the Suez Canal Company, which was owned by the British and French. In response to the provocation, the British and French planned to take back the canal while the Israelis attacked from the east. Israel's objectives in entering the war were to 1) open the Gulf of Aqaba to shipping; 2) be able to use the Suez Canal; and 3) get the Egyptian Army out of Gaza. When, on October 25, a joint high command was established to control the Egyptian, Syrian, and Jordanian armies, Israel did not wait for the inevitable attack.

On Monday, October 29, 1956, Israeli forces swept into Gaza and the Sinai, breaking the Red Sea blockade by occupying the port city of Sharm el-Sheikh. One hundred hours later, the war was over—but not before the Egyptians had blocked the canal by sinking ships in it. France and Britain occupied Port Said and Ismalia, then handed the canal over to the U.N. forces, who, in turn, returned control to the Egyptians. Ultimately, under international pressure, Israel withdrew from the Sinai and Gaza on the condition that no Egyptian troops enter those areas. The outcome of the war was that Egypt still retained control of the blocked Suez Canal, while Britain and France gained nothing. Israel, on the other hand, achieved her objectives of opening the Gulf of Aqaba shipping to her port city of Eilat, and the Egyptian army was no longer a threat from Gaza and the Sinai—at least for the present.

In the early days of the war, as soon as the Israelis had taken Gaza, Bob drove there to check on colleagues at the Baptist Hospital in Gaza City. (When Gaza was under Egyptian control, there had been virtually no contact between Baptists serving in Israel and those serving in Gaza. When Bob approached the entrance to Gaza City he was stopped at an Israeli check point. Only those involved in what were deemed essential services were allowed into Gaza. So, in typical Bob Lindsey fashion, he retreated gracefully and parked his car. He then convinced the driver of a truck entering Gaza with the daily newspapers to take him along as his helper. He learned that all the Baptists serving there had survived the conflict. Dr. Young and the three nurses, along with the Arab staff, were too busy with battle casualties to talk very much. Bob returned several times during the war and the following period of Israeli control to assess the need for assistance and encountered no difficulty entering Gaza other than the first day.

Consequently, as the Lindseys followed news reports from the Middle East in the spring of 1967, they uneasily noted the remarkable similarity to events preceding the 1956 war. Toward the end of May, President Nassar expelled the United Nations Emergency Force from Gaza and the Sinai, remilitarized the Sinai, and blockaded Israel from shipping in the Tiran Straits. The blockade of Israel's port on the Red Sea was sufficient to precipitate a war, but when troops, tanks and other armaments began massing in Gaza along the border with Israel, war seemed inevitable.

On the other side of the border at the Baptist Hospital in Gaza, the staff also believed that war was unavoidable. In preparation, Dr. Merrill Moore, Jr. formulated a disaster plan for the hospital. Incoming casualties would be divided into five groups: 1) minor injuries; 2) injuries which could wait for delayed treatment but requiring admission; 3) urgent cases requiring immediate surgery and intensive care for survival; 4) hopelessly injured cases needing comfort and pain medication; 5) those dead upon arrival. Hospital business manager and chaplain, Ed Nicholas, stockpiled supplies. The wives and children of the international staff, were evacuated to Beirut by a United Nations plane on May 28. Accompanying the group was a surgeon, Dr. Jean Dickman, who preferred to stay in Gaza where she felt she would soon be needed. However, she reluctantly agreed to go and help care for the families, while Dr. Moore, Dr. David C. Dorr, and Marilyn Shaeffer, R.N. stayed behind along with the Arab staff. As preparations intensified, all elective surgeries were cancelled.

On June 3, the Egyptians had massed 1,000 tanks along Israel's border with Gaza were. The Jordanian Army was ready with 5,000 men and 250 Patton and Centurion tanks. Syria moved troops and armaments into the Golan Heights as an Iraqi division moved into Jordan. The UN Security Council took no action as Israel exhausted every possible diplomatic avenue to avoid war.

The war started June 5 as Israel initiated pre-emptive strikes against Egypt, Jordan, Iraq, and Syria. Israel destroyed Egypt's air force on the ground. Jordan entered the war before noon. Early in the day, while on furlough in Norman, Oklahoma, Bob and Margaret heard that Israel was at war. They anxiously followed the unfolding events on radio and TV. He stayed in touch by phone with friends in the U.S. who had some connection with Israel to try to gather any extra information about the situation there and the fate of colleagues and friends affected by the hostilities. The Baptist Hospital in Gaza which normally had 85 inpatients a day was admitting from 170 to 250 cases daily. On June 7 the Israeli forces drove the Jordanians across the Jordan River, and Jerusalem was reunited. The Egyptian forces also retreated on June 7 and the next day the war with Egypt was over. Israel had captured the Egyptian oil fields (which they later developed extensively), occupied the Sinai Peninsula, and the Gaza Strip. The Syrian troops on the Golan Heights retreated to Damascus and the Iraqi division did not even enter the conflict. The war officially ended the evening of June 10. The next day Bob phoned Dr. J. D. Hughey, their Area Secretary at their Board in Richmond, requesting that they be permitted to return to Israel right away.

The six-day war ended with Israel successful beyond all expectations. Never had Israel so dominated the Middle East. They had destroyed 430 combat aircraft and 800 tanks, killed 15,000 Arab troops and captured 5,500. They occupied the Golan Heights as far as Kunetra, the whole of the Sinai to the east bank of the Suez Canal, and the entire West Bank (land west of the Jordan River). The Israeli Army now occupied 26,476 square miles of land, which the Arabs previously had held. Israel lost 40 aircraft and 676 soldiers. The Americans and other western countries supported the cease-fire lines. Israel was determined not to return any land taken, rather keep it until the Arabs would agree to an enduring peace.

The stinging defeat perhaps was felt most deeply by the Egyptians who were confident of their military might and battle plan. Nasser's successor, the late President Anwar el-Sadat, wrote in his autobiography *In Search of Identity* (New York: Harper & Row, 1977, p. 174) regarding the reason the Israelis were able to obliterate the Egyptian Air Force on the ground.

> On the day of the disaster itself—June 5—as I learned afterwards, the plan which had been endorsed by Nasser had been completely changed by [Field Marshall Abdel Hakim] Amer. That too was obvious, for Israel was able to occupy Al-Arish in the evening of that day while she could not do so in 1956 when our

forces were vastly weaker than in 1967.

On Monday June 5, Amer, accompanied by all commanders, took an aircraft and flew off on a "tour of inspection" to Sinai. It was natural that when the commander-in-chief was in the air, orders were issued to all SAM and antiaircraft batteries to hold their fire. And it was during that tour that Israel attacked all our airfields and hit our aircraft on the ground. We can thus say that the war began and ended while Amer was in the air.

Tensions in the region did not subside but continued to escalate with attacks mounted from outside Israel's borders as well as from within the occupied territories. Following the six day war, Israel was faced with a dilemma: if they ignored international law and annexed the territories as spoils of war, there would be an Arab majority in Israel, in which case they could not have a Jewish state and still be democratic. Consequently, they opted not to incorporate the occupied territories into Israel, but to construct settlements at strategic locations for purposes of national defense. Moreover, Israel believed that she could someday negotiate a meaningful peace by surrendering land. (Some Israelis opposed surrendering any land, as some Palestinian Arabs opposed any settlement that allowed the continued existence of Israel.) The increasing number of settlements along with the slow pace of the negotiations proved a source of bitter frustration for the Palestinians as well as for many Israelis.

As the Israeli military government attempted to maintain order, periodic attacks were directed at the occupying forces as well as at the Jewish settlers. Although the Baptists had served in Israel since the British Mandate, none had been seriously injured or killed. That changed dramatically on the evening of Sunday January 16, 1972. The Lindseys' daughter Lenore, her husband Ken and their two children were in Jerusalem for a visit from Gaza where they served at the Baptist Hospital. The phone rang and Ken answered. After a few seconds he exclaimed, "No, no, not Mavis, not Mavis!"

Earlier that evening, around 6 p.m., Ed Nicholas left Gaza to take his three daughters back to boarding school near Tel Aviv. Mavis Pate, a nurse at the hospital, went along to visit friends in Israel, and planned to drive a car back to Gaza. Near the Jabalyah refugee camp in Gaza, Arab guerrillas ambushed the party with machine gun fire from a citrus grove beside the road. Because Gaza was under curfew after dark, it would be assumed that anyone going into Israel in the evening would be Jewish—military, government employees, or settlers. At the sound of gunfire, Ed instinctively stepped on the accelerator in an effort to get out of range even though he could tell the tires had been hit.

When Ed stopped the van, his daughter Mary Ann got out and tried to stop one of the many taxis with workers returning to Gaza from jobs in Israel. Without exception the vehicles slowed slightly and then sped away without stopping. Perhaps, the dark hooded sweatshirt Mary Ann was wearing caused them to mistake her for a female Jewish soldier. Eventually, an Israeli army patrol arrived and radioed for a helicopter to take Ed and Mavis to the army hospital in Beersheba. Ed had sustained wounds in the thigh and lower left leg. Though the wounds were painful and required months of physical therapy, they were not life threatening. Mavis was placed on life support and was taken to surgery. She had sustained massive head and chest wounds and attempts to save her proved fruitless. About forty-five minutes after her arrival at the hospital, she was pronounced dead at forty-six years of age. Mary Ann and Joy Nicholas escaped injury while their sister Carol Beth sustained a small wound in one foot requiring crutches for about a week. Several years later Carol Beth had her foot x-rayed after an injury and discovered that a bullet fragment from the attack was still in her foot. The van was riddled by some fifty bullet holes.

A funeral service for Mavis was held in the hospital chapel. Muslims, Jews, and Christians sat together, mourning the loss of their friend and colleague, truly a *nurse of mercy*. Bob Lindsey spoke on Matthew 10:28, *"Do not be afraid of those who kill the body but cannot kill the soul. Rather, be afraid of the One who can destroy both soul and body in hell."* Her body was buried in a specially prepared plot beside the nursing school and dormitory. Mavis, a Louisiana native, had supervised the operating room of the hospital ship *SS Hope* on its first voyage, which went to the South Pacific. Appointed by the Southern Baptists in 1964, she served in Bangladesh and Thailand before going to Gaza in 1970.

A week after the funeral, with her baby daughter only three weeks old, Lenore Lindsey Mullican assumed Mavis's responsibility as surgery supervisor and instructor for the surgical technician program. About the same time the hospital received a message from the Palestine Liberation Organization (PLO), assuring the hospital that the attack was a mistake and that Baptist Hospital personnel had not been their target.

Attacks against Jewish Israelis were not limited to the country of Israel. On August 26, 1972 the Olympic Games began in Munich, Germany. The event was hailed as the *Olympics of Reconciliation.* Before sunup on the morning of September 5, the Palestinian terrorist group known as Black September broke into the Olympic village and killed two Israeli athletes outright, then at the airport killed nine more whom they had taken hostage. There was grief, shock and outrage in Israel as they buried their dead. Dreams of reconciliation were shattered as the Israelis got on with their lives.

Autumn 1973 found the Lindseys with their daughter Debbie in Ruschlikon, Switzerland, where Bob was teaching in the International Baptist Seminary during the September-December term. The *Yom Kippur War* caught the Israelis by surprise in October, 1973. The Egyptians launched a massive attack across the Bar-Lev line guarding the Suez Canal on Yom Kippur (the Day of Atonement), the most holy day to Jews, thus the name *Yom Kippur War*. With only token forces at posts along the borders, most soldiers were on leave. Radio, television, and telephone were shut down requiring the military to drive through the streets with loud speakers, calling the troops to duty, losing valuable time as the Syrians swept across the Golan Heights in a coordinated attack. From Switzerland Bob and Margaret listened anxiously to the radio and TV following the losses and gains. At first, Israeli forces suffered very heavy losses but then recovered to inflict crushing defeats on both Egypt and Syria.

The Lindseys were back in Jerusalem by Christmas. A cease-fire agreement was signed with Egypt in January of 1974 and with Syria in May, 1974. Israel agreed to withdraw from parts of the Sinai and Golan. Unfortunately, thousands of Israelis criticized their government over the conduct of the war, leading to the resignation of Golda Meir's Labor government in April 1974.

Once again, the Lindseys faced the daunting task of ministering to the spiritual, emotional, and physical needs of those about them following another major conflict. In marked contrast to the jubilation of the post war period of 1967, they noted that the spirit of the entire country was one of mourning due to the heavy loss of life in spite of the military victory. The Lindseys were indeed grateful that they sensed a spiritual strength and ability from the Lord in a manner they had not experienced during and following previous wars.

CHAPTER 25

EMPOWERED

In the early 1970s, a mighty wind of spiritual renewal was blowing around the world and was being experienced in numerous churches of various denominations, both Catholic and Protestant. As the wind of renewal blew across Israel, the Lindseys listened with growing interest as some of their respected Christian friends related their encounter with the Holy Spirit in a fresh new way. Both Bob and Margaret had been seeking a deeper, more intimate relationship with the Lord and had a strong desire to serve him more effectively.

Being filled with the Holy Spirit was not a new concept to Bob. Since childhood he had been influenced by the preaching of his Norman, Oklahoma pastor, E. F. "Preacher" Hallock, who advocated being filled with the Holy Spirit as essential to living the Christian life. His home church had seasons of refreshing from time to time wherein the Spirit of God moved upon the church with great power bringing strong conviction as well as joy in the Lord to the people. As a young man, Bob had been influenced by R. A. Torrey's book on the Holy Spirit.

Bob had been very impressed by a sermon he had heard in Europe, delivered by a colleague and friend, Dr. William L. Wagner. He stressed the necessity of praising God both in private as well as in public worship services, simply concentrating on God and praising him in prayer, song, and testimony.

During this time two young women serving at the Baptist Hospital in Gaza visited the Baptist Church on Narkis Street. Since they had brought a guitar with them, they were invited to present some special music during the service. They told the congregation that singing songs of praise, many taken directly from scripture, had become very meaningful to them. They then asked the congregation to open their Bibles to Psalm 19:7-10 KJV and sing along with them.

> The law of the LORD is perfect, converting the soul:
>> the testimony of the LORD is sure, making wise the simple.
> The statutes of the LORD are right, rejoicing the heart:
>> the commandment of the LORD is pure enlightening the eyes.

> The fear of the LORD is clean, enduring forever.
>> the judgments of the LORD are true and righteous altogether.
> More to be desired are they than gold, yea than much fine gold:
>> sweeter also than honey and the honeycomb.

As they became familiar with singing this and other songs of praise, a new dimension of freedom to praise God was experienced by the congregation. It was nothing revolutionary at first. The people simply felt more open to the Lord's presence and experienced more freedom to participate in the services with their entire being. People began to tell of experiencing a new enabling power within their lives as they participated in a more intimate, renewed relationship with the Lord through the infilling of his Spirit.

Baptists believe that the Holy Spirit enters one's life when one invites Jesus to become Savior and Lord. It is the work of the Holy Spirit to cleanse, seal, and empower. Regarding this tenet of faith, Bob Lindsey had no doubt. And yet, what these people, many longtime believers, were experiencing with regard to the infilling and empowering of the Holy Spirit in their private and public worship was undeniable and significant. It seemed to be related to the degree of one's willingness to yield oneself completely to the moving of the Spirit, without reservation or concern for propriety.

Bob and other pastors in Jerusalem began having home prayer and praise meetings each week. As the numbers increased, they outgrew the houses and began meeting in their churches. In fact, this was happening in the lives of ministers and church people all over Israel and the Middle East and beyond. It was as if God were calling his people everywhere to prayer and praise. With prayer came confession of sin, the seeking of forgiveness for offences, and a stronger love and concern for fellow believers as well as for nonbelievers.

An East Jerusalem Arab Baptist pastor, Fahid Karmut, shared with Bob his experience of "speaking in tongues" as part of his worship experience. Although this was not part of the Baptist experience and was generally relegated to the realm of the Pentecostals, Bob's feeling was that anything the Lord does for somebody is great. Consequently, he was sympathetic with his fellow pastor even though the experience was foreign to him personally. He had already determined to endeavor to be completely open to virtually anything the Lord wished to accomplish within him or through him, regardless of how strange it might appear.

One day in 1972, Pastor Karmut told Bob about a recent experience in Bethlehem. An Arab man told his Lutheran pastor that because of her strange and sometimes violent behavior, he wanted to divorce his wife, Therese. The pastor agreed to visit her and see what could be done to help the situation and consequently sought assistance from Pastor Karmut. He learned she was twenty four years old and had two small children. He also discovered that she helped her father who made and sold magic charms that were placed on or near a sick person in an attempt to bring healing. Use of charms is a common practice all over the Arab and Oriental world. The pastors cast eight demons out of her that day, but she condoned her father's charm business which may account for her failure to be totally free of the demonic presence.

This type of ministry was totally new to Bob and he found it fascinating. Pastor Karmut invited him to accompany him on his next visit, and Bob eagerly agreed. When they arrived, Therese served coffee to Bob and Fahid. After a while during a time of ministry to her, Fahid spoke in Arabic to the demon in Therese, "Come out, come out of her in the name of Jesus!" The demon screamed in Arabic, "No! No!" Bob and Fahid took turns — one praying while the other rebuked the demon. The demon spoke to Fahid in Arabic, but to Bob it said accusingly in Hebrew, "You are a Jew! You are a Jew!" to which Bob responded, "I am a believer in Jesus!" The woman then jumped up and ran around the table while this heated shouting match continued for several minutes. The pastors rebuked and prayed while the demon quoted verses from the Bible and argued. At this point Therese picked up a large, heavy clay jar and raised it above her head. As the demon contorted her face in a snarl, it spoke to Bob in English,

"I'm going to take her to hell along with you and Karmut!" Bob was standing across the room from her as she prepared to throw the jar at him. He was praying aloud in Hebrew, when suddenly, from his mouth he heard himself speaking with great authority in totally unfamiliar sounds that appeared to be some sort of language that was directed at the demon. The words were spoken with absolutely no effort on his part and he had no idea of their meaning. Therese stopped short with the jar still over her head, and the demon responded to Bob angrily in a variety of different languages, one of which sounded like a Chinese dialect. Bob continued to feel a new sense of authority well up within him as he rebuked the demon in the new language that flowed effortlessly from his lips. After a few moments, Therese abruptly relaxed and her face returned to its normal appearance as she set the jar on the floor and sat down.

Unfortunately, Therese was not totally released on that occasion either, perhaps because of her continuing inability to renounce the charms she helped her father make. On the way back home, Pastor Karmut parked his car and entered a market, leaving Bob in the car. Bob started praying aloud and again that same utterance came out. His verbal expression was on a plane transcending his consciousness. Bob recognized that his experience was like his wife Margaret's, and that of respected Christian friends who likewise spoke in tongues.

Margaret had first experienced the phenomenon of speaking in tongues some three years earlier in 1969. She later wrote of the occasion:

> I was very discouraged. I had the feeling that there was no point in our labors. I was fed up with everything—it seemed so black and useless. One day while alone in our house, I lay prostrate on the floor and prayed, "If you are there, God, do something or I want to die." Then I heard my name called at a far distance. The name was repeated, "Margaret! Margaret!" and got closer and closer. I felt the presence of the Lord, and opened my mouth to say, "Jesus," and out came this strange language; it was my prayer language. I was extremely conscious of the presence of the Lord. After a while, I walked around the house praising God.

I wanted to tell someone, so I left the house and went down to the main part of the city toward Baptist House. On the street I met my friend Liz Kopp who had a Pentecostal background. I started telling her of my experience and she seemed almost disinterested as if that was to be expected. She was not excited at all. Then I went to Baptist House and told my colleague Eddie Fields and was comforted that she knew exactly what I was talking about. Later that day when I told Bob, he accepted it. From that day on I could pray in English, Hebrew, or my prayer language at will.

The phenomenon of "speaking in tongues" is called *glossolalia* by theologians. It is considered by those in the renewal movement to be a spiritual gift in which the Holy Spirit actually controls the speech of those endowed and that the speech is not in any language known by the speaker. There have been many cases in which one speaks in a language unknown to the speaker, but which was recognized by another person present who knew that language. Some believers speak in tongues after much seeking, desiring, and praying for this glossolalia. Others, as in the case of Bob and Margaret Lindsey, did not especially seek or try to speak that way, but they were joyfully surprised when it happened. An important facet of the experience is that one can pray or sing in tongues whenever one wants. When one is speaking or praying in tongues he can still carry out various functions such as ironing clothes or driving a car. Then he or she can quit at will.

Bob and many others believed that in the scriptures there are two different kinds of tongues. One is mentioned in Acts 2:4-12, and relates what happened at Pentecost, when God gave men the ability to testify about Jesus in languages they did not know. There were people present from at least fifteen different countries who heard the Apostles speaking in the languages of those countries without the Apostles having learned them. The second type of tongues is mentioned by Paul. "For anyone who speaks in a tongue does not speak to men but to God. Indeed, no one understands him; he utters mysteries with his spirit," 1 Corinthians 14:2. "For if I pray in a tongue, my spirit prays, but my mind is unfruitful. So what shall I do?

I will pray with my spirit, but I will also pray with my mind; I will sing with my spirit, but I will also sing with my mind," 1 Corinthians 14:14-15.

Spiritual gifts are called "grace gifts" which is the meaning of *charismata*. The lists of grace gifts in Romans 12:6ff and 1 Corinthians 12 are not exactly the same. This leads many to believe the gifts mentioned are not meant to be a definitive list, so they would include the gift of music and other God-given abilities as well.

In May of 1974, Bob and Margaret flew to London and took the train to Oxford where Bob conferred with several scholars about biblical matters. As several professors were carrying on their discussion around a table, Bob became aware that his left ear was hot whereas his right ear was normal. In the following months and years, his left ear would often get hot, particularly during meetings. Bob believed that this phenomenon was from God and that it meant, "Bob, I'm here. Pay special attention." That was not the conventional interpretation of the phenomenon, but on the other hand, being non-conventional was nothing new for Bob.

Flying back to Israel, a young couple seated in front of the Lindseys caught Margaret's attention. This couple seemed to be enjoying each other in a delightful, natural way. They appeared to be about twenty-five years of age, were speaking Hebrew, and seemed to be Kibbutzniks (common term for members of a collective farm or settlement in modern Israel). Margaret was surprised to see the girl take out a scarf and quickly tie it around her head, orthodox style, then take out a little book and start to read. The young man also began reading it and they pointed here and there discussing the writing. It appeared to Margaret to be a New Testament, but she couldn't see it clearly so she asked Bob, "See if you can see what they're reading." After a glance, he replied, "They are reading Matthew." Margaret whispered, "It's a new day." Perhaps at last people were realizing that they could still be observant Jews while accepting Yeshua (Jesus) as their Messiah.

Early in the morning of April 2, 1975 Bob drove from Jerusalem along the twisting road to Lod Airport. He mused to himself that this was certainly one opportunity he did not want to miss. He was planning to meet a tour group from South Africa that he had learned would arrive that morning. The group was led by Reverend Eric Uys, but Uys was not the man Bob was eager to meet. Rather, the man destined to impact the congregations and Christian leadership in Israel with a message of healing and deliverance was a member of the tour group. Ralph van Kooij, pastor of the Hatfield Baptist Church in Pretoria, had come expecting to tour the Holy Land for two weeks and then to return home.

As he drove along, Bob thought back to an earlier experience that had moved and excited him and that ultimately was responsible for this morning's trip to the airport. Anna Venter, a South African friend, had been diagnosed with a fatal illness and had left Israel to return home to South Africa. Then, unexpectedly, she had returned to Israel a few months later—totally cured. She was literally glowing with excitement as she told Bob and Margaret about her healing experience. Upon her return to South Africa, she had shared her physical problem with Pastor van Kooij. He then had read to her several New Testament passages about healings, faith, and forgiveness, and had put his hands on Anna's head and had prayed that God would heal her. A miraculous healing had taken place, and subsequently had been confirmed by Anna's doctors. Pastor van Kooij, she explained, had ministered to many people in that way. When Bob learned that van Kooij was planning to come with a tour group to Israel, he decided then and there that he must spend some time with him.

As the members of the tour group claimed their baggage and emerged from the airport someone pointed out van Kooij to Bob, who then went over and introduced himself. After exchanging greetings, Bob explained earnestly to van Kooij, "We have no such healing ministry as yours in this country, and I, as well as many colleagues and national pastors will gratefully receive any help or instruction you can give us." Pastor van Kooij replied, "I would indeed be happy to do anything I can to help the work here, but I must first see whether the leader of my tour would permit me to leave the group and help you." Eric Uys said, "I consider it to be the hand of the Lord if Brother van Kooij feels called to give a helping hand to Christians in Israel."

Bob sensed that this encounter with van Kooij was God ordained and literally rejoiced as he excitedly took him to his home in Jerusalem. Within a few hours, Bob had contacted many colleagues and pastors and started arranging meetings where van Kooij would teach and preach. Although interest in this kind of spirit-filled ministry grew rapidly, Bob did arrange for van Kooij to be with his tour group about a week. The group finished their tour and returned to South Africa—without van Kooij. His planned two weeks in Israel grew to four weeks, then six and finally to nearly two months. Hundreds heard him teach and preach. During the days he ministered to the needs of individuals one after another—primarily burdened pastors, church leaders, and Christian workers and their family members—then met in churches with groups several evenings a week.

"Many Christians don't experience the joy of walking in the Spirit because of tenacious old bad habits, both fleshly habits and also damaging mental habits," explained van Kooij. All during his stay in Israel, individuals would phone for an appointment with him. After one would tell him he had come because of an unbreakable, tenacious habit, or doubts about God, or unexplained fears or compulsions, van Kooij would read scriptures indicating that the war was not against flesh and blood, but with supernatural evil powers. He explained that in the case of believers, they were in need of deliverance, not from possession, but from oppressive spirits. "You must confess your known sins before effectual prayer can be offered for you," he counseled. After confession by the seeker, van Kooij would pray for him or her and then exercise authority over the spiritual power responsible for sickness or negative behavior. Bob knew many of these seekers before and after their session with van Kooij and testified that the changes in their lives were genuinely positive.

Pastor van Kooij was asked many times, "Why should a Christian have these problems?" He replied again and again, "My friend, something happens the moment we get serious about following Jesus as Savior and Lord, and submit ourselves to the empowerment of the Holy Spirit. We find that we are not wrestling with flesh and blood and with ordinary problems, but with spiritual powers of wickedness operating on a supernatural level. The Bible tells us the devil goes about like a roaring lion and even more often as an angel of light and he is out to oppress us. We have to live victoriously by the power of Christ but this often means we must take radical action against any powers Satan has managed to get operative within us. Only then can the power of the Lord effectively come in and heal us and make us whole." Many times van Kooij explained the gospel to those who sought him for healing, because although culturally they were Christians, they had never made a personal choice to follow Jesus as Savior and Lord. Once they had cleared up that matter, they were in the best position to receive their healing or deliverance.

Bob learned a lot from the practical ministry of Pastor van Kooij. It was with a reluctant but grateful heart that he bade him good-by as he returned to South Africa. The memories of their time together became even more poignant two months later when Bob learned of Pastor van Kooij's fatal heart attack. He took comfort, however, in the knowledge that the people touched by his dear friend's ministry now endured as a living memorial to van Kooij's selfless attitude and willingness to set aside his own plans in order to bring healing and deliverance to them during the final months of his life.

Before van Kooij arrived, all but one of the Arab Baptist pastors were either Charismatic or deeply sympathetic with the movement. Almost all the new converts among the Arabs tended to be more Charismatic than their pastors. However, some of the Lindseys' Southern Baptist colleagues, as well as a few members of the Jerusalem Baptist congregation, were quite disturbed about Bob's practicing a Charismatic ministry.

Unfortunately, some new believers who received the Lord in the Charismatic environment were not fully informed regarding what the Bible actually teaches about the work of the Holy Spirit and about grace gifts. Some went so far as to say that if one didn't speak in tongues he was not filled with the Holy Spirit, and some even doubted the salvation of those who did not speak in tongues. Conversely, Bob and Margaret Lindsey never advocated any particular grace gift, nor did they believe that everyone should have all the grace gifts. They did not believe that speaking in tongues was the only proof of being filled with the Holy Spirit, nor that it was proof of salvation. To Bob and Margaret, tongues is a gift from God, edifying to the believer experiencing it.

Most of Bob's Southern Baptist colleagues were sympathetic to his Charismatic experience and practice and many shared in the experience—but not all. Two couples felt strongly enough about the issue, that they chose to serve in other countries. Even Bob himself struggled over matters of faith and practice that were new to his experience. Bob's Baptist colleague Charles Worthy recalls the struggle:

Aristotelian logic and the Semitic mind—I remember Bob saying again and again, "Charles, I was taught to think logically—I call it Aristotelian logic; everything must make sense. That is not the Semitic way, the Biblical way. The Semitic mind sees miracles and wonder, demons and angels. I must begin to think Semitically, not logically." I could see Bob wrestling with this again and again, especially as he continued his critical work with the synoptic gospels and with the Charismatic Movement at the same time. This is very important in the theology, thinking and practice of the great intellect of Bob Lindsey.

Wes Brown and Wayne Buck both provided significant support for Bob in the church in Jerusalem during this time. Wes was an American Baptist who had served in Africa and understood the talk about demons and that sort of thing. He seemed sympathetic to Bob's new understanding of the Holy Spirit—this energized Bob and gave him support. Wayne Buck, another of Bob's Southern Baptist colleagues, became Bob's music man— no one could lead "Charismatic worship" like Wayne. Bob relied heavily upon him and found him to be very supportive.

In spite of the opposition he faced, Bob was grateful for the empowerment of God's Spirit to more effectively minister to the needs of those who sought help. As word spread that one could experience the healing, delivering presence of God at the meetings Bob held, the small congregation which he served experienced phenomenal growth. He prayed for divine wisdom, guidance, and empowerment as he endeavored to serve those who had entrusted themselves to him. He had no way of knowing that on the horizon loomed a conflagration that would test the faith and resolve of both Bob and his growing congregation. Bob was also greatly encouraged and strengthened by the expressions of appreciation and solidarity from a variety of individuals who had been associated with the Lindseys during their three decades of service in the land.

CHAPTER 26

THIRTIETH ANNIVERSARY

Bob and Margaret Lindsey's thirtieth anniversary of their appointment to service in Palestine and Israel greatly interested their board. In 1974, the Southern Baptist Foreign Mission Board commissioned The Radio and Television Commission of the Southern Baptist Convention to write and film the story of the Lindseys service in Israel. A competent film team from Germany was engaged and shadowed Bob and Margaret for approximately three weeks. In addition to filming Bob and Margaret as they went about their daily routine, the team interviewed several prominent Israelis who knew the Lindseys well, including Professor David Flusser of Hebrew University and Mayor Teddy Kollek of Jerusalem.

Filming, editing, and voice-over resulted in an interesting and enjoyable film of about thirty minutes in length. Unfortunately, during the time between the Board's asking the Commission to make the film and its completion, the Board had received some letters of complaint about Bob's ministry. Some Southern Baptist tourists who had attended services at the Baptist Church in Jerusalem were quite concerned about Bob's stressing the grace gifts such as anointing the sick with oil and praying for their healing, and casting out demons. In other words, Bob and Margaret were considered *Charismatics*. Although there was nothing in the film to suggest this, the executives at the Board decided not to distribute it. The Radio and Television Commission, however, did broadcast it on television.

The Baptist representatives working in Israel comprise an organization known as the Baptist Convention in Israel, or BCI. The

Lindseys' colleagues chose to honor them on their thirtieth anniversary of service by devoting an entire issue of their in-house paper, the *BCI Intercom,* to tributes to the Lindseys. Editor Elizabeth Smith describes the newsletter and how the material was collected:

> During the years that I was the press rep for the BCI, I decided to begin writing and publishing a monthly in-house newsletter. Some of us lived rather isolated from other BCIers, while others lived in clusters. The *BCI Intercom* would be a way to keep each other informed about our various ministries. I enlisted "stringers," colleagues with a nose-for-news, who would telephone me when something special was happening in the ministries in his/her area. He/she could write the article and send it to me or give me the details and I would write it for the next issue of the *Intercom*. Charles Worthy was my stringer in Jerusalem. He and the other stringers enthusiastically tackled my assignment about a special issue to celebrate the Lindseys' 30th anniversary of service in Israel. That issue would be delivered at the BCI annual meeting in July. I was glad Charles was able to get statements from such people as Kollek and Flusser along with tributes from our BCIers in his area. I received tributes from the other areas as well as from people abroad. All these I happily included in the special edition, with the first copy given to the Lindseys during the BCI meeting at Green Beach Hotel in Natanya (July 7-10, 1974).

The following selected assessments by colleagues and friends provide valuable insight into the personality and character of the Lindseys and the esteem in which they were held in Israel by some of those who knew them best.

> Rabbi Stephen Wise once said that many scholars try to be men and many men try to be scholars but it is rare that one person is both a man and a scholar. Bob Lindsey is both. And Margaret is both a woman and a helpmate.

You can't have one without the other, and who would want to, and that's the way it's been for thirty years in Israel for the Lindseys. Margaret has been right there helping, pulling (not pushing), cheering and decorating. She's all woman too, producing six fine specimens of humanity, five already out of the nest and one on the nest edge.

It all began in 1939 when Bob came to Palestine to study Hebrew and geography. Thirty months later he married Margaret Lutz and brought her to Jerusalem in 1945. Those were Mandate days and not so pleasant. Margaret remembers the lines, the shortages and...the dangers in the streets. What do the people of Jerusalem think of the Lindseys? Read the comments of some well-known and not-so-well-known Jerusalemites.

Charles Worthy
Colleague

I have known Bob Lindsey for a long time and know him to be a true friend of Israel and the Jewish people .

Teddy Kollek
Mayor of Jerusalem

Many people think that because I am a friend of the Lindseys that I am a believer in Jesus. I am not; I am Jewish, but before I met the Lindseys, I didn't even believe in God. Now I do.

Manasseh Genoshor
Jerusalem Musician

I understand Bob's Theory of Gospel Origins and agree with it. Most scholars don't understand it or agree with it because they do not have a thorough knowledge of Hebrew and Greek and have not taken the time and effort to investigate what Lindsey is saying.

David Flusser
Hebrew University Professor

We, as a mission, want to add our word of tribute to Margaret and Bob. Those of us who were in Gaza before 1967 had heard many and varied tales of the exploits and adventures of Bob Lindsey from our friends in Lebanon and Jordan. We had the idea that he must be some sort of nine-feet-tall giant to do and be all that some told us he was. It was a joy to get to know him and to find that he really is an extraordinary person in many ways, if not quite in the way we had imagined. All of us in Gaza appreciate so very much the tremendous contributions made by Margaret and Bob to the work of sharing the Good News of Jesus in the Middle East.

Colleagues at the Gaza Baptist Hospital

In a given lifetime the average person knows and associates with very few really *great* people. After all, greatness in a human is illusive in description and always peculiar in quality to the individual. I guess I could say that Bob and Margaret Lindsey are *illusive and peculiar* if I follow my train of thought, but I am trying to say that they are two of the really *great* people whom God has allowed me to know, love and work with during my lifetime.

There is a genuineness in the Lindseys—*the whole clan*—that stubbornly refuses to be poured into a mold. They are void of pretense, dedicated to seeing the best in those about them, self-sufficient without a trace of conceit and amazingly consistent in plodding toward a goal in their lives' work.

What Ben Gurion was to the State of Israel in pioneering through to success, Bob Lindsey has been to Baptist work in this land. We who have shared in his dreams and worked along side…have felt a strength and depth that is not unique; it is *great*. My life has been immeasurable blessed by their having been a part of it and for this I shall be eternally grateful!

Marjorie C. Rowden
Colleague

Bob amazes me in his ability to think deeply and discuss ideas on a scholarly level and then moments later, wrestle with small children who tease him to play with them. He and Margaret graciously open their home to people of all walks of life.

Carolyn Worthy
Colleague

Any attempt to commemorate Bob and Margaret will fall short due to the zest with which these two live their lives. If *zest* seems too stilted a term, perhaps *full-throttled* would be more precise. Leaving such exquisite performance in the rarefied stratosphere of textual scholarship or uniqueness of theories to others to expound, I would rather underline one Lindsey activity, though humble, that is both typical and demonstrative—fishing.

To go fishing with Bob Lindsey is more a *happening* than an activity. One finds oneself raiding strange secluded yards for worms or dashing hither and thither after grasshoppers. One knowledgeable in productive worm beds or prolific grasshopper fields attains importance in Bob's eyes, an importance surpassing that of one who uncovers a new Dead Sea Scroll or undeniable proof of the primacy of Luke.

One accompanying Bob fishing has not to do with casting rods, trolling lines, or fly lures and such; that person has to do with floating within a tire tube, simple rod and line in hand, hope in heart and patience.

Fishing of course, is merely symbolic of an opportunity for fellowship with rather rare individuals in a world sodden with sameness and mediocrity. If art would be profound, it first must be simple. It is not maudlin in the Lindseys' case...to assert that their peer group does not match their profundity because it does not match their simplicity, with apologies to Wellington for distorting his appraisal of Napoleon, *With God* (rather than by God) *they do living honor."*

Chandler Lanier
Colleague

Through the Lindseys I have grown closer to our Lord Jesus Christ.

Pat Hoaldridge
Colleague

Uncle Bob and Aunt Margaret were very warm towards each of the Home Kids. The nineteen of us and their six kids were like one big happy family. They made our life at Baptist Village enjoyable and fun. For example, Uncle Bob always took us on trips and camping. These adventures were as memorable as listening to Uncle Bob's *band.*

Aunt Margaret, as principal of our school, was patient and attentive to each child. She gave each one special and individual treatment. We felt like one of her own children and not a *separate* group. During the Lindseys' stay the Village became a real community, with home, farm, church, school, and camps. We were glad to be part of all the activities. All the Kids feel a deep love for the Lindsey family, parents and children. We had evidence that they were ready to sacrifice for us personally and for the Home. We still feel that way.

Rhadia Shurrush [Qubti]
For the "Home Kids"

One of my first memories of Bob after we arrived here is his sitting in the church wearing a bright red shirt, playing a *mean* piano. His ability to be perfectly at home in all situations is a sign of deep self-acceptance which in turn enables him to minister in a real way to people of all backgrounds. What a great inspiration Margaret has been to me! I have been drawn closer to God through her quiet, gentle spirit and her personal, deep relationship with God.

Mary Anne Burnham
Colleague

Gets more thrilled over digging up big fat worms than a kid finding a $10 bill. Likes to build boats that float halfway under the water resulting in the police at Tiberias telling him to "get that thing off the lake!" Would rather sing, or blow a trumpet than anything.
When asked a question, gives an honest, straightforward answer. Unpretentious, inspiring. We love them.

Dale and Anita Thorne
Colleagues

I personally believe no fisherman can be all bad, even if he looks so...but fishing with Bob is unlike fishing with anyone else...the gems of wisdom and knowledge on the trip going and coming are marvelous. His apparatus is unbelievable, but his hiding his wooden leg in the bushes is totally unforgettable. So fish or no fish, the trip is memorable. And you know...now that I get to thinking about it, it was a raft I slept on in the Lindsey's cabin at Poriah...

Jim Burnham
Colleague

They are the epitome of gracious hospitality, love, concern, intellect—all wrapped up in one twosome!"

Wayne Buck
Colleague and Jerusalem Tourist Chaplain

While hardly fulfilling the fond *ad mea va esrim* wish, the 30-year milestone...is at least a better beginning toward that noble goal than the rest of us have made to date. I certainly recognize that a few penned lines of appreciation is scarcely a decent substitute for the column that could be written about the devotion and dedication of Margaret and Bob to the growth and maturing of the Baptist Convention in Israel. Thirty years is a long time...and it gives us much satisfaction to know that we are not mounting these testimonials as terminal tributes. In thinking of Bob and Margaret I am attracted to the words of Brutus, but with a dual application; We have not come to bury Caesar, but to praise him.

We not only praise the Lindseys, we love them. Also, none among us would deny that love flowed from their lives to each BCI brother and sister at all times, but especially when needed.

Actually, that they are easy to love, esteem, and greatly respect are, to my mind, the finest of many attributes. Bob is skilled at defusing trouble, tension and frustration by his relaxed listening, and to them both, all lines of communication are open.

Others can write and speak about Bob's scholarship, Margaret's many-splendored talents, their spiritual powers and leadership, but I like best to recall their warm-hearted openness and their loving, human responses.

Dwight Baker
Colleague

Bob and Margaret Lindsey were deeply touched by the kind expressions of appreciation by friends and colleagues. They had chosen to invest three decades of their life, living their faith in service to all who came within their sphere of influence. The response in honor of their thirtieth anniversary was beautiful indeed. But life is not always beautiful—sometimes it is ugly. The Lindseys discovered, however, that in the midst of ugliness, God works through other people to give beauty in exchange for ashes.

CHAPTER 27
BEAUTY FOR ASHES

To appoint unto them that mourn in Zion,
to give unto them beauty for ashes,
the oil of joy for mourning,
the garment of praise for the spirit of heaviness;
that they might be called trees of righteousness,
the planting of the LORD,
that he might be glorified.

—Isaiah 61:3

Bob and Margaret retired for the night just before midnight on Thursday October 8, 1982. They were awakened from a sound sleep by the telephone about an hour later. As a pastor, it was not unusual for Bob to receive calls any time of the day or night. When Bob sleepily answered he was jarred awake, however, by the shocking news delivered by a friend, "Bob this is Ben-Chorin! Your church is on fire!" Bob quickly replied, "We'll be right over!" They hurriedly dressed and within minutes were driving toward the church.

As they maneuvered their car around the fire trucks and parked, the night sky was illumined by flames leaping from the roof, doors, and windows of the chapel. The entire structure was engulfed, including the temporary shelter built on the east side for overflow crowds. The firemen were unable to save the chapel but they were able to contain the fire and keep it from spreading to the adjoining Baptist House. Rabbi Tovia Ben-Chorin of a nearby synagogue and his wife spotted Bob and Margaret getting out of their car. The Ben-Chorins immediately came over and stood speechless with their arms around them and tears in their eyes. After a few moments, the rabbi spoke in a serious tone, "It's arson. The firemen and others who arrived first smelled a strong odor of petrol." Everyone knew intuitively that it was the work of Jewish extremists. The bookstore in Baptist House had sustained heavy smoke damage in a previous arson attempt when firebombs hurled through a broken window failed to ignite a fire but only smoldered, sparing the building but covering the bookstore and its contents with thick black soot.

As the chapel burned, many Jewish friends from the neighborhood gathered around them, their faces illuminated by the flames and with tears in their eyes, expressed their deep regret. Upon later reflection, Bob thought it ironic that some of the same people who had watched as their synagogues were burned by people bearing the name "Christian" during the Holocaust in Europe were capable of shedding tears at the loss of a Christian house of worship in Jerusalem. Indeed, perhaps it was because of what they had suffered that they were capable of such empathy.

After some two hours the chapel was reduced to smoldering ruins with only its stone walls left standing. As the firemen were dousing the remaining embers, a Jewish lady entered the gutted chapel, and laid a rose on the ruined but recognizable piano. When nothing more could be done, the Lindseys and their friends returned sadly to their homes.

During this time, Christians from all over the world had gathered in Jerusalem to join in the celebration of the Jewish Feast of Tabernacles. Bob invited Jamie Buckingham, who was in Jerusalem for the celebration, to preach on Saturday. The regular congregation was joined by about six hundred of those attending the Feast of Tabernacles as they gathered outdoors around the ruins. In typical fashion, Bob evoked a big laugh from the crowd when he commented, "I was praying for fire, but not that kind. However, *Gam zu letova*—this too is for good. We desperately needed a larger chapel to accommodate the attendance of three hundred and fifty or four hundred people, and saw no way to get one. Now that an arsonist graciously destroyed the small chapel, we see the way open to build a larger one." An offering was taken to start a fund for the new church building, and the crowd's generosity produced $12,000.

Jerusalem Mayor Teddy Kollek vigorously condemned the loss of the Baptist Chapel, and opened several accounts in various banks to which those who wished could contribute toward a new building. He stated emphatically that the Baptists would be given a building permit to construct a new facility. In spite of the mayor's strong support, however, the bureaucracy of various government offices blocked the approval of the permit for a number of years.

Even if the permit had been issued immediately, everyone knew that it would take several years to raise the necessary funds and to complete construction. In the first attempt to provide a meeting place for the congregation that would provide some protection from the elements, the men of the church set up a large canvas tent. It's size soon proved to be inadequate so the church decided to erect a large, tent-like structure consisting of a metal frame covered with vinyl. As Bob and the other men began erecting this temporary enclosure on the site of the former tennis court, someone asked, "What are we going to say if the building inspector comes around here and asks what we are doing?" Bob responded, "We'll tell him that we are erecting a *succah*." The workers broke out laughing, since it was already past Succoth, the Feast of Tabernacles, when observant Jewish families build a *succah*, a temporary place to celebrate, remembering the time of wilderness wandering during the exodus from Egypt. For as long as the temporary structure was in use, the church called it a tabernacle, or an *ohel moed*, the Hebrew words for the tent the Israelites used to house the Ark of the Covenant.

Work on the tabernacle was completed by Christmas. It had a wooden floor, vinyl walls and vinyl covered wooden roof and was illuminated by electric lighting. Two large electric blowers provided heat when necessary, but most of the year, when the three hundred and fifty to four hundred people packed into the structure every Saturday, heat was not a problem. By the time construction was complete, the local congregation had spent $11,000 on the tabernacle, and the building fund contained an additional $50,000.

A few months after the fire, Moshe Felber, a Jewish man of Reform affiliation who lived on Narkis Street not far from the Baptist church, wrote an article in Hebrew for a small newspaper that was circulated in the neighborhood of Rehavia. His article, *My Ecumenical Street*, described his neighborhood on the Sabbath. Narkis Street starts on the west side of the city and runs some five blocks to its juncture with

King George Street in the heart of west Jerusalem. On this street there are four synagogues (Ashkenazi, Orthodox, Reformed and Yemenite) and the Baptist Church. Mr. Felber humorously wrote that he enjoyed sleeping in on the Sabbath, but was always awakened by his neighbor early in the morning going from door to door calling on Jacob or Rachamin to join the *minyan*, ten men needed to start the Jewish prayers. He would slowly get up and ready, then stroll along to his synagogue. About the Baptists he facetiously writes that they don't have the problem of *minyan*, since they draw what appears to be no end of worshippers, coming from all over the city and even outside the city. Behind their burned-out chapel they fill a courtyard.

> Even though they are Christians and Gentiles they meet on the Jewish Sabbath. The Baptists sing their prayers, a part of which are in Hebrew and sung to Israeli tunes, accompanied by a piano and cornet. By the volume of the singing which fills the street, there must be about a thousand Baptists inside. [It is more like 400]. As many Jews leave their synagogues to walk home, they stop on the sidewalk to enjoy the singing, "without fear of the missionary danger or of hobnobbing with idolaters." They stand in a kind of demonstration of solidarity with the Baptists and with revulsion at the sight of their burned chapel. They even linger and greet the Baptists when they leave, many of whom are Israelis, some are foreigners or tourists.

According to Felber, the only objection to religious activity on Narkis Street is by the Orthodox complaining about the excessive noise and fumes of the cars that bring the Baptists to their church and Reformed Orthdox folks to their temple on the Sabbath. Felber ends his article:

> If all these different kinds of people have lived in peace so many years and even prayed in so many different ways in my street, surely the sound of the Redeemer's steps must already be heard. Indeed can we not talk of this hill where my street ascends and descends, the rain falling

some to this side and some to that, as somehow fulfilling the vision of Isaiah (2:3) when he saw the multitudes of people from many nations coming up to Jerusalem and could prophesy, "out of Zion shall go forth the law, and the word of the Lord from Jerusalem."

Early in 1983, Rabbi Tovia Ben-Chorin of the Har-El synagogue walked around the corner to the Baptist property with a request for Bob. He told Bob his congregation wanted to present the Baptists with a large Hebrew Bible at a Friday evening service. He sheepishly said, "I didn't have the nerve to ask you to speak but my people insisted." It turned out well. Bob and some of the Baptists were present in the synagogue when, after Hebrew prayers and recognitions, Bob delivered a sermon and received the Hebrew Scriptures for the church. Inside the Bible's cover, written in English and Hebrew were the words, "This Hebrew Bible is presented to the Baptist congregation of West Jerusalem by your neighbor Har-El congregation of Jerusalem (Israel Movement for Progressive Judaism) as a token of friendship and encouragement after the fire which destroyed your house of prayer." Bob commented, "The warmth of the people is so genuine and beautiful."

Shortly after the fire, a local Jewish teacher took an hour with each of her High School English classes to speak about the arson and her long-standing friendship with Baptists. She was compelled to "...educate them for total living and not teach them an academic subject." In the following months hundreds of letters and gifts were sent to the Baptist church by local people. Money came from various individuals, churches and synagogues, school students, civic clubs, and merchants' associations. The workers in the local butcher shop sent over a gift. Members of the local Baptist congregation itself gave generously. One local Christian gave $3,000 he had been saving to have his teeth fixed.

Gifts were also received from individuals and groups around the world. German Baptist and Evangelical churches gave sizeable gifts as did an American Baptist group. As might be expected, the largest contributions were from "our landlord," as Bob called it, the Southern Baptist Convention in the U.S.A.

The process of constructing a new building was long, tiring, and tedious. The church had to decide whether to build on the property they owned or to relocate. They chose to stay on Narkis Street and worked with a local architect, Ze'ev Baran, who submitted plans to the various building commissions many times. The church decided not to go into debt, but rather to attempt to have all the needed money before construction began. From the day of the fire until the new building was in use was over ten years. Bob was active in the planning until he retired, but was not there during the construction.

In retrospect, he was indeed grateful for the beauty God had given in place of the ashes, foremost being the expressions of concern, kindness, and generosity by their neighbors in Jerusalem and others around the world. He treasured the beauty as he faced the sometimes ugly challenges of life that made him feel like he was swimming upstream against the current.

CHAPTER 28
SWIMMING UPSTREAM

It often seemed to him that he had been swimming upstream against the current of popular opinion throughout his entire life. Bob Lindsey's parents had wanted him to become a doctor—but he had chosen to become a pastor. His mother had chosen a popular local girl that she had hoped her son would marry—but he had chosen to marry Margaret Lutz whom he had met in Japan as he was returning to the U.S. from Palestine. In fact, the very reason he had been in Palestine was due to his decision to pursue truth no matter where the path might lead. In his pursuit of biblical truth, he followed the advice of his pastor in equipping himself to be able to read the Bible in its original languages. After majoring in Classical Greek at the University of Oklahoma, he traveled to Palestine where he studied Modern Hebrew and other subjects at the Hebrew University in Jerusalem. This foundation would prove invaluable when he entered seminary where he studied the Biblical Hebrew of the Old Testament (or Hebrew Bible) and the "Koine" Greek of the New Testament. In later years, his familiarity with these languages enabled him to "feel" Greek and Hebrew in much the same way as one feels the correctness of word order or idiom in one's own native language.

As a university student in Palestine, Bob spent much of his free time in talking with the people of the land, particularly with the young people—Jews, Arabs, and expatriates. He had an almost insatiable desire to understand their perspectives on the important issues of life.

Bob Lindsey was a visionary, but he was also a pragmatist. He was always alert for new ways to meet the needs of those he served, both on a grand scale as well as on an individual basis. And as with most if not all visionaries, he faced numerous obstacles, with opposition coming from numerous quarters, sometimes including his own Baptist colleagues. Fortunately, he had learned early in life that flexibility and adaptability are essential to one's survival, but he didn't give up easily on issues that were important to him. On a particular occasion one of his colleagues lamented in a letter to their area director: "It is impossible to argue with Bob Lindsey because he will not consider another point of view. He is insensitive. People won't argue with Bob because he responds so strongly that they yield and are wiped out." In response to the accusation Bob simply replied, "It certainly is not my desire that I should wipe out my opponents by emotional response to criticism, but I think I am too much inclined to a good fight on issues I think are important." He then added wryly, "I do manage to fight my inclinations along this line with occasional success, however."

Bob generally attempted to answer his critics, often taking hours to compose a letter. He did not take criticism easily although he did take it seriously. He cared deeply that he and his actions should be understood accurately by people locally as well as by the constituency in America.

One of the ideas for which he fought was for a Baptist Center built around an agricultural cooperative that would be located near Petah Tikva. (Petah Tikva is outside Tel Aviv on the Sharon Plain). Bob was impressed by the potential offered by a Christian agricultural settlement in keeping with the *kibbutz* and *moshav* settlements that were so prominent in the early years of Israel's development. This system of communal farms was pivotal in the formation of Israel. Every group who had anything in common formed a *kibbutz* or *moshav*, the majority being agricultural in nature because food was so scarce. In fact, the black market was rampant due to the scarcity of food (and nearly everything else). Consequently, the country depended on the *kibbutzim* and *moshavim* to provide food, not only for their own settlements, but for those who lived in cities and villages as well. Much of the agricultural attention was focused on the Sharon Plain, which was known as the "breadbasket" of Israel. It is not surprising, therefore, that Bob chose farmland in this area near Petah Tikva for a Baptist cooperative farm. In a fund-raising effort he wrote of the plan he envisioned:

It is becoming increasingly clear that the Arabs of Israel will shortly be using Hebrew as their second tongue, and this one fact means that future vacation camps, conferences, and Bible school training may be conducted in that language. This fact should serve to unite the work as a whole, and thus Baptists who are both Jews and Arabs will be able to join in a mutual witness for Christ to the country.

Perhaps more should be said about the settlement and center planned near Petah Tikva. There is a nucleus of several Baptist workers now engaged in a cooperative agricultural venture on the outskirts of this city. Located only eight miles from Tel Aviv, this cooperative runs a small truck-farm which has at its disposal nearly forty acres, all of which are eventually to be intensively cultivated and irrigated. In this area, three and sometimes four crops may, by rotation, be raised on the same land during the year.

The plan calls for a number of different units of workers and families cooperating in every way possible to build up a settlement characterized by mutual aid and friendly relations. One unit is to be a cooperative largely for young people, some of whom would be full-time workers, others of whom would be receiving part-time work on the farm while going to the Bible school. Not all of these are to be dedicated Christians, as there are always people interested in what Baptists teach, and who may be called "inquirers."

Other units would be family acreages. Here families predominantly interested in truck-farming would buy small plots of land on which they can build homes and share in cooperative farming, implements, and advice. The agricultural couple is to be on hand to help in the planning of these units and in continued advice for those who are new at farm work.

Located in the immediate vicinity, the Bible school would have one resident couple whose responsibilities would be the development of a congregation composed of members of the settlement and any others from nearby built-up areas such as Petah Tikva.

Such a plan, it is believed, should help to strengthen Baptist work as a whole. For one thing it will show the interest Baptists have in the working population which is, of course, the largest in Israel. It will make possible the training of laymen for the congregations growing up slowly in the cities. It will provide work for some of those who may lose employment because of their faith. Again, it will provide the physical possibilities of a local congregation. The difficulties of achieving all of these goals will be readily recognized. Good workers will be needed. Enthusiastic laymen will be necessary. The economic problems of such a group will not be easy. Yet, given sacrificial personnel and the help Baptists can (and we believe will) send, such an institution should help greatly to make the cause of New Testament Christianity better known and appreciated.

Unfortunately, the formation of an agricultural cooperative as Bob had envisioned it ultimately failed, due primarily to a decision by the Board in the U.S. that to develop the property as a cooperative would prove too costly in light of other priorities in countries around the world. In this and similar situations, one always faces the difficulty of how to effectively translate a vision for a project in some remote part of the world to those making funding decisions in America. In fairness, one must acknowledge that the task of those making funding decisions is generally complicated by the fact that there are insufficient funds for all the worthwhile projects proposed. While it was a great disappointment to Bob and to the Baptist couple from America that had been appointed to develop the cooperative, the Baptist Center did become a reality although different from that originally proposed. The George W. Truett Children's Home from Nazareth relocated there, a local Baptist congregation was organized, and a campsite was constructed for summer Bible camps for families and young people. The camps provided opportunities for Baptists of both Jewish and Arabic backgrounds from all over the country to come together for a time of relaxation, fun, learning, and worship. And Bob Lindsey moved on to envision other endeavors such as the Dugit Art Gallery and Bookshop, and the Dugit publication center in downtown Tel Aviv.

Bob Lindsey frequently found himself swimming upstream with regard to his pastorate. Perhaps the most vigorous criticism (as well as the most enthusiastic support) came from Southern Baptist tourists from America that visited the Baptist Church in Jerusalem. Some were critical because they had expected to find in Jerusalem a Southern Baptist Church transplanted from America. What they found was an indigenous church that was shaped by the culture and needs of the congregation. For example, worship services were held on Saturday rather than Sunday for the practical reason that Saturday was the day that most of the congregation was off from work. The vast majority of Baptist visitors from abroad, however, voiced their approval and support of their worship experience at the church on Narkis. The number of unsolicited letters praising Bob far outnumbered the complaints.

On the Sabbath after the church was burned, many of the church's Jewish neighbors came and silently joined in the outdoor service in a show of solidarity. Upon returning to the U.S., a tourist who had been present at the service complained to the board that Bob had not "given an invitation" at the conclusion of the service when so many strangers, particularly Jews, were present. Bob was well aware, however, that an evangelistic emphasis asking those present (including Jews) in that particular service to come forward and publicly accept Jesus as the Messiah would have been highly offensive and unproductive. In his regular church services, Bob sometimes gave a public invitation but usually did not. He generally preferred to invite those who wanted to know more about Jesus to speak with him after the service or during the week. Bob believed that when the Holy Spirit was working in someone's life, all was not lost because he didn't offer a public invitation.

He also was criticized for holding services that were too open to the Holy Spirit with the style of the service being Pentecostal, Charismatic, too lively, too loud. There was too much emphasis on the reality of evil, Satan, and Satan's demonic horde. In reality, while it is true that many people would raise their hands in praise to God (which is biblical), many did not. There was complete freedom in that matter. They anointed the sick with oil and prayed for healing. They also were open to the testimony of anyone who received a word of encouragement from the Lord for the church.

Bob was criticized for preaching in non-Baptist churches in America and was accused of not really being a Southern Baptist, or questioned whether he had ceased being a Southern Baptist. To some Southern Baptists it appeared that for one of them to be different was an unbearable threat. On the other hand, a certain well-known Charismatic leader voiced the opinion that Bob was not completely a Charismatic either. There were certain practices in Charismatic churches during the 70s and 80s that were not permitted or encouraged in the Jerusalem church. Consequently, he did not seem to fit any particular religious mold. Some found that disquieting — others found it refreshing. In spite of the criticism he received from some, he was held in high esteem by others. He was named *Alumnus of the Year* in 1984 by The Southern Baptist Theological Seminary National Alumni Association.

When the executives at the Southern Baptist Foreign Mission Board received complaints, they would try to defuse the issue by explaining that the church's style fit well in the multi-cultural environment of Jerusalem. They also maintained that Bob, Margaret and the congregation were building a great church and that in Baptist churches around the world there are dozens of different styles of worship. They normally would write something complimentary about Bob (and send him a copy of the correspondence) as seen in the following example:

> Bob and Margaret Lindsey have been under appointment of the Foreign Mission Board for forty years. He is one of the recognized scholars in the world in the Hebrew language. His knowledge of Greek is also excellent. Even in ordinary conversation he quotes scripture and verse with exact wording in three languages with greater frequency than some preachers mention the Bible in their sermons. He and Margaret have poured out their lives in service to our Lord and to the Jewish people in particular but without limitation to

them exclusively. He grew up under the preaching of Preacher Hallock in Norman, Oklahoma. Here is a man who for four decades has served our Lord, witnessed to people, prayed and wept over lost souls. The church where he serves back a few years ago was running 15 or 20, whereas now 400 is not unusual.

Some visitors were disturbed to discover that Bob offered a choice of either wine or grape juice to worshipers during the Lord's Supper (Holy Communion). Southern Baptists from America are encouraged to abstain totally from alcohol while Baptists from Europe and other areas face no such restriction. In addition, Christians from other denominational backgrounds also were represented in the congregation. To most participants, their tradition of using either "real" wine or only red grape juice was very dear and to be offered a different form of the fruit of the vine would have interfered with their spiritual experience.

Even the best attempt to accommodate both traditions was not without its challenges. One Friday, Bob realized they were out of wine for the Lord's Supper to be celebrated the next day. Being busy with other tasks, he requested, "Margaret, please take a bottle to the wine-shop for more. It's cheaper if you take your own bottle!" So Margaret took a bottle with her and dutifully told the shopkeeper she wanted a bottle of red wine. He filled it, she paid him, and took it home. Early the next morning Bob poured the grape juice and the wine into the respective communion cups for each participant, and then prepared the plates of unleavened bread. The service went well and it ended with the Lord's Supper. As people were leaving, however, several insisted to Bob that he had served cognac rather than wine. He was somewhat perplexed until he checked the bottle which both he and Margaret thought had been refilled with wine. It happened that Margaret had given the shopkeeper a bottle with a cognac label, so he had totally disregarded her instructions to fill it with red wine and had given her cognac instead!

Neither did Bob Lindsey fulfill the usual expectations when people came to visit the recognized Greek and Hebrew biblical scholar. Sometime after the publication of *A Hebrew Translation of the Gospel of Mark*, two prominent pastors from America made an appointment to visit Bob while they were in Jerusalem. When they arrived at Baptist House, they were conducted not to Bob's office but through the kitchen and out into the side yard. There they found Bob kneeling over an open sewer grease trap, shirtless, with muck up to his elbows. He was dipping out accumulated sludge in an attempt to restore proper drainage to the kitchen sink. This "man of many talents" engaged a clogged sewer line with as much energy as he might engage a Gospel passage in Greek in a quest for the Hebrew undertext!

Bob had a couple of suits with wedges of cloth in a contrasting color sewn into the lower trouser legs forming "bell bottoms." This was done to facilitate putting on his trousers over his prosthesis. He customarily would wear a suit until it was nearly threadbare. Consequently, on several occasions after speaking in a large church in America, someone would give him a couple of expensive suits. He would wear them in the U.S. but, invariably, he would give them to someone in Israel that he felt needed them more than he.

His well worn suits were always adorned with a memorable tie. Many people wondered if he were colorblind, but he was not. In reality, he merely was quite fond of bright colors and unusual designs—shirts, ties, sweaters, and socks. It became a sort of Bob Lindsey trademark. He seems to have adopted a Middle Eastern appreciation for color. The landscape in much of the region is predominantly a monotonous brown much of the year. Consequently, the indigenous people traditionally have painted their homes and buildings with bright colors, and adorned their clothes, saddles, tents, walls—almost everything—with a splash of color.

Bob's pursuit of biblical truth led him to research the first century mode of baptism. For a long time he wrestled with the Greek verb meaning "to baptize" compared with the meaning of the Hebrew equivalent because the implications were not exactly the same.

The acceptable mode for Baptists is total immersion of the fully clothed candidate that is administered by a fully clothed ordained minister in a special baptismal tub or pool at the front of the sanctuary. Christian paintings depicting the baptism of Jesus by John the Baptizer usually show both individuals standing in the river up to their waists with John pouring water on Jesus' head. The paintings reflect the theology of the painters, however, and totally ignore the fact that both Jesus and John were first century Jews and would have used the Jewish mode of baptism.

Two important points should be noted about the Jewish mode of baptism in which Jesus participated:

1. It was self-administered. The person officiating was a witness who certified that the baptism was properly performed including total immersion of the entire body including hair.
2. Baptism in "living" or "running" water was highly esteemed; consequently, John chose to baptize in the Jordan River.

A wall painting depicting the baptism of Jesus that was discovered in the catacombs of St. Callixtus in Rome probably more accurately reflects the actual mode. In this painting, a fully clothed John is standing on the bank of a stream and reaching out to assist a naked, dripping Jesus who is coming up out of the water after having fully immersed himself. This picture is consistent with the Jewish mode of baptism. John's role was to call people to repent and to get ready for the Messiah's coming. As a sign of their repentance they took off their clothes and entered the water to dip themselves in the river (like the Indians at the Ganges). John stated the terms and oversaw the baptisms as the people immersed themselves.

Consequently, Bob initiated this mode of baptism in his church in Jerusalem. (Some of his colleagues humorously noted that he did not discover that the one baptizing stood beside the water until after he had a prosthetic leg and could not enter the water with it!) He liked to baptize in the Wadi Kelt located in the Judean Wilderness a few miles from Jericho. Wadi Kelt is a beautiful, though somewhat austere, area, where, according to tradition, the ancient prophet Elijah was fed by ravens while in hiding. Bob officiated at the baptisms he conducted by standing beside the pool formed from a mountain spring while the candidate entered the pool and at the appropriate time immersed himself or herself (fully clothed).

During his decades of service in Israel, Bob Lindsey faced many challenges, perhaps none greater than the challenge brought about by the Charismatic Renewal that swept through many churches and denominations around the world in the early 1970s. While trying to guide his church and Baptist work in Israel away from some of the excesses of the movement, he always tried to remain open to any genuine spiritual experience that the Lord might want to bring about within or through him. He was particularly interested in spiritual experiences that touched the lives of those to whom he ministered in the area of their life in which they experienced a need. As he and the church prayed in power for the needs of people and witnessed seemingly insurmountable obstacles melt away with people healed, delivered, and other needs met, the church experienced a literal explosion in attendance.

By 1985, the core of twenty to forty people in attendance during the 1950s, 60s, and early 70s had grown to an enthusiastic crowd of 350 to 400 people who were coming each Saturday to worship in the temporary structure known as "the tent." The 9 A.M. Hebrew worship service was followed by an English service at 10:30. The worship was joyful and included much singing accompanied by a variety of instruments. After about forty-five minutes in the English service, the children would go out to Bible classes. There were twelve classes for children, including nine in English and three in Dutch. On Sunday evening there was another English-language service whose primary purpose was ministry to those in need of prayer for healing, etc. The spiritual life of the church was directed by elders that were called *ro'eem*, which is Hebrew for "shepherds" (not to be confused with the so-called "Shepherding Movement.") The *ro'eem* shared in every area of pastoral responsibility, including preaching. Whenever the senior pastor was absent, he could rest assured that the church was not lacking in leadership. As the time of his retirement approached, Bob took comfort in the conviction that the church possessed capable leadership that would continue after he was no longer present.

Bob Lindsey had little patience with the proponents of end time prophecy. Although many Baptists have a so-called "premillennial view" of the end times, Bob's view was "amillennial (no millennium). The premillennialists essentially expect a seven year period of world tribulation followed by the return of Christ who sets up his headquarters in Jerusalem and reigns over the earth for a thousand years before the final judgment of mankind. Bob, on the other hand, believed the apocalyptic genre of literature of the New Testament Book of Revelation is figurative rather than literal. He believed in the "sudden" literal return of Christ (Messiah) followed by the final judgment of mankind.

Having been in the land longer than many Israelis, it is no wonder that Bob had adopted many of their attitudes. Israel is well known for its extensive bureaucracy with the inevitable bureaucratic delays that reach into virtually every area of life. He knew that rules theoretically existed in an attempt by various authorities to retain control and to curb abuse. But he knew that the endless rules, many whose purpose was long since forgotten, made it difficult, if not impossible to minister in an effective manner to the needs of those who depended upon him. Consequently, he would keep or circumnavigate a particular rule according to which best served the need on any given occasion.

During a time of food scarcity in West Jerusalem in 1948, for example, friends reportedly saw Bob go through no man's land on a motorcycle wearing what appeared to be a clerical collar since priests were the only ones who could freely cross into East Jerusalem without a hassle. He later returned with his saddle bags full of food for those living at Baptist House.

David Bivin tells of accompanying him to the port in Haifa in later years where Bob needed to visit a person on board a ship. When they arrived at the port, Bob parked the car, reached into the back seat and retrieved a stevedore's jacket from a sack, donned it and walked on board without being questioned.

On another occasion, Bob needed to take a visitor from America to visit someone in the hospital in Jerusalem but it was past visiting hours. He simply donned his white doctor's coat and the two proceeded to the patient's room. As they walked along the hall, he was greeted several times with, "Good evening, doctor."

Perhaps most indicative of how Israeli Bob had become may be illustrated by what happened one morning when he met a tour bus on a narrow Jerusalem street. Since there was insufficient room to pass, the bus driver began impatiently honking the horn and motioning for Bob to back up. But in a very Israeli manner, Bob simply honked and motioned for the bus driver to back up. The bus driver continued to honk and became quite verbally abusive. With that, Bob simply opened his car door, swung his feet out, and sat there reading his newspaper. After several more minutes of honking and verbal abuse, the driver backed his bus out of the narrow street and Bob calmly folded his newspaper and drove on.

Jerusalem seems to act as a magnet that draws numerous mentally troubled individuals there each year, many believing they are biblical figures such as prophets. As many as fifty or more per year require admission to a psychiatric hospital in Jerusalem. They wander the streets loudly proclaiming their message. Usually they are harmless, but may become quite agitated—such as the two Elijahs who happened to meet in a local market one day and came to blows, each claiming to be the "real" Elijah and the other to be an imposter. For these mentally troubled individuals, Bob had compassion and attempted to help them when appropriate.

Bob's concerns for the needs of others was not limited to his congregation but extended to the country at large. At the end of September, 1986 the country was in the grip of a severe drought. Bob announced that on the first Sabbath of October, the church would have a special prayer for rain. He then challenged, "If you believe God will answer your prayer, bring your umbrellas." Their prayers for rain attracted the attention of *The Jerusalem Post* that published an article with the caption, "Baptists to Thank for Rain Bounty." The story was that the Baptists started praying for rain on Sabbath Day, October 4 and everyone knelt to pray. In a few days it rained a little. The next Sabbath the Baptists were back praying for more rain. That day Bob walked about the platform under a raised umbrella singing, "Praying for the Rain," substituting his own lyrics to the song, "Singing in the Rain." Bob later commented, "Our prayers for rain were one way the congregation was going back to its biblical sources." A woman in the congregation was from Hollywood and knew the actor Gene Kelly who made the song famous in a movie by the same name. She wrote Kelly that her Jerusalem Baptist pastor was improvising and singing his own words to the tune. It pleased and amused Kelly so much that, a few days later, Bob received an autographed photo of Gene Kelly dancing and singing in the rain under his umbrella.

Bob was delighted when he received the photo of the actor who had starred in one of his favorite movies. Although he had not personally met Gene Kelly, through the years life presented him with the opportunity to meet a number of other high profile people.

CHAPTER 29
HIGH PROFILE PEOPLE

Perhaps the most revealing description of Bob Lindsey would be that he was a "people person." He was genuinely interested in meeting people and getting to know them. If one were seated next to him on an airplane, by the time the plane landed he probably would know a great deal about you—and you probably would know very little about him. It was not that he was such a private person—it was that he was more interested in talking about you than about himself.

Throughout his lifetime he met a great many high profile people and became friends with a number of them. Although he valued these friendships, he was not a "name-dropper." His own sense of self esteem was not dependent upon whom he knew or did not know. His friendly, caring, unpretentious nature coupled with his genuine interest in people regardless of social status enabled him to enjoy friendships with people from all strata of life. As with anyone, his relationships ranged from single or occasional encounters to enduring close personal friendships. Through his attention and interest, he possessed the ability to make each person feel important. Bob always seemed surprised when anyone attempted to speak of his importance. A common characteristic of the truly great seems to be that they are totally unaware of their greatness and are somewhat uncomfortable when such is suggested.

From the many high profile people in Bob Lindsey's life, the following examples were selected from the areas of government, religion, and scholarship.

Mayor Teddy Kollek

In various capacities, Bob became well acquainted with a number of government officials. One of those he most admired was Teddy Kollek during his long tenure as mayor of Jerusalem. In a letter to Bob dated March 19, 1979, Mayor Kollek wrote:

Dear Dr. Lindsey:

At the close of President Carter's visit to Jerusalem, I wish to convey to you my appreciation and gratitude for your inspired choice of Psalm 122 as the central theme of the Sunday Service Sermon at St. Andrew's.

You have again manifested your true love and concern for Jerusalem for which we are proud and grateful.

Yours sincerely,
Teddy Kollek

He was often present at receptions at Baptist House and on New Years Eve 1986 he presented Bob with the Mayor's Medal of Appreciation for more than four decades of community service contributing to harmonious relations between the Christian and Jewish communities of Jerusalem.

Mayor Kollek commented on his relationship with Bob in an interview for the 1975 documentary film *The Lindseys of Israel* produced by The Radio and TV Commission of The Southern Baptist Convention for the series *The Source*. When asked to characterize Bob, the mayor replied, "In our view, Jerusalem and Lindsey are inseparable!"

Evangelist Billy Graham

The roots of friendship between Bob Lindsey and Billy Graham reach back to the childhood of their wives when Margaret Lutz

Lindsey and Ruth Bell Graham (both daughters of missionaries) attended the same mission school in Pyongyang, Korea.

As 1959 drew to a close, the Christians of Israel had been praying for about five years that Billy Graham might come to preach in their country. In a letter dated December 21, 1959 to Milton Murphy at the Baptist Center near Petah Tikvah, Dr. Graham wrote:

Dear Mr. Murphy:

A note to say that it is possible that I will be arriving in Israel approximately March the 20th, and am looking forward to meeting you personally. We are taking an intensive tour of Africa beginning about the middle of January and hope to go to Cairo and Jordan before coming to Israel.

My thoughts in coming to Israel were primarily for sight-seeing and rest, as I will probably be exhausted by the time I reach there. However, our mutual friend, Bob Lindsey, was in my home today, and he urged me to consider the possibility of meetings in Israel. I deeply regret that it was impossible for me to stop on my way from Australia; but, due to the fact that Queen Elizabeth had invited me to be her guest at Buckingham Palace for that period, I felt it was of strategic importance throughout the British Commonwealth that I accept her invitation, even though it meant cancellation of my plans in Israel.

The reason I am writing to you is that I understand from Bob that you were the chairman of the committee last year. We would be delighted to accept two or three public meetings, perhaps in Jerusalem, Nazareth and Tel Aviv, along with at least one meeting for missionaries and national Christian leaders, if the brethren so desire. I would like to hear from you as soon as possible after you have given thought, prayer and consultation with the other brethren to this matter.

In addition, I would like to have the privilege of meeting some of the leaders of government. I have before me a letter, dated November the 23rd, 1959, from Mr. Aba Khoushy, the Mayor of Haifa, inviting me to be his personal guest while in Haifa. During the past few years I have received a number of inquiries from the Israeli government as to the possibility of taking a tour of Israel.

Thus, if the Christians can use me in any way to further the cause of Christ in Israel while I am visiting there, I should be delighted to put myself at your disposal. In any plans made, however, I should appreciate you keeping in mind that I would like to sight-see and rest as much as possible.

With warmest personal regards, I am
Most cordially yours,
Billy Graham

Securing permission to rent auditoriums large enough to accommodate the expected crowds coming to hear a high profile Christian evangelist such as Billy Graham proved to be a somewhat daunting task. Bob describes some of the difficulties they encountered:

The United Christian Council (UCC), representing all the churches in Israel, had invited him [Billy Graham] to come. Milton Murphy, our Baptist pastor and leader in Petah Tikva, had worked with many other leaders as the chairman of the committee on arrangements. They had spent many hours in planning the four public meetings and the closed meeting for Christian workers which Billy would address.

Two weeks before Billy arrived it became clear that a great number of Israelis who were not committed believers in Christ wanted to hear him. But where? There were not even three Protestant, much less Baptist, churches in the country large enough to hold more than 700 people.

The UCC approached the management of the Mann Auditorium in Tel Aviv, explained the situation, and asked if they might rent the hall for the Tel Aviv appearance. The management of the hall, which holds 2,700 for every kind of high-brow and low-brow performance normal in any part of the world, did not know whether to allow a Baptist evangelist to preach there or not. After all, Mann Auditorium is a public hall in what is supposed to be an all-Jewish city.

The committee decided it would be best to take the rental up with Israel's Foreign Ministry. The Ministry immediately wished to help. Meantime, however, the story reached the newspapers. Within three days public opinion was excited. Would Israel let the famous evangelist preach in her best hall?

The Foreign Ministry, like many a government department in other parts of the world, was by now not completely free to decide this issue. Two dozen Israeli newspapers were following the developments and two conducted polls of well-know citizens to find out what they thought should be done. Most of those polled said that no democracy should imagine closing a public hall to as great a man as Billy Graham, a man long known for his interest in Israel. In the end a telegram was sent to Mr. Ben Gurion, Israel's Prime Minister who was at that time in the United States, asking his opinion. The report was that Mr. Ben Gurion replied that if Billy did not preach for conversion or mention the name of Jesus there should be no objection. The committee on arrangements declined. Meetings were planned in Nazareth in an open forest, in Haifa and Jaffa in churches, and in Jerusalem in the YMCA auditorium.

Baptist colleague Jim Smith recalls going with a number of pastors to Prime Minister Ben Gurion's office in Jerusalem to request Graham's use of the Mann Auditorium in Tel Aviv. Teddy Kollek, who was then the director of the prime minister's office, conveyed their request to Ben Gurion in the U.S. via telegram. When they returned for Ben Gurion's response, Kollek quoted the prime minister as saying that it would be fine with him for Billy Graham to speak in the Mann Auditorium if he would not mention Jesus or read from the Bible! The pastors then asked Kollek, "What then, could Graham say?" Kollek answered by saying that the prime minister would like for Billy Graham to speak about his world travels.

Among the wide ranging opinions expressed in newspaper editorials, perhaps the most enjoyable and enlightening is that expressed by Israel's foremost humorist, the late Ephraim Kishon in his welcome to Billy Graham. Bob apparently translated the following from one of the local Hebrew language newspapers:

SHALOM, BILLY GRAHAM!

I am not sure you will remember me? We met the first time when you were preaching and I was sitting in front of a tiny 7-inch television set watching and trying to catch every word you said: "It is still not too late! You have a little while before the end! You can still say to Jesus, I am coming, Lord!" Truthfully, I did not step forward. I am not sure why, perhaps because the screen was so little, perhaps because I did not understand every word, perhaps because I did not know what to do—the important thing was that I remained a Jew.

I know you did not ask me to change my religion. You never ask anyone to be Christianized. But you must understand that I cannot believe in Jesus without a change in my *status quo*. Besides that, I am still afraid of Jesus. Maybe Father Patech is to be blamed for that. There were three of us Jewish boys in his class in Budapest— Garros, Previart, and I. A boy named Sakrash came up to me at recess time and said, "You crucified Jesus!" Father Patech immediately called all the boys together and told them that it was not Garros, Previart, and I ,but the Jews of Jesus' day who killed him.

We Jews have had some trouble with Jesus. But that did not keep me from enjoying your preaching. You are young, handsome, sincere, speak with grace, with a voice like that of Lawrence Olivier, a personality effusing love and friendliness. The words of Paul are as aptly applied to you: "I did not fall short of the very chiefest apostles…" All come to you. You have harvested in all the world. Yet—not among us.

Blessed is your coming to Israel. We have few friends and you have constantly been our friend. We are happy to have you. If anti-Zionist Jews have been welcomed here, surely you should feel doubly welcome. Your friendship stems from the Book you quote (to which we have the copyright!) and that is surely good. But don't preach to us, please.

Not because we are afraid of apostasy; because you will fail. We would not like to see a friend like you disappointed. We shall hear you standing in the Mann Auditorium, preaching, "The hour has come. You have no hope of life, even tomorrow. And you cannot take anything with you. How will you fare when you stand before the Throne of Judgment? What can you say?" and all the time we will be sitting there thinking, "What is going to happen next week? Will Nasser cross over our southern border or the northeast one?" and when you make the plea to come forward there we will be sitting. No one will be coming—nobody.

Truth is that people become Christians here too. For simple juridical reasons, income tax, or hot summers. But they do it quietly, on the sly. We citizens of Israel are vaccinated against apostasy. First, why? Secondly, we are not so impressed; we organized the firm, so to speak— Jesus and the disciples were Jews (only Father Patech had not heard about that). We have learned so much in history about the real world that all we can think about today is water for the Negev, or cheap jet fighters. Believe me, Mr. Graham, nothing but the pain of disappointment would await you in Mann Auditorium. We have our rabbi, tried and ragged.

But perhaps still in time our Foreign Ministry will intervene and save you! Since in little countries nobody dares to get entangled with the affairs of the Almighty, the management of Mann Hall, worried stiff, turned to the Hebrew University, they in turn to the Workers Council in Haifa, thence to the Central Language Committee in Jerusalem, and finally, they turn it over to the Foreign Ministry who forbid your failure (forgetting that a certain personality of ours [Ben Gurion] has completed a tour of the large halls of America calling for volunteers to leave America for Israel).

After translating for Billy Graham, Bob returned to Wake Forest, North Carolina to continue his work on translating the New Testament into Modern Hebrew. In an undated letter written the day after his return to the U.S. he expresses his appreciation and evaluates Dr. Graham's visit:

Dear Billy:

Finally returned to N.C. yesterday and naturally was happy to be home again.

People will continue to talk about your visit to Israel for a long time to come. It meant a great deal to the evangelical groups who, as you know, are working under many difficulties. Your very presence has strengthened our Baptist work vis-à-vis the official organs of government.

I have heard since the meeting in Jerusalem that many members of the Knesset and some very spiritually-minded professors of the Hebrew U. were present at the YMCA. At a recent meeting of our folks I collected a considerable number of stories which I will send on to you when the translation of some of the important articles in the Hebrew press are completed and also ready to send.

Margaret and I, with the family, have been promised peace and quiet if we return to Israel this summer. It appears we shall stay in Tiberias in a Church of Scotland house. If you and Ruth plan to spend some time in the vicinity and we can get together let me know. We are planning to drive from England through Turkey in July and should be in Petah Tikva through August, moving to Tiberias the first of September.

Hoping you have had a good rest the past two weeks and with many, many personal thanks for having helped to answer our prayers about your coming to Israel, I am

Your Servant in Christ,
(Signed)
Bob

Evangelist Kathryn Kuhlman

In November of 1974, Kathryn Kuhlman was scheduled to hold a miracle service at a sports stadium in Tel Aviv in connection with the second World Conference on the Holy Spirit. Most of the thousands in attendance were Christian participants from all over the world, but a concert by the Christian musical group, *The Living Sound*, prior to Miss Kuhlman's appearance had attracted about two thousand Israelis to this open event. Conference organizers Dan Malachuck and Ralph Wilkerson had arranged for sufficient translation headsets for the eight main language groups represented by the conference participants, but there were not enough for all of the local, Hebrew-speaking Israelis. Exceptional news coverage by the press resulted in more local interest than had been expected. Consequently, Dan Malachuck approached Miss Kuhlman prior to the service with the news that they had no choice but to ask her to work side by side with a Hebrew-speaking translator. She was not at all pleased with the prospect because she felt it would be a distraction to the working of the Holy Spirit through her. When Dan insisted that they had an obligation to the Israelis since it was their nation and they had come to hear her, she inquired about the translator. Dan motioned for Bob Lindsey to join them and introduced him as a Spirit-filled Southern Baptist who had lived in Israel for almost thirty years. Lindsey had translated for Billy Graham when he had come to Israel in 1960. He was perhaps one of the best Hebrew scholars in the world and had earned the respect of the Jewish community.

A quick glance told her all she needed to know. While she was wearing a long, flowing white dress and her piano accompanist, Dino

Kartsonakis, wore a tuxedo, Lindsey was wearing a regular business suit, colorful tie, and—*Earth Shoes*! He had chosen the shoes because they worked comfortably with his prosthetic leg. Their rough leather exterior, however, stood in stark contrast to Dino's highly polished black shoes. She could not change. There was no way she could minister beside a man wearing *Earth Shoes*—even though half the Israelis in the audience were wearing the same thing.

She shook her head and said, "I'll tell you what we'll do. You have Dr. Lindsey come to the platform before I do and he can bring greetings to the Israelis in their language. He can tell them that I will speak only ten minutes and then we'll go directly into the miracle service."

In spite of her intention to preach only ten minutes, she preached an hour and fifteen minutes. She could not make the miracles of healing at will—she could only continue to speak until the Holy Spirit moved. Finally, she called out healing after healing but by this time, more than a thousand Israelis had gotten up and walked out, shouting at the ushers and slamming doors as they left.

Most of those experiencing healing were Christians but several Jews were also healed. One of those who came forward to confirm his healing was a Jewish man from a kibbutz. He had been deaf in one ear and was now able to hear. Bob Lindsey came with him up onto the stage where Miss Kuhlman was questioning those who claimed healing. As she approached them, Bob suddenly fell backward and was caught by one of the men assisting and gently lowered to the floor. After lying there several minutes, he arose and translated for the Jewish man as he told of his healing. In describing the experience, Bob told of being "zapped" by a blast of energy that knocked him backward and enveloped him with a great sense of warmth, peace, and God's love.

Bob had been very curious about this phenomenon of "resting in the Spirit" ever since he had observed it the previous year at the first World Conference on the Holy Spirit in Jerusalem. At that event, the pastors and church leaders of various denominations in Israel along with some of the conference speakers were seated onstage since virtually every seat in the auditorium was taken by participants from abroad. At one point while she was speaking, Kathryn Kuhlman asked the pastors and speakers on stage to stand. She then started on one end and gently touched the forehead of each man in turn. One by one they fell backward and were caught by workers who were positioned for that purpose. This was in spite of the fact that such practice was not part of the theological practice of many of these men. At last there remained only Bob Lindsey and David DuPlessis, one of the key men in bringing together Pentecostals and Roman Catholics and who was know affectionately as "Mr. Pentecost." As Miss Kuhlman stepped in front of them, she looked squarely at both, then turned abruptly and returned to the center of the stage and continued speaking. Bob and DuPlessis looked at each other, then at the stage littered with the pastors "resting in the Spirit" and then sat down. Bob was extremely disappointed that he did not get to experience the phenomenon, but now, one year later, his curiosity had been satisfied at last.

It was several years before Bob learned of the real reason for Kathryn Kuhlman's refusal to let him translate for her. He had accepted her explanation that she felt the translation would be a distraction and hinder the flow of the Holy Spirit. Even when he learned that the real reason was her refusal to minister alongside a man wearing *Earth Shoes*, Bob Lindsey had only kind things to say about Miss Kuhlman.

Three days after her return from Israel she held her final miracle service at the Shrine Auditorium in Los Angeles. After completing the service, she complained of feeling ill. Her health continued to deteriorate over the following weeks and she died of complications following open heart surgery.

Professor Anson F. Rainey

Bob was associated with numerous high profile scholars during his career, but perhaps none more closely than Anson F. Rainey and David Flusser.

Professor Rainey is Emeritus Professor of Ancient Near Eastern Cultures and Semitic Linguistics, Tel Aviv University and has been a full professor since 1981. He is adjunct professor of Historical Geography, Bar Ilan University and Ben Gurion University of the Negev. An American by birth, he has spent most of his adult life in

Israel. He is a prolific writer with numerous books, textbooks, journal articles, items in encyclopedias, papers presented at scholarly meetings, popular articles, and other publications. Professor Rainey recalls:

> I first met Bob when he visited Brandeis University before I got to Israel. Then I would see him from time to time. He drove me and my ex-wife to Haifa harbor to leave by boat for the U.S.A. and then he drove to Jerusalem to make his famous crossing to rescue that kid from East Jerusalem. The next thing I know, his story was in the newspaper when I reached the U.S.A. two weeks later.
>
> After I completed my Ph.D. and came back to Jerusalem in 1962, he and Margaret came to pastor the church on Narkis Street. After that we spent considerable time (not enough) discussing his theory of the Synoptics and I did some work for him color coding the synoptic text in 1963-64. I had started teaching at Tel Aviv University and Bob knew I needed extra money so he gave me this job. I remember setting aside a few hours on Friday evenings to work on that. When I finished, we spent some really high quality time together going over Luke/Matthew agreements against Mark. The two were usually in good translation Greek while Mark was not! It was amazing and convinced me that Bob was on the right track.
>
> Bob's field trips with the Bible inspired the Baptist Seminar I taught and its field trips from which I got the idea for the field trip program of the American Institute [of Holy Land Studies; later renamed Jerusalem University College]. I had a commitment to learn the cutting edge data in documents and archaeology to make the Institute trips seriously academic. My atlas is a result of these forty years.

Professor David Flusser

Bob Lindsey's long friendship and scholarly collaboration with the late David Flusser, Professor of Comparative Religion at Hebrew University in Jerusalem, has been alluded to earlier. Both men were born in 1917, Bob on August 16 in Norman, Oklahoma and Professor Flusser on September 15 in Vienna, Austria.

Flusser could converse fluently in nine languages and read literature in an additional seventeen. He authored over 1,000 scholarly articles in Hebrew, German, English and other languages. Among the books he authored are *Jesus* (3rd ed., 2001) and *Judaism and the Origins of Christianity* (1988). Paradoxically, his book *Jesus* has been translated into eleven languages, but not into Hebrew. He was a member of the Israel Academy of Sciences and Humanities and was frequently recognized for his scholarship. His awards include the Israel Prize (1980), the State of Israel's most prestigious honor, as well as the Rothschild Prize for Jewish Sciences (2000).

He was a founding member of the Jerusalem School of Synoptic Research, and was one of the world's leading Jewish authorities on Early Christianity. His pioneering research on Jesus and Christianity's relationship to Judaism won him international recognition. His collaboration with Bob Lindsey, beginning in 1961, inspired a new approach to the synoptic gospels.

His relationship with Lindsey is expressed succinctly in the autographed copy of the first edition of this book Jesus in 1969:

To my friend, teacher, disciple—R. Lindsey

David Flusser

President Jimmy Carter

When United States President Jimmy Carter and his wife Roselyn visited Israel on a state visit in March of 1979, he indicated that they would like to worship at a church service. Since the Carters were Baptists, Bob Lindsey was contacted about the matter but authorities in charge of security determined that the location of the Narkis Street Baptist Church precluded that option. Two other sites were investigated—the West Jerusalem YMCA near the King David Hotel and St. Andrew's Church of Scotland. The latter was selected and its pastor, Reverend Tom C. Houston, agreed to share the service with Bob. The church was located on the edge of a hilltop across the Hinnom Valley from Mt. Zion and the walled Old City of Jerusalem. The 150 seats in the church sanctuary were much fewer than what was needed for the diplomatic party as well as the two congregations and Israeli dignitaries. Consequently, the limited number of people from the two congregations who were permitted to attend were chosen by lot in an attempt to avoid controversy.

The Houstons and Lindseys welcomed the Carters and their party on the steps of the church in a scene described by the Lindseys' Baptist colleague, Elizabeth Smith.

> Margaret presented Roselyn Carter with a Bible inscribed with the best wishes of the Baptists in Israel. She told the American First Lady that Baptists were praying for them and for the success of their peace mission. In response, Mrs. Carter thanked her and exclaimed over the 'lovely' olive wood cover on the Bible.

In describing the worship service that followed, Smith said in part:

> Bible readings included Psalm 2 from the O. T. and Luke 22:24-30 from the N. T. The worshippers also sang a metric version of Psalm 122 which included the words, "Pray for the peace of Jerusalem...Peace be within thy walls..."
>
> Preceding his sermon, Dr. Lindsey led in intercessory prayer for the peace negotiations and for President Carter's part in them.
>
> In his sermon, Dr. Lindsey read his own paraphrase versions of Psalm 122 and Luke 22:24-30. He pointed out that in Christian thought Jerusalem is often visualized in spiritual terms. But, he stressed, the prayer for the peace of Jerusalem was for the physical city, with its 360,000 souls.

The "thrones" mentioned in Ps. 122:5, Dr. Lindsey explained, are places where people on pilgrimage gather before the Lord to worship and where God is going to act in deliverance and redemption. Referring to the Luke passage, Lindsey said that, contrary to popular interpretation, the disciples were not arguing about who would have first place in the Kingdom. Since Jesus had told them that He was going away, the disciples were in panic and wondering who was strong enough to lead the movement when Jesus was gone. Jesus' example of service at the table [during "the Last Supper"] was the answer to the question of authority. "As Christians we are given authority, but we must use it in service for others as Jesus did in getting up and down to serve the reclining guests at that Passover meal," Lindsey explained.

After the offering and the singing of the Doxology, the service ended with the Baptist minister reciting the threefold priestly blessing [Aaronic Benediction] in Hebrew. Mrs. Carter had requested that Dr. Lindsey include the blessing in the church service when she had been with him at the official welcoming ceremony at the entrance to Jerusalem. Lindsey, along with the heads of the various religious communities in the capital city, had been invited by Mayor Teddy Kollek to witness the special blessing of bread and wine offered by Rabbi Moshe Porush. The basis for this ceremony is found in Genesis 14 when Melchizedek blessed Abram and the most high God.

The congregation remained standing while the Carters left. The President smiled as he passed the worshippers and said, "Thank you for praying for me. Please continue to pray." As they left the church building together, Dr. Lindsey told President Carter, "I am sorry that we couldn't work it out for you to worship at our Baptist church." President Carter remarked that he was sorry also, but that those decisions he had to leave to others. He then asked about the Baptist congregation.

The pastor told him that about 300 people attend every Shabbat but there were between 60 and 65 actual members. The President laughingly responded, "That's about the opposite of what is in our country."

Outside the church, President and Mrs. Carter paused briefly in the church yard to pose for dozens of photographers against the background of the walls of the Old City. President Carter then kissed his wife good-bye as they separated to proceed to different locations—he to official talks with the Israeli Prime Minister and she to visit an absorption center for new Jewish Immigrants.

One thing President Carter did not hear was Bob Lindsey's comment to Pastor Houston after the service. Earlier, since the pastor of St. Andrews traditionally wore a clerical robe while preaching, he requested that Bob do the same. Although this was totally foreign to Bob, he agreed to wear one of Pastor Houston's robes. Following the service, Bob commented to the Presbyterian minister, "This is the most uncomfortable robe I have ever worn." As he removed the robe, he discovered the problem: he had failed to remove the wire coat hanger from the robe and it had been in the back of the robe all during the service!

The land of Israel in general and Jerusalem in particular have been magnets that have attracted innumerable high profile people as well as people from all strata of life throughout history. Bob was so focused on interacting with the various people that entered his life in that arena, however, that he hardly noticed the years passing swiftly by. But steadily and surely the day was approaching when life would dictate—a change of pace.

CHAPTER 30
A CHANGE OF PACE

Near the end of 1986, Bob and Margaret affirmed their decision to retire when Bob reached the age of seventy in August of 1987. On the last day of December he resigned his position as senior pastor of the Jerusalem Baptist Church and Pat Hoaldridge was named to that position. Termination of his various responsibilities necessitated by retirement and permanent relocation to the United States required considerable attention. They had much to accomplish in the next five months.

In May, 1987, friends and colleagues held three retirement parties for the Lindseys: one at the Jerusalem Baptist Church, one at the Baptist Village, and another at a meeting of the Baptist Convention in Israel. Almost everyone who knew the Lindseys well were at one or more of the receptions—and everyone had something to say about them. A few representative comments follow; most speakers are unidentified:

Teddy Kollek, Mayor of Jerusalem reiterated what he had said previously: "Bob and Jerusalem are inseparable."

Bruce Ya'akobi told about meeting Bob on a ship in the Mediterranean in 1945, on the way to Palestine, seeing Bob teach the "Home Kids" Christmas songs in Hebrew in 1948, and that he made Bob's first prosthetic leg.

One man said, "Bob stayed up one night until 4 A.M. answering my questions."

Another said, "When I started attending the Baptist services, some of the people thought I was a spy. Because of Bob I came to believe that Jesus is Messiah."

"I was in Margaret's Bible Study group," a young woman volunteered, "and I learned about Christian love and got a deeper knowledge of our Lord."

Other comments include:

"Once Bob took me up Masada off the trail, which was nearly impossible, but Bob was one for stepping outside normal boundaries."

"Bob was innovative, had tenacity, love, perseverance—he was my mentor."

"When Bob spoke, people listened."

A number of friends wrote humorous songs and sang them: "Luke was First," "The Kingdom of God is At Hand—It's Already Here in the Land," and "He's a Charismatic." Bob and Margaret enjoyed them all, especially the one called "The Lindsey Bob" which was a parody on Bob's mode of baptism. It was sung with body motions to the tune of "The Hokey Pokey." Although not theologically accurate, at least it rhymed and everyone had a good laugh!

> Put your left foot in—then your right foot in,
> Duck yourself completely and you wash away your sin,
> While you're in the water he is standing on the job,
> Doing the Lindsey Bob!

About two months before leaving Israel, the Lindseys moved what furniture and personal belongings they wished to keep (mostly books) to their small vacation cottage in Poriya. The apartment that they vacated on Nablus Road in the Sheikh Jerah section of East Jerusalem had been their home for sixteen years.

They boarded a plane for the United States on May 18, 1987, after having served in Palestine and Israel for forty-three years and six months. The decision to settle in Moore, Oklahoma (located between Oklahoma City and Norman), probably was due to the fact that it was the city with the largest concentration of their grandchildren. Sons David and Danny lived there with their families. Bob and Margaret joined First Baptist Church in nearby Norman—the church which Bob had attended as a child and youth and which had maintained close personal ties with the Lindseys along with contributing to their financial support.

They were hardly settled before Bob began to receive invitations to speak in churches and at seminars around the country. Trinity Broadcasting Network broadcast a total of fifteen programs for their series *Understanding the Gospels* in which Bob spoke on various aspects of *The Messianic Consciousness of Jesus*.

Even though Bob had retired, his interest in Gospel research had not waned. Several times Bob jokingly made the statement, "Sometimes I wonder if God has been hiding somewhere a copy of Matthew's Gospel written in Hebrew, along with the Hebrew documents used by the writers of the gospels of Matthew, Mark, and Luke. They may be in a jar in a cave somewhere in Judea. I would like to be living when they are found. If or when they are discovered, I'll catch the next plane to Israel."

Bob and Margaret did not wait for the scrolls to be found, however, before returning to Israel in mid-1988. When they arrived in Tel Aviv, they sensed that they had been gone far too long and it was wonderful to be home again. At their cottage in Poryia they killed the scorpions and spiders, cleaned and dusted and made it their home for the next two months and ten days. They visited friends all over the country and friends came to see them in Poryia. They attended different worship services, participated in various functions and kept quite busy. As is frequently the case in retirement, however, being back in Israel as a retired person was not quite what they had envisioned and was particularly difficult for Bob. He missed the direct involvement and responsibility he had known for so long. Also, much of what had been meaningful in their life was centered in Jerusalem and they felt somewhat isolated in the Galilee. Bob particularly missed the regular weekly Bible seminars with Professor Flusser and other Bible scholars and students. Bob was invited to preach and speak from time to time but it simply was not the same. The Lindseys initially had planned to spend half a year in Israel and the other half in the U.S., but they actually stayed in Israel an average of only two months during each of the five years following their retirement.

In 1990 he wrote a 111-page book entitled *The Jesus Sources: Understanding the Gospels* (Tulsa, OK: Hakesher). This academic work describing the technical aspect of his gospel research was a revised text of *The Lindsey Lectures* given in Jerusalem in 1983 that had been transcribed and formatted by colleague Jim Burnham. The same year he completed a 227-page book that he wanted to entitle, *Jesus: How We Misunderstood Him.* However, his friends and colleagues prevailed upon him to select a more positive title. It was released as *Jesus, Rabbi & Lord: The Hebrew Story of Jesus Behind our Gospels* (Oak Creek, WI: Cornerstone). It is written in popular format and consequently is a valuable resource for anyone wanting to know what Bob believed and taught.

Bob strongly believed in two traditional Baptist doctrines: the priesthood of each individual believer; and, the autonomy of the local congregation. He was quite troubled by developments within the leadership of the Southern Baptist Convention that he had observed for some years previously. One day, four years into his retirement, a friend asked him, "Bob, are you still a Southern Baptist?" He replied somewhat sadly, "I am still a member of a Southern Baptist Church. The average Southern Baptist in the pew has not changed, but in the past few years the ones who took control of the Convention have been doing some things that are neither Baptist nor biblical!"

One area of controversy regarding the Bible relates to the terms *inerrant* and *infallible.* When asked whether or not he believed in the inerrancy of the Scriptures, Bob would normally answer, "In the first place, when discussing the accuracy and authority of the Scriptures, it is best to use the words used by the biblical writers in describing the Scriptures. The word *inerrancy* is not one of them. How about these words? 'For the word of God is *living* and *active. Sharper* than any double-edged sword, it *penetrates* even to dividing soul and spirit, joints and marrow; it *judges* the thoughts and attitudes of the heart' (Hebrews 4:12). Or in this verse: 'All scripture is *God-breathed* and is *useful* for teaching, rebuking, correcting and training in righteousness, so that the man of God may be thoroughly equipped for every good work' (II Timothy 3:16). There is no glory in making claims about the Bible which the Bible doesn't make about itself. Many people today wave the "inerrancy flag" which only serves to divide people into two groups—the fundamentalists and the heretics.

"Some claim that the original *autographs,* those parchments or vellums originally written, are inerrant. What good is a theory about the originals, when the best manuscripts we have today are all copies of copies, and there are scribal errors in all of them? Also, there are many places in any translation where the original thought is lost, or is meaningless in the language of the translation. No one can judge the original autographs because no one has them. I have been studying the Scriptures almost all my life, preaching from them, using them in worship, and claim no other than the Bible for my doctrine and message. When it comes to knowing the essential things a person should know, he or she can find these things in any edition of the Bible in any language he or she can read. Man's need is to be instructed in the ways of the Lord, have his sins forgiven, be saved and sanctified and go to heaven. The scribal errors do not detract from the essential message."

Although his interest in biblical research and study remained strong, Bob began to face significant physical limitations. In 1969 he had been diagnosed with adult-onset diabetes. At first he was able to control it with weight loss, diet, and oral medication. Eventually, he required insulin injections and careful monitoring of his blood glucose levels.

One of life's mysteries is how someone who is brilliant in one area can simultaneously be stubborn and totally illogical in another area. Bob refused to let Margaret monitor his blood glucose consistently. He was convinced that he could tell when he needed to adjust his insulin dose. In reality, by the time he was able to detect physical symptoms (on several occasions requiring hospitalization), damage would already have occurred to his body. By the time of his retirement he was already experiencing some neuropathy manifesting as numbness and tingling in his hands and foot. It became increasingly difficult for him to type or to play the piano.

Even more devastating than the neuropathy was the small blood vessel disease he acquired secondary to the diabetes that affected primarily the small blood vessels supplying the brain. This condition became apparent in early 1993 when he suffered a major stroke. A number of mini-strokes followed, each one stealing a little more physical and mental ability. Following the first stroke, Bob was quite frustrated and angry when he would attempt to say something and a totally different word would be voiced. For example, he might want an apple and he would ask for an egg. He knew that what he was hearing was not what he wanted to say—and there was nothing he could do about it. With each successive mini-stroke, he became more passive. He retained a limited ability to speak until the last few months before his death.

In the spring of 1993 Bob and Margaret relocated to an apartment near their daughter Lenore's home in Tulsa, Oklahoma. He remained at home during his extended illness with family and friends assisting Margaret with his care. Only in the final weeks did he require a visiting nurse for certain procedures. Even after he was no longer able to speak, he would smile and show signs of recognition. He had fought a good fight, he had finished his course, he had kept the faith. In spite of considerable discomfort, he was a man at peace as he waited to meet his Lord.

CHAPTER 31
HENAY ANI ADONAI

On Saturday morning, June 3, 1995, word of Bob Lindsey's death had already spread among those in attendance at the Narkis Street Baptist Church in Jerusalem. Pastor Pat Hoaldridge led in "remembering Bob." Accompanied by a piano, flute, cornet, drums and guitars, the large congregation sang numerous choruses in Hebrew and English that Bob had written.

Numerous individuals came to the microphone to recall their memories of Bob and Margaret Lindsey. One said, "Behind every great man is a great woman, and behind Bob was Margaret. She loved him and 'balanced him out.' " Some credited Bob with leading them to the Lord, stimulating them to study the Bible, to be more Christ-like. Others spoke about his scholarship and about his emphasis on the Kingdom of God as a present reality.

Along with the serious and spiritual, the speakers spoke of the mundane. One said, "At Bob's house he always had a pot of soup on, and offered soup to anyone who entered." Another said that when the Lindsey's sixth child was born the Board sent a telegram that said only "CONGRATULATIONS STOP." Yet another recalled how he liked to lie on the floor and take off his prosthetic leg to use for a pillow. Someone else remembered his outlandish color combinations and wild neck ties—and on and on.

Before the sermon a man in the congregation blew two long blasts on a *shofar*, or ram's horn, usually sounded in Israel on most solemn occasions.

A memorial service was held in Jerusalem at the Narkis Street Baptist Church on June 7. The auditorium was bright and cheerful. In addition to singing in Hebrew and English and Bible reading, eighteen different long-time friends shared memories of Bob and his family. Among those sharing, Pastor Pat Hoaldridge remarked, "Bob eagerly waited for the coming of the Lord." Ray Register told the large gathering that Bob had given him a new understanding of Jesus as a baptizer in the Holy Spirit. Mayor Teddy Kollek knew Bob as "a man whose actions and what was deep in his heart were the same." Other speakers included Rhadia Qubti (one of the "home kids"), several Southern Baptist colleagues working in Israel, Professor David Flusser with whom Bob had worked closely on synoptic gospel texts, Rabbi Tovia Ben-Chorin of the neighboring Reformed Synagogue, and Reverend Tom C. Houston, pastor of St. Andrew's Church.

Elia Qubti, a teacher at the Baptist School in Nazareth and Chairman of the Association of Baptist Churches in Israel, eloquently expressed what was felt by many of those present:

> Jesus tells in John 15:13, "There is no greater love than
> this—that a man should lay down his life for his
> friends." Dr. Robert Lindsey was willing to do this
> because of the love of God that directed the course of
> his life.
> He loved our land and its people.
> He gave us the best of his days.
> He came to this country an energetic young man and
> left old and sick.
> He gave us the vitality of his youth and the wisdom of
> his age.
> To many he was a graceful father, a caring brother, but
> a friend most of all.
> He was a friend to the Arab and to the Jew.
> He was a friend to the young and to the old.
> He was a friend to the rich and to the poor.
> He was a friend to the educated and to the unschooled.
> He was a friend to those in key positions and to the
> common.
> He was a friend to the afflicted and to the whole.
> He was a friend to all.
> I can imagine his soul, when it left his body, did not go
> directly to the Father. It traveled thousands of miles in

the twinkle of an eye to float high above the land and the people he loved most. His soul hovered over the Holy Land, from Dan to Eilat, and from the River to the Sea, and from the City of Jerusalem—it ascended to the New Jerusalem.

On behalf of all Baptist congregations in Israel, I send our deepest condolences to our dear sister Margaret and to their children and grandchildren. Our prayer is that you find consolation in knowing that he is with the Lord, and realizing that his name is so precious to us, and his memory shall always be in our hearts.

Most appropriately, the service ended with the singing of the Lord's Prayer.

A large crowd attended Bob's funeral at the First Baptist Church in Norman, Oklahoma, on Monday, June 5. 1995. His wife, Margaret, was present with their six children, thirteen of their fifteen grandchildren, and many other relatives and friends. The service was a celebration of his life and reflected the extraordinary manner in which he dealt with the ordinary matters of life.

Dr. Gene Garrison said, "If he is happy in Heaven, it's because he found out the Hebrew source for the synoptic gospels."

Cliff West, one of Bob's cousins who had grown up with him, described his youth. "He was never mean or ornery—he didn't have a temper. Bob was genuinely concerned for people. He was easy to get along with as long as his mother would leave him alone. She wanted him to be a neurosurgeon, but, against her wishes, Bob wanted to be a preacher. In time she gave in and said, 'Well, if you are going to be a preacher, be a good one!' "

Aida Payne (one of "the home kids") spoke about "Uncle Bob": "We were the unwanted who were wanted by those of the Mission. Uncle Bob and Aunt Margaret and others present sacrificed for us."

Rema Gilcreast (another of "the home-kids") said: "He taught me by example to take the second mile when he went to rescue Edward and got him back but stepped on a land-mine."

Five of Bob's Baptist colleagues who had served with him in Israel spoke. Milton Murphey recalled the time when a reporter, who was writing an article about Bob, phoned him for a few details. He asked Milton exactly what was Lindsey's full name and he told him it was R.L. Lindsey. When the article appeared in the newspaper, however, his name was given as Ariel Lindsey. In Hebrew, Ariel means "Lion of God ." "That's what Bob was," concluded Murphey, "God's lion in Israel."

Marcus Reed spoke of his twenty-seven years of service with Bob. He remembered Bob as "an honest, brave man, an all-around great person."

Chandler Lanier recounted, "Late in the 60s and 70s, Bob and Margaret had some deep experiences and we became friends with the Holy Spirit and Bob was our leader. He was a giant among giants."

Dwight Baker shared, "No tie could be better or more real, no closer than our family had with the Lindseys. Bob always had a charged mind, a high level intellect; he was sharp and innovative. Ideas crackled in his mind, and some of those sparks touched me."

Almost everyone who spoke brought out something humorous about Bob. Jim Smith said that Bob was one of the most uninhibited and unpredictable men he and Elizabeth had ever known. Smith told how he invited Bob to come to Nazareth to preach in 1955. Bob often paid little attention to what he would wear. When he arrived at the church, after having stopped at the Baptist Center to fish in the Yarkon River, Bob asked Smith to loan him a Bible and something appropriate to wear for the church service. During the song service Smith noticed that Bob was writing notes in Hebrew on a scrap of paper for his sermon (in an Arabic Baptist Church)—the seven sayings of Jesus while on the cross. Then Smith held up a forty-year-old memento—Bob's sermon notes that he had left in the Bible that he had borrowed from Smith!

Susan Daniel Miller, the first Baptist student union director for Oklahoma University students in Norman back in the 30s, knew Bob when he was still in high school. Bob once attended a noonday prayer service for university students in the student union. He liked the idea and so he started one in his high school. Consistent with almost everyone who spoke at the funeral, she told of a humorous experience in which she and Bob with several friends went into a drug store where Bob bought a double-dip ice cream cone. "Realizing he was the only one with ice-cream, he said to the rest of us, 'Have some,' and passed it around and we all took a generous lick."

The funeral service was serious yet light, interspersed with Hebrew words and phrases. There were solos, duets, and congregational singing along with spoken and silent memories of Bob. There were tears and laughter. After an hour and a half, it was time for the church's pastor, Dr. Lavonn Brown, to speak.

> Yesterday the family was arranging the order of this service and they asked me to bring the message. When I saw the list of those who were speaking, I said, "Put me down for closing remarks."
>
> Bob was a world-class scholar. Consequently, his presence in a congregation could be intimidating to a minister. Over the past twenty-five years, Bob and Margaret have come back to this church many times. I would look out over the congregation and see Bob sitting there. Biblical scholarship and humility were wrapped up in one person—they are seldom found together. Bob was always a good listener and intense worshipper, and never confronting to a pastor who does not walk barefoot through the Greek and Hebrew as he did. I always appreciated him for that.
>
> Bob was always quite spontaneous, so you always had to be prepared for anything. Once when visiting Israel, we went with Bob to a baptism at a pool in Wadi Kelt. He invited me to speak on Romans 6 with no previous warning.
>
> In April of 1990, I preached an Easter sermon entitled, "Relax, He is Risen." I got the title from Bob's book, *Jesus, Rabbi & Lord*, where he tells an interesting little story. His very close friend, Professor David Flusser, had come to the United States and while going through customs he got very nervous. One of the customs officials noted how nervous he was and said, "Mister, don't be nervous; relax." Flusser had never heard that American phrase before so meditated on the meaning, and later shared with Bob, "You know, that's what Jesus is all about. Jesus

says to people, 'Relax.' " Then Bob wrote the comment in his book, "If you think about it a bit, that's indeed the tone of the events and words of Jesus at the first Easter. He kept saying, 'Don't be afraid; don't be amazed. Peace be with you. Relax—I have risen.' " And I think that would be Bob's message to us this afternoon. "You can relax now because He is risen. "

The eulogy was delivered by Bob Lindsey's son-in-law, Ken Mullican:

We have gathered here today to celebrate the life, ministry and home going of the Reverend Doctor Robert Lisle Lindsey, more affectionately known to people throughout the world as "Bob" or "Uncle Bob." He was born to J. L. and Elsie Lisle Lindsey on August 16, 1917, in Norman, Oklahoma. He went to be with the Lord on Wednesday, May 31, 1995, following a long illness. He is survived by his wife, Margaret, and six children and fifteen grandchildren. We are confident that he is now free of the shackles that took away his physical health and in the final stages took away his ability to communicate. All who knew and loved him will miss him dearly but we rejoice in the knowledge that although he is absent from us he is present with the Lord.

Words are extremely inadequate to express the meaning of the life of anyone, and particularly anyone of the stature of Bob Lindsey. As with most, if not all, truly great people, he remained totally unaware of his greatness. He was one of the most humble men I have ever known. He was quick to brush aside praise, and to turn the conversation to the other person. If you should have chanced to meet Bob, when you parted he would have known much about you and you would have known very little about him. He had no hidden agenda; he was simply genuinely interested in other people. Many people knew and loved Bob Lindsey and benefitted personally from his ministry, or knew him through his books, articles, tapes and seminars. He wisely chose to invest his life in the lives of others and those touched by his life continue, in turn, to touch the lives of others, thereby multiplying the labor of his lifetime many times over.

Bob Lindsey possessed great curiosity. I have heard him say many times as he grappled with a question of scripture, particularly in the gospels, that he could hardly wait to get to heaven and ask the writer personally what was intended in a particular passage. In fact, he had questions for most, if not all, of the personalities of the Bible. Perhaps already he is getting a chance to ask some of those questions.

Bob had a great sense of humor—he enjoyed life! And as he studied the words of Jesus, he also discovered that Jesus had a very sharp wit and used humor to great advantage in his theological discussions. We had a great time at the First Baptist Mission House last night where family, missionary associates from Israel, and other friends gathered to watch videos of Bob and share personal remembrances of him—most of them humorous. We celebrated his life—and that is what I hope you will join us in doing today—celebrating the life of one who loved life and managed to spread a great deal of humor during his time on the earth.

No one loved the land of the Bible and the people of the land, including Jews, Arabs, and expatriates, more than Bob Lindsey. He first came to the land of Palestine in 1939 and stayed for a year and a half to study Hebrew while living with a Jewish family in Jerusalem. On the way back to the U.S., he traveled through the Orient and, in Japan, met the young woman who would become his wife. Margaret Lutz was the daughter of missionaries to Korea and had booked passage on the same ship as Bob on her way back to the U.S. to complete college. After completing seminary he returned to the Holy Land in 1945, under appointment by the Southern Baptist Foreign Mission Board, with his wife and two small children, to become pastor of the Narkis Street Baptist Church in Jerusalem. He functioned in many different capacities while serving in Israel until his retirement in 1987, but he is perhaps best remembered by more people in his beloved role as senior pastor of the church in Jerusalem.

The Lindseys were sponsored by First Baptist Church of Norman, Oklahoma, Bob's home church, and have continued a close relationship through the years. Bob always pointed to the strong influence of Dr. E. F. Hallock (affectionately know as Preacher Hallock), longtime pastor of this church, as the major influence in his life that not only led him into the ministry, but imprinted indelibly upon his mind the necessity of a thorough knowledge of Greek and Hebrew in order to gain a clear understanding of the Bible.

The Lindseys' association with Israel covers all its modern history. They were there for the partitioning of Palestine into Israel and Jordan and the birth of those respective nations. They agonized with Jews and Arabs through wars and attacks of various types. They endured the firebombing of the Baptist Bookstore and later the firebombing of the church which destroyed the building but not the church itself. In fact, after both attacks the outpouring of love and concern by the Israelis, both Jews and Arabs, more than compensated for the physical loss. The action of a few zealous religious extremists actually backfired and served to bind the Lindseys, their congregation, and their associates more closely to the people of the land. The numerous expressions of concern and acts of kindness were overwhelming. At these and other times of crisis, we were privileged to get a small glimpse of the countless individuals whose lives have been touched by Bob and Margaret Lindsey through the years and who continue to hold them in highest admiration.

Bob Lindsey was a world class scholar with an impressive list of publications. But, above all, Bob Lindsey had a pastor's heart. Except for a few brief periods through the years, the time for his scholarly pursuits was made up of a few hours here and a few hours there or a short "vacation" at the little cottage in Galilee away from telephone and pastoral duties. Bob's primary scholarly interest was the synoptic gospels of Matthew, Mark and Luke. His concern for publishing the life and words of Jesus in easy to understand Modern Hebrew led him to do his translation of the Gospel of Mark from Greek to Modern Hebrew. He also contributed to the effort of the United Bible Society's publication of the New Testament in Modern Hebrew.

An indication of the respect with which Bob Lindsey's scholarship was held is the fact that on several occasions he was invited to serve along with such well known people as David Ben-Gurion (first Prime Minister of Israel) as a judge at the International Bible Contest in Jerusalem. Young people from all over the world come to this contest to compete in answering extremely detailed questions about the people and events of the Bible.

Music was always a part of Bob Lindsey's life. He played several instruments and delighted in composing scripture choruses in both English and Hebrew which he taught to the Jerusalem congregation. Bob had his own particular style of playing the piano which I like to call "Ragtime-Gospel." Whenever he and Margaret would come to our house for a visit, soon after walking through the door, he would sit at our piano and play and sing rather lively renditions of favorite hymns or the latest scripture worship chorus he had composed.

Because music was always so much a part of his life and because he loved Jesus so much, I think it was very appropriate that as the time of his home going drew near he was comforted by the worship choruses that he had written. On Wednesday evening, May 31, Bob lay peacefully with a tape playing of him singing his songs to the Lord that had been recorded in Jerusalem. The last song on one side of the tape is in Hebrew and is entitled "Henay Ani Adonai" which may be translated either "Behold, I am the Lord" or "Here am I, Lord." His daughter, Lenore (my wife), and I entered his room and were standing beside his bed as the song ended with the words, "Henay Ani Adonai!"—and the instant the tape clicked off, he stopped breathing. He beheld the Lord— and the Lord took him.

I think nothing describes the life of the Reverend Doctor Robert Lisle Lindsey better than the words at the end of the Book of Acts that describe the Apostle Paul: "He welcomed all who came to him, preaching the Kingdom of God, and teaching about the Lord Jesus Christ…"

Epilogue:
The Legacy

In the realm of finances, the expectation one has of funds invested wisely is that benefit may come not only to the investor but to his or her heirs as well. Similarly, when one's life is wisely invested in service to others, it is not unreasonable to expect that those who follow may benefit as well. The legacy of Bob Lindsey's life and work is expressed in a variety of ways.

The Jerusalem School of Synoptic Research
(JSSR) is a consortium of Jewish and Christian scholars who are examining the synoptic gospels (Matthew, Mark and Luke) within the context of the languages, land and culture in which Jesus lived. This Jewish-Christian collaboration is unique and unprecedented historically. The results of these scholars' research confirm that Jesus was an organic part of the diverse social and religious landscape of Second Temple-period Judaism. He, like other Jewish sages of his time, taught in Hebrew and used specialized teaching methods to teach foundational Jewish theological concepts such as God's abundant grace. Nevertheless, Jesus' teaching was revolutionary in many aspects, particularly in three areas: his radical interpretation of the biblical commandment of mutual love; his call for a new morality; his idea of the kingdom of Heaven (David Flusser, *Jesus*, p.81).

The late Dr. Robert L. Lindsey, a founding member of JSSR, pioneered, together with the late Professor David Professor David Flusser, the methodology upon which the School's synoptic research is based. Research projects of Jerusalem School members are directed toward the publication of: 1) a series of academic volumes utilizing the School's distinctive methodology; 2) an idiomatic translation of the gospels and Acts with annotations highlighting the text's Hebraic nuances and briefly explaining the significance of Jesus' words and deeds; 3) the Jerusalem Synoptic Commentary, a detailed commentary on the synoptic gospels. *www.JerusalemSchool.org*

Jerusalem Perspective

Jerusalem Perspective was begun in 1987 by JSSR founding member David Bivin, as an independent magazine published bimonthly in Jerusalem. It features the work of Jewish and Christian scholars, particularly the scholars of the Jerusalem School of Synoptic Research. Publisher and editor Bivin switched to a larger, color format published quarterly from 1994 to 1999, after which *Jerusalem Perspective* has been published online at *www.JerusalemPerspective.com*.

The Center for Judaic-Christian Studies

This center, directed by Dwight Pryor, began in 1984 as a nonprofit organization that seeks to cultivate among Christians an appreciation of their Hebrew heritage. The Center, headquartered in Dayton, Ohio has produced a thirteen-part television series, "The Quest: The Jewish Jesus," and co-published books, such as the award-winning *Archaeology of the Land of the Bible* (Mazar, Doubleday), the bestselling *Our Father Abraham: Jewish Roots of the Christian Faith* (Wilson, Eerdmans); and *Understanding the Difficult Words of Jesus* (Bivin and Blizzard, Destiny Image). CJCS produces a variety of audio and video teaching materials and presents lectures nationally and internationally. *www.jcstudies.com*

The Centre for the Study of Biblical Research

The Centre, directed by Dr. William Bean, was incorporated in 1985 to augment the work of JSSR. CSBR houses materials incorporating results from the latest New Testament research and Middle Eastern archeological and linguistic findings. The Centre is affiliated with or works in conjunction with many organizations in Israel and the USA that conduct, support, and apply New Testament research. Dr. Bean is on the USA Board of Advisors of the Dead Sea Scrolls Foundation. CSBR endeavors to assist ministers and lay people in utilizing the work of biblical scholars. Their effort reaches beyond academics into the practical application of the principles taught by Jesus in a ministry of helps, care for the needy, and care for children. CSBR, located in Redlands, California, has established several synoptic gospel study groups that meet monthly in Southern California. *www.csbr.net*.

Gospel Research Foundation is dedicated to the scholarly exploration and spiritual restoration of the Jewish roots of the Christian faith. Founder and President Brad H. Young received his Ph.D. from Hebrew University in Jerusalem under Professor David Flusser. Dr. Young is also a founding member of the Jerusalem School of Synoptic Research.

GRF operates from Tulsa, Oklahoma with the following objectives:

- Seeks to interpret properly the teachings of Jesus in their authentic context, giving fresh vitality to Christian experience. The Judaism of Jesus is the root which nourishes the branch.
- Promotes interfaith understanding between Christians and Jews through mutual respect and appreciation.
- Works to place the best of scholarship in the service of people who want to learn.

GRF is committed to long-term projects which accomplish the founding purpose:

- Preparing a Hebrew Heritage Study New Testament which will explore the Jewish background of Christianity. Teachings from Judaism in the time of Jesus reveal fresh insight.
- Preparing a major scholarly commentary on the New Testament based upon the comparative study of rabbinic literature, the Dead Sea Scrolls, historical writings, archaeology and ancient Judaism. Comparing the teachings of Jesus with Jewish texts reveals fresh perspective.
- *www.gospelresearch.org*

Jerusalem Cornerstone—Biblical Studies in Israel.
The Biblical studies in Israel is a year abroad program for Christian

undergraduate students majoring in biblical studies or related fields. It is directed by Dr. Randall Buth in cooperation with the Rothberg International School of the Hebrew University of Jerusalem. BSI is ideal for students who want to develop strong language skills along with introduction to the cultural and geographical backgrounds of the Bible. *www.JerusalemCornerstone.org*

Biblical Hebrew Ulpan of the Biblical Language Center.

This is an intensive language immersion course offered in the summer at Yad ha-Shmona, Israel, by Dr. Randall Buth and a staff of teachers. Biblical Hebrew is spoken in class so that students learn at an accelerated rate and retain the language with the highest efficiency. Students have come from many countries, ages, and walks of life for this unique approach to Biblical Hebrew. All share a desire to learn to read the Hebrew Bible that Jesus read with his followers.

Texts and Land, an intermediate Biblical Hebrew course in the Land of Israel, is also directed by Dr. Buth. It is an intermediate level, intensive program for continuing studies of Biblical Hebrew in its geographical setting. There is a double focus: 1) to learn to interpret the literary and grammatical signals in a text, and 2) to relate the stories to their geographical and historical settings. *www.biblicalulpan.org*

Home for Bible Translators in Jerusalem, Inc.

HBT assists native speakers involved in translation projects to improve their Biblical Hebrew language skills as well as their knowledge of biblical geography and culture. Located in the Mevasseret Tzion suburb of Jerusalem, translators and scholars can study while living in the Land of the Bible. Opened in 1994 by Halvor and Mirja Ronning, this program has proven to be quite effective in contrast to the usual translation method in which a non-native scholar attempts to learn the target language in order to create a native language translation. By providing living and study accommodations for Bible translators and scholars from around the globe while offering special in-house and Hebrew University study programs, HBT aims to improve the accuracy and efficiency of the many Bible translation projects throughout the world. *www.BibleTranslators.org*

Emmaus Educational Services

EES is an initiative intended to assist students, clergy and laity to engage and understand the biblical world. Travel on the biblical stage together with on-site study of the Scripture illuminates the richness of God's unfolding drama of redemption. EES began in 1993 as a collaborative effort between Linda Edwards, who was then a lecturer in Religious Education at King's College, University of London, and Dr. Steven Notley, who resided in Jerusalem.

Notley lived in Jerusalem for sixteen years where he earned his Ph.D. under the direction of the late Professor David Fusser. During his years in Israel, Notley was extensively involved in directing travel and field study for students and laity in Israel, Greece and Turkey and continues to direct trips through EES. He served as the chairman of the department of New Testament Studies at the Jerusalem University College from 1996 to 2001. Currently he is Professor of Biblical Studies at the New York City campus of Nyack College.

A new era for EES began in 2002 with the combining of efforts between Dr. Notley and Dr. Wink Thompson, who himself has studied and taught the physical settings of the Bible both in the U.S.A. and in Israel over the last thirty years. Notley and Thompson have committed to bring their strengths and respective areas of academic focus to serve those who travel and study on the Emmaus programs. *www.EmmausOnline.net*

HaKesher, Inc.

HaKesher,Inc. was founded as a nonprofit corporation in 1987 by Ken and Lenore Lindsey Mullican in Tulsa, Oklahoma, with the following objectives:

1. To promote an awareness of the Hebraic heritage of the Christian faith through the teaching of Hebrew language and culture, thereby developing a deeper, more mature and meaningful faith.
2. To support the research of biblical scholars whose aim is to illuminate more clearly the social, historical, religious and linguistic context of Jesus' teaching.
3. To be a unifying, cohesive force both locally, nationally, and

internationally, utilizing the expertise of various individuals and organizations that are committed to the advancement of Judaic-Christian studies.

4. To offer books, audio- and videocassettes, and other study materials by mail order, including self-study Hebrew language courses.

5. To promote an understanding of biblical equality in gender and ethnic interpersonal relationships.

6. To combat anti-Judaism through mutual understanding and respect.

7. To promote a balanced relationship of the church with both Arabs and Jews in the Holy Land.
   www.hakesher.org

Church Growth

Four congregations have been birthed primarily by language group from the original Baptist Church on Narkis Street in Jerusalem. Korean, Russian, and Hebrew congregations are thriving as well as an international congregation with services in English. Charles "Chuck" Kopp is pastor of the international congregation known as the Narkis Street Congregation. Kopp served as a church elder during Bob Lindsey's tenure as pastor. He also serves as international director of Jerusalem Cornerstone Foundation. Under his leadership, the church continues the tradition of addressing physical as well as spiritual needs of the people of the land. Food and clothing are collected to assist the needy in the West Bank and Gaza as well as Israel. They also cooperate with other ministries such as Shevet Achim (www.shevet.org), a Christian ministry that brings Arab children from Gaza, the West Bank, and Iraq to Israel for heart surgery. Most of the Arab children are Muslims that are treated by Jewish doctors at no charge with hospital billing only half the usual charge. Because the Palestinian Authority has failed to pay the hospital charges, Narkis Street Congregation and other Christian groups and individuals have endeavored to collect funds to cover the charges. Compassionate people are reaching out to address the needs of others, regardless of ethnic or religious background. May the seeds of peace ultimately bear a bountiful harvest!

Other Organizations and Individuals

Numerous other organizations and individuals who have been influenced by the life and work of Bob Lindsey are multiplying his efforts many times over in ever increasing spheres of influence. A hallmark of his life was the ability to translate his academic research of the life and teachings of Jesus into practical experience. For Dr. Lindsey, it was never a matter of academic study for the sake of study alone, but his goal was to better understand what Jesus said and the context in which he taught in order that he might share that understanding with others. This same spirit is evident in the life and service of those who are the legacy of a life well lived. May the reader be inspired to "go and do likewise."

ENDNOTES

[1] When the New Hadassah Medical Center in Jerusalem was dedicated in 1960, the road to the center was named Henrietta Szold in honor of one of the founders of the Hadassah movement. The former Henrietta Szold Street that ran in front of the Baptist property was renamed Narkis Street, in honor of Mordechai Narkis, director of the Bezalel Art Museum and School which is located around the corner from Baptist House.

CPSIA information can be obtained at www.ICGtesting.com
Printed in the USA
LVOW12s2317100214

373114LV00001B/3/P